# TENNESSEE FAMILIES

## A Bibliographic Listing

*of* **Books** *about* **Tennessee Families**

*by*
*Donald M. Hehir*

HERITAGE BOOKS
2014

# HERITAGE BOOKS

*AN IMPRINT OF HERITAGE BOOKS, INC.*

## Books, CDs, and more—Worldwide

For our listing of thousands of titles see our website
at
www.HeritageBooks.com

Published 2014 by
HERITAGE BOOKS, INC.
Publishing Division
5810 Ruatan Street
Berwyn Heights, Md. 20740

Other Heritage Books by Donald M. Hehir:

*Carolina Families: A Bibliography of Books about North and South Carolina Families*

*CD: Delaware Bible Records, Volumes 1-4*
Donald O. Virdin and Donald M. Hehir

*Delaware Bible Records, Volume 4*

*Georgia Families: A Bibliographic Listing of Books about Georgia Families*

*Kentucky Families: A Bibliographic Listing of Books about Kentucky Families*

*Missouri Family Histories and Genealogies: A Bibliography*

*Ohio Families: A Bibliographic Listing of Books about Ohio Families*

*Tennessee Families: A Bibliography of Books about Tennessee Families*

International Standard Book Numbers
Paperbound: 978-0-7884-0517-4
Clothbound: 978-0-7884-7569-6

Dedication:

To Jeanne McAdam Hehir

# ACKNOWLEDGEMENTS

Particular thanks are due to Karen Ackermann at Heritage Books for her very helpful advice on putting together this and previous works, to Donald Odell Virdin for his always helpful suggestions and encouragement, and to Robert Dean Larson for his help on accessing the Library of Congress on the Internet.

# TABLE OF CONTENTS

# INTRODUCTION

The works in this bibliography, covering over 1500 family names, deal with families who have some connection to Tennessee. A separate section lists family histories and genealogies on microfilm at the Library of Congress as of mid-1993. A brief introduction to that section of this book may be found on page 161. At the end I have included a brief guide to accessing family histories in the Library of Congress via the Internet.

By far the largest portion of the works covered in this book can be found at the Library of Congress in Washington, D.C., the National Genealogical Society (NGS) Library Arlington, Virginia, or in the Daughters of the American Revolution (DAR) Library in Washington, D.C.

Also included are a significant number of books from more than 15 historical associations and public libraries from Massachusetts to California, including the New York Public Library, the Allen County Public Library (Fort Wayne, Indiana), and the San Francisco Public Library.

The reader should remember that no work of this kind can ever be complete. Many family histories are privately printed and never make their way into large collections. Similarly, many newer works will not have been published, or cataloged, in time for inclusion in this book. It is neither possible, nor practicable, to review individual bibliographies and family histories. For this reason, family names included here may, or may not, be primarily or exclusively associated with Tennessee and some works, published in Tennessee and included here, may occasionally refer to non-Tennessee families, with the only reference to the state being the fact that the bibliography or history was published there. These have been included in order to cast as wide a net as practicable to include all possible references to families with

some association with Tennessee. By the same
token, there may be other published material on
Tennessee families in works relating to other
areas of the country, but they are not included
here, because there was no way to identify a
relationship to Tennessee. Many of the books
cited here include references to other states
and countries.

This work follows primarily, but not
exclusively, the Library of Congress system for
cataloging names, so, for example, a work on
"Cline" might be shown under the Library of
Congress Family Name Index of "Kline" even when
"Kline" is not mentioned in the title or the
description of the book.

Similarly, since different libraries catalog
publications with slightly differing
classification systems, family names may have
different spellings, depending on the system
being used. As a result, there are listings in
this book, which may in some cases be
duplicative of other listings, since it was not
always possible to determine if references were
to the same book, to different editions, or to
different books.

In compiling the bibliographies and family
histories listed, I have attempted to err on the
side of including, rather than excluding, works
with similar titles and publication dates where
the possibility exists that the books are, at
least, different editions of the same work.

The Cross-Reference Index will show the page
location in this book of all families mentioned
in the descriptions in the original source
documents.

Among the various sources, the use of the terms
"pages" and "leaves" is not always consistent
from library to library, so that the same book
in different libraries may be shown as having
"n" leaves, or "n" pages. Similarly, different
catalogers may use different styles to indicate

pagination . . . 47 pages in one source may
appear as 2 1, 44 pages in a different source
but both are indicating a total of 47 pages.
This adds to the problem of determining whether
different catalogers were reporting on the same
or different editions of the same book . In
the interests of simplicity I have shortened
some lengthy pagination descriptions so that,
for example, a pagination description of p.
1, 14p, [1]p, 2 4p, is generally rendered here
as 1, 44p, [1].

Another area, which may present difficulty to
the reader, occurs when cataloguers indicate the
pagination as, for example, 160 [i.e. 124].
Usually this means that there are 160 numbered
pages altogether than there only with the added
possibility of additional blank pages and some
sheets numbered on both sides. In such cases,
the bracketed figure generally indicates the
total number of pages in the volume. This,
fortunately, does not often occur.

Where different library catalogers have used
different descriptions for the same work, the
more detailed description has generally been
followed, and in some cases, differing
descriptions have been combined to provide the
user with as much information as possible about
the content of an individual work.

FORMAT:    The description of bibliographies
and family histories contained in this volume
generally follows the format indicated below:

FAMILY NAME -- Author (Compiler or Editor).
*Title*. *Subtitle*. Place of Publication, Date of
Publication.    Number of pages or leaves.
Additional Descriptive Material, if any.
[Source abbreviation. Library catalog or page
number in that source for the referenced work
may also be given, e. g. L600 shows that the
genealogy is listed as item 660 in *Genealogies
in the Library of Congress*].

Note that in the Section dealing with Histories
and Genealogies on Microfilm at the Library of
Congress, the last item will be the catalog
number for the Microfilm which contains the
book, chart, or other document cited.

## ABBREVIATIONS FOR SOURCES

Each source cited and its abbreviations used in
this work are as follows:

A      -      Appendices to KAMINKOW, Marion J.
Genealogies In The Library of Congress.
Baltimore, Maryland, 1972.

C      -      KAMINKOW, Marion J. Genealogies In The
Library of Congress, Second Supplement 1976
- 1986. Baltimore, Maryland, 1987.

D      -      MICHAELS, Carolyn Leopold and Kathryn
S. Scott. DAR Library Catalog, Volume One.
Second Revised Edition, Family Histories
and Genealogies. Washington, DC, 1983.

DC     -      GRUNDSET, Eric B. & Bebe METZ. DAR
Library Catalog, Volume Three Centennial
Supplement: Acquisitions 1985-1991.
Washington, DC, 1992.

DS     -      MICHAELS, Carolyn Leopold and Kathryn
S. SCOTT. DAR Library Catalog, Volume One
- Supplement - Family Histories and
Genealogies. Washington, DC, 1984.

G      -      GENEALOGIES Cataloged in the Library of
Congress Since 1986. Washington, DC, 1992.

L      -      KAMINKOW, Marion J. Genealogies In The
Library of Congress. Baltimore, 1972. 2.
v. A-L and M-Z.

NG     -      National Genealogical Society Library
Book List, 5th Edition. Arlington,
Virginia, 1988.

NGS   -   *National Genealogical Society Library
Book List, 7th Edition Supplement.*
Arlington, Virginia, 1989.

N-A   -   *National Genealogical Society Library
Acquisitions, December 1989 through
December 1994.*   Arlington, Virginia,
National Genealogical Society, 1995.

T     -   TOWLSTON, Marion J.   *Genealogies in the
Library of Congress, Supplement 1972-76.*
Baltimore, 1976.

VV    -   VIRKUS, Scott & al.   *Virginia Genealogies
and Family Histories.*   Bowie, Maryland,
Heritage Books, Inc., 1990.

VP    -   VIRKUS, Donald O.   *Pennsylvania Genealogies and Family Histories.*   Bowie,
Maryland, Heritage Books, Inc., 1990.

X     -   KAMINKOW, Marion J.   *A Complement To
Genealogies In The Library of Congress.*
Baltimore, 1981.

XA    -   Appendix to KAMINKOW, Marion J.   *A
Complement To Genealogies in The Library of
Congress.*   Baltimore, Maryland, 1981.

In the above sources the numbers following the
entry in the text refer to the number assigned
to the entry in the source publication and not
to a page number:

         A - C - S - D - DC - DS - T.

In other sources, the number refers to the page
number where the genealogy or family history is
located in that source, e.g. NG123 shows that
the genealogy is located on page 123 of the
National Genealogical Society Library Book List.
In the case of "G" entries, the page number and
column location of the citation are given, e.g.
G81:2 indicates the entry is on page 81 in
column 2 of that page.

         NG - NGS - NGN - VP - VV - X - XA

                        XI

## EXCEPTIONS:

Works acquired by the Library of Congress since 1991 which were taken from the Library's Computer Listing are an exception to the above rules. No catalog of these works has been published by the Library. In these instances, the Library of Congress call number for the work is given, e.g. "LC CALL NUMBER CS71.P3000 1994."

Also, works listed as NGN, indicate the volume, the number, and the year in which the items were listed in the National Genealogical Society Newsletter, e.g. [NGN17-1-92] indicates newsletter issue: volume 17, no. 1, 1992. Six issues were published each year. Starting in January 1994, the newsletter designation was changed by the NGS so that a listing shown in the January/February 1994 newsletter will read [NGN JAN/FEB 94]. Unfortunately, the NGS Newsletter entries do not indicate the place or date of publication, nor the pagination, only the date the acquisition is shown in the Newsletter. These works are, with some exceptions, available through the NGS Library Loan Service. Instructions for borrowing the books can be obtained by sending a self-addressed, stamped envelope to: NGS Library Loan Service, 4527 17th Street North, Arlington, VA 22207-2399. Currently, the phone number for the NGS Library is 703-525-0050.

While most citations are to specific library collections, the Virdin Virginia (VV) and Pennsylvania (VP) genealogies are not contained in any specific library. Library collections for entries followed solely by [VV] or [VP] may be in some of the other library collections cited, but the user is advised to consult other libraries and historical and genealogical societies in the states concerned. All other source references are to libraries and genealogical societies located in the Metropolitan Washington, DC area, except those marked "X-_____ or XA-_____".

Note that the entries for the *Complement to the*
*Genealogies in the Library of Congress*, "X" and
"XA", are for genealogies and family histories
not in the Library of Congress at the time "A
Complement..." was written and many are not in
the Library of Congress collection to this date.
The coding at the end of each entry will
indicate if any particular "X" or "XA" entry is
also shown as being in the Library of Congress
collection. The X is followed by the initials
of the Library or Libraries where the
genealogy or family history is located, e.g.

(X-FW) Allen County Public Library, Fort
Wayne, Indiana

(X-NY/SL) New York Public Library and St.
Louis Public Library.

Library Designator used with the "X" (and "XA")
entries are:

| | |
|---|---|
| AH | Alaska Historical Society |
| BA | Boston Athenaeum |
| CH | Cincinnati Historical Society |
| DP | Denver Public Library |
| FW | Allen County Public Library, Fort Wayne, Indiana |
| GF | Genealogical Forum of Portland, Oregon |
| IG | Idaho Historical Genealogical Library, Boise |
| KV | Kansas State Historical Society, Topeka |
| LA | Los Angeles Public Library |
| LI | Long Island Historical Society, Brooklyn, N. Y. |

| | |
|---|---|
| MH | Minnesota Historical Society, St. Paul |
| NJ | Gloucester County Historical Society, Woodbury, N. J. |
| NY | New York Public Library |
| OH | Ohio Historical Society, Columbus |
| OL | The State Library of Ohio, Columbus |
| OS | Oregon State Library, Salem |
| PH | The Historical Society of Pennsylvania, Philadelphia |
| PP | Library Association of Portland, Oregon |
| SF | San Francisco Public Library |
| SP | Seattle Public Library |
| SL | St. Louis Public Library |
| SU | Sutro Branch of the California State Library, San Francisco |
| SW | Spokane Washington, Public Library |
| WR | Western Reserve Historical Society, Cleveland, Ohio |

Unfortunately, neither the Library of Congress, the DAR, nor the National Genealogical Society have published catalogs of their holdings in recent years. The last published catalogs were in 1991 for the Library of Congress, 1992 for the DAR, and 1989 for the National Genealogical Society. You should contact these libraries if you have specific questions about whether they have materials on the family history or genealogy of a particular name you may be interested in.

# GLOSSARY

? - Indicates a doubt by the compiler of this work as to the accuracy of the material shown in the original source. Also, indicates a conflict in the date shown in different sources when referring apparently to an identical work.

! - Indicates a doubt by the compiler of the source document as to the accuracy of the material shown in the referenced work.

c. - Circa. (About, ca.)

ed. - Edition

enl. - Enlarged.

l. - Leaf (Leaves).

NAS - No Author or Compiler shown in the source listing.

NP - No Place of Publication indicated.

n.d. - No Date of Publication indicated.

numb. - Numbered.

p. - Page(s).

pni - Pagination Not Indicated

rep. - Reprint.

rev. - Revised, Revision.

sic - Used to indicate that the previous word or phrase has been copied precisely from the original source even though apparently misspelled or incorrect.

unp. - Unpaged.

v. - Volume or Volumes.

# TENNESSEE FAMILY
# HISTORIES & GENEALOGIES

## A

ABERNATHY -- Abernathy, Elizabeth Derry. *The Abernathy Family.* Pulaski, TN. Abernathy, 1935. 35p. [L33, 512].

ADAMS -- Johnson, Clara Klare. *Ancestors of Adams.* Adams, Proctor, Rudd. Ten Mile, TN. Johnson, 1977. ii, 104p. [O4: BRI: OCLC].

ADAMSON -- Dixon, Ben F. and Alice L. (Dwelle) Dixon. *The Adamson Source Book, A Genealogy of the Descendants of Rachel Williams Adamson (1775-1850) of Surry County, NC, Jefferson County, Tenn. and Lawrence County, Indiana.* Washington, DC, 1942. 56 leaves. [PG16].

ADAMSON -- Dixon, Ben F. and Alice L. (Dwelle) Dixon. *The Adamson Source Book, A Genealogy of the Descendants of Rachel Williams Adamson (1775-1850) of Surry County, NC, Jefferson County, Tenn. and Lawrence County, Indiana.* Washington, DC 1942-1961. 3 vols. Benjamin Franklin Junior Historical Series, no. 1-4. Part 2 has title: Rachael Williams Adamson and her Hoosier Clan & Imprint: San Diego, CA. [K6-FW/HV/SU].

ADCOCK -- Southern, Martin & Marguerite White Williams. *William Adcock an Sallie D'Howell of Knox County, Tennessee.* Knoxville, TN, 1970. 8, 86 l. [819].

ADDINGTON -- Addington, Hugh M. *Addingtons Family in United States and England, Vol II: Including a Multitude of Related Families.* Kingsport, TN. Franklin Printing Co. 1960. 59p. Continuation of the Author's History of the Addington Family in the United States and England. [L133].

ADDINGTON -- Addington, Hugh M. *History of the Addington Family in United States and*

*England.* Nickelsville, VA, Service Printery; Kingsport, TN, Franklin Printing Co., 1931. 1960. 2 v. (98; 59p.) [L133; D77].

**ALBERT** -- Albert, Ethel Evans. *Links With The Past.* Kingsport, TN, Albert, 1972. ix. 497p. X gives no date. [D94; X8-FW].

**ALBERT** -- Albert, Linzy D. *The Alberts of La Fourche, A Profile of Acadian Heritage.* Memphis, TN, Albert, 1979. ii, 112 leaves. [C7].

**ALBERT** -- Albert, Linzy D. *Genealogy and Historical Sketch of the Nicolas Albert Family of France, Acadia, and Bayou Lafourche in Louisiana, 1726-1985.* [Also Albert, Berbudeau, Benoit Fams]. Memphis, TN, L.D. Albert, 1985. iv, 125 leaves. [G6-3; C7].

**ALBRIGHT** -- Albright, A. G... *Some Data on the Albright Family.* Memphis, TN, Press of S.C. Tool & Co., 1915. 83p. [L171].

**ALDRIDGE** -- Aldridge, Franklin Rudolph. *Aldridge Records.* Nashville, TN, Aldridge, 1966. 167, 19p. [D129].

**ALDRIDGE** -- Aldridge, Franklin R. *Aldridge Records.* Nashville, TN, Printed by Commercial Letter Shop, 1966-75. 2 Vols. Vol 2 has subtitle: Variants: Alldredge, Aldredge, Aldred, Allred, Alred, Arledge. [X11-FW,IG,NY].

**ALEXANDER** -- Alexander, Charles C. *Alexander Kin.* Columbia, TN, Alexander, 1965, iii, 173p. S gives iii, 73p. [L228; S39; D130].

**ALEXANDER** -- Alexander, Charles C. and Virginia W. *Alexander Kin.* (Columbia, TN), The Authors, Greenville, SC, Southern Historical Press, 1965, 1980. 2 v. A complete index of names abstracted by James Bullagh Moore. [S39; DC48].

ALEXANDER -- Andrews, Vera B. *Alexanders of Cannon Co., Tn.: A Family History and Genealogy Covering 1848-1989 Plus Some Earlier.* Elkhart, IN, V.B. Andrews, 1989. 152, 48p. 1. Alexander Family. 2. Tennessee-Genealogy. [G8-2; DC51].

ALEXANDER -- Moore, Ralph Erskine. *The Alexander, Carson, Moore Genealogy.* Sweetwater, TN, Moore, 1967. 121p. [D149; X12-SW].

ALEXANDER -- Peterson, Ruth S. *Descendants of Captain William Alexander and Elizabeth King of Lancaster County, Pennsylvania, Guilford and Roncolph sic Counties, North Carolina, Green County, Tennessee.* NP, 1952. 94 leaves. [D151].

ALLDREDGE -- Sausaman, William Amel. *Nathan Alldredge (1739-1862) of North Carolina and Tennessee and His Descendants.* Springfield, IL, Sausaman, 1971. 129p. D gives 113p. X shows ALDRIDGE. [NG15; D161; X11-FW].

ALFORD -- Hailey, Naomi. *The Alford - Drake Family of Middle Tennessee, with Ancestors, Descendants and Allied Families.* Nashville, TN, N.M. Hailey, 1982. vii, 53, 12 leaves. [C9].

ALLEN -- Allen, Bulah Oyama. *Allen House and Some of Its Allens.* Nashville, TN, B.O. Allen, 1980. xxvi, 599p., 1 leaf of plates. [C9].

ALLEN -- Allen, Cornelius T. *A Genealogical Statements.* Knoxville, TN, S.B. Newman & Co., 1895. 48p. [X13-LI,NY].

ALLEN -- Allen, William A. *History of George Hunt & Mary Ogilvie Allen and their descendants and Related Families Ogilvie, Ewing, and Fonville. Prepared for the Allen Family Reunion August 8-11, 1985, Caney Spring, Marshall County, Tennessee.*

Brentwood, TN. W.A. Allen, 1985. 62 p.
LC CALL NUMBER: CS71.A43 1985b

**ALLEN** -- Goddard, Margaret E. *Annals of an Allen Family in Maryland, North Carolina, Tennessee, Indiana, Minnesota, and Iowa.* Cottonwood, AZ, The Author, 1985. 2 v. [DC63].

**ALLEN** -- Hill, Irene Allen. *The Isaac Allen Family of Tennessee and Kentucky.* Salt Lake City, UT, I. A. Hill, 1990. 258p. 1. Allen family. 2. Allen, Isaac, 1789-1856-Family. 3. Tennessee-Genealogy. 4. Kentucky-Genealogy. [G9].

**ALLEY** -- Allen, Maud B. *Alley - Osbourne Genealogy... of Va., Ky., Tennessee and Indiana.* NP, n.d., (various pagings). [X16-LA: VV3].

**AMIS** -- See below: CAMPBELL. [L2939; D2108].

**ALLISON** -- Morton, Margaret C. M. *Uriah Sherrill Allison and Nancy Clark Cox, Their Ancestors and Descendants, 1500-1975.* Rockwood, TN, 1975. 264p. [X17-FW].

**ANDERSON** -- Anderson, Beverly Bright. *Anderson: Ancestors and Descendants of Walter Roy and Edith Mae Clark Anderson.* Oak Ridge, TN, B.D. Anderson, 1985. ii, 423p. 1. Anderson family. 2. Anderson, Walter Roy, 1893-1933-Family. [G12-3].

**ANDERSON** -- Battey, George Magruder, III. *... The Andriessen (Andriezon, Anderson) Family of East Tennessee, Pennsylvania, Delaware and Elsewhere.* Washington, DC, 1940. 1, 11, 4 numbered leaves. Typewritten. [L386; VP5].

**ANDERSON** -- Battey, George Magruder, III. *The outlaws of North Carolina and Tennessee, the Hamiltons and Campbells of Virginia and*

*Tennessee as related to their inlaws, the Andersons of Pennsylvania and Tennessee.* Washington, DC, 1940. 1p., 5 numbered leaves. Typewritten. [L387; VP6].

**ANDERSON** -- Anderson, S. T. *Isaac Anderson, Founder and First President of Maryville College...* Maryville, TN. Priv. Print. 1932. 168p. [X21-DP].

**ANDREWS** -- Andrews, Mrs. Forrest. *The Descendants of John George and Ephraim Andrews, Sons of Mark Andrews of Williamson County, Tennessee.* Knoxville, TN, 1966. 969p. [L429 & L434].
_____ *The Descendants of A211 Sarah Locke Andrews and Elliott R. Waddey* Knoxville, TN, 1968. 6p. [L429 & L434].
_____ *McCurdy Chart. Basic Research.* Edited by Mrs. Forrest Andrews. Knoxville, TN, 1968. 4p. [L429 & L434].

**ANGLE** -- Anglea, Robert W. *A Band of Angleas: A History of the Anglea, Angel, Angell, Angle, etc. Family.* Cullman, AL. Gregath Pub. Co., 1991. xii, 408 p. 91-182901
LC CALL NUMBER: CS71.A585 1991

**ARCHER** -- Randolph, Wassell. *George Archer I of the Umverslade Archers of Henrico County, Virginia and His Descendants.* Memphis, TN, Randolph, 1965. vi, 63, 20p. X lists as ARCHERI and gives 63p. [D341; X27-SV; VV5].

**ARMISTEAD** -- Cate, Margaret Randolph and Wirt Armistead Cate. *The Armistead Family and Collaterals: among others: Anderson, Cate, Harrison, Mayo, Nelson, Phipps, Tabb, Waller.* Nashville, TN, 1971. vii, 319p. 1. Armistead family. [G19-2; S74].

**ARMOUR** -- Armour, Quinnie. *William Armour and His Known Descendants.* Bolivar, TN, Q. Armstrong, 1975. S gives: 1972 - and "Cover Title: The Descendants of James Armour." 1 volume in various paginations. [S76; DC106].

ARNOLD -- Arnold, Howard L, Pauline Scott, Pauline Miller. *Arnel's [sic] /Arnold's [sic] of North Carolina and Virginia, Family History.* Milan, TN, H.L. Arnold, 1988. vi, xx, 319p. 1. Arnold family. 2. North Carolina-Genealogy. 3. Virginia-Genealogy. [G19-3; DC110].

ATCHLEY -- Atchley, Paul L. *Maud Horn's Atchley Family History, Including Long, Maples, Scoggin, and Griffith Families.* Knoxville, TN, Atchley, Thompson, 1965, xiii, 530p. [D396].

ASBILL -- Bennett, George T. *A Family History.* Pulaski, TN, 195_, 176p. [X31-FW].

ATKINS -- Hazelwood, Louise V. and Jeremy L. Benson *Descendants of Winston Atkins of Pittsylvania County, Virginia and Grainger County, Tennessee.* NP, 198_? 21 leaves, 2 leaves of plates. 1. Atkins family. 2. Atkins, Winston, b. ca. 1773-Family. [G23-1].

ATKINSON -- Stanfill, Suzanne Latayne. *Atkisson Ancestry of West Tennessee, Featuring Grandmother Annie, Her Family, and Her Poetry.* Glendale, CA, Heirloom Press, 1993. vi, 128p.
    LC CALL NUMBER: CS71.A87 1993

AULD -- Grady, Jamie Ault. *Michael Ault, A Revolutionary Soldier and His Descendants.* Knoxville, TN, Grady, 1979. iv, 220p. 8 leaves of plates. [C24].

AUSMUS -- Ausmus, Harry L. *Ausmus Family History, 1711-1962.* Johnson City, TN, Ausmus, 1963. xvi, 112p. [L632; D422].

AYERS -- White, Paul Richard. *Taproots, A Virginia and Carolina Legacy.* 2nd ed. Nashville, TN, P.R. White, c1986. xv, 860p. 1. Ayers family. 2. Blackwell family. 3. Virginia-Genealogy. DC lists under AYRES. [G26-2; DC143].

AYRES -- Ayres, Nellie F. *Ayres Kin and Kin to Kin*. Memphis, TN, Ayres, 1961. 416p. [D458].

AYRES -- White, Paul Richard. *Taproots, a Virginia and Carolina Legacy*. Nashville, TN, White, 1978. v. 320p. (p. 318-320 blank). [C26].

## B

BABB -- Tice, Mrs. Robert D. and Jessie Taylor Webb. *Benjamin Babb*. Memphis, TN, The Authors, 198?. 105p. [DC145].

BALL -- NAS. *The Ball Family*. Chattanooga, TN, 1917. 2p. (Notable Southern Families). Detached from the Lookout. [L800].

BAILEY -- Bailey, Thomas H. *Bailey - Britton History and Genealogy*. Kingsport, TN, Bailey, 1962. vi, 459p. [D501].

BAILEY -- Lambeth, Mary Weeks. *Memories and Records of Eastern North Carolina*. Nashville, TN, 1957. 252p. [L757].

BAIN -- Bain, Ethel M. *The Bain Family: Ancestors and Descendants of Peter Bain of Tennessee, 1775-1980*. San Angelo, TX, E.M. Bain, 1980. x, 320p. [C30].

BAIRD -- Catchings, Fermine Baird. *Baird and Beard Families: A Genealogical, Biographical, & Historical Collection of Data*. Nashville, TN, Baird-Ward, 1918. 230, 10p. D gives underscored part of title and 230p. [L781; D516].

BAKER -- Baker, Emerson R. *Nathan I. Baker, 1824-1911. Born and Married in Candor, Tioga Co., New York, came to Michigan in 1872 and went to Tennessee in 1907*. Matlacha, FL, E.R. Baker, 1987, c1988. 1. Baker family. 2. Baker, Nathan I., 1824-1911-Family. [G30-2].

BALTHROP -- Bumpus, Anne Shirley. *The Balthrop Family from Bute County & Warren County, North Carolina.* Columbia, TN, Bumpus, 1978. 48p. [D588].

BARGER -- NAS. *Arkansas Barger Family Tree (Time Scale Chart) Originating in Henry Barger - Matilda H. Mitchell in Tennessee and Searcy, Arkansas.* Assembled and Charted during 1958-59. Washington, DC, 1959. 1 v. (loose-leaf). [L994].

BARKLEY -- Fischer, K. B. *The Barkley Brigade: The Story of John Barkley of Smith County, Tenn., and His Descendants 1753-1994.* [NGN MAY/JUN 95].

BARNES -- La Forge, Robert M. *Family and Relatives of Robert M. La Forge.* Knoxville, TN, 1987. vi, 62 leaves. 1. La Forge family. 2. La Forge, Robert M. (Robert Mallory). 3. Barnes family. 4. New York-Genealogy. [G35-2].

BARNETT -- NAS. *The Barnetts of Smith County, Tennessee; Some Ancestors and Descendants.* Lubbock, TX, 1963. iii, 123 leaves. [L1057].

BARRETT -- Pyron, Ron. *John Clinton Barrett, Tennessee Settler in the Ozarks: Life and Times of John C. Barrett, His Family and Descendants with Notes and Excerpts of Findings on the Families of Wm. C. Baldwin and Thomas F. Allen.* Greenville, TN, R. Pyron, 1980. x, 127p. [C38].

BARRETT -- Pyron, Ron. *The Descendants of Thomas and Winnie Barrett. Compiled with Notes on the Origins of the Hawkins County, Tennessee Barretts, Newspaper Clippings, Selected Letters, Wills, Bible Records, and Complete Index.* Greenville, TN, R. Pyron, 1981. 55, 17 leaves. [C38].

BARTON -- Barton, William Baynard, Dr. and Mrs. *A Genealogical Study of the Descendants*

of Anthony Barton, the First American Barton
of This Record, An Emigrant from England to
America. Kingsport, TN, Collier's Print Co.,
1983. v. 216p. 12 folded leaves of plates.
Cover title: The Bartons of Carolina. Spine
Title: The Bartons of South Carolina. [C40].

BATCHELOR -- Williams, Lyle Keith. *The
Batchelor Family: Bachelor in Virginia,
Batchelor in North Carolina, Bachelor-
Batchelor in Tennessee, Missouri and Texas,
Batchler in Texas, and Bachlor in Oklahoma and
California.* Fort Worth, TX, L.K. Williams,
c1991. vi, 345p.
LC CALL NUMBER: CS71.B366 1991

BATES -- Bates, James E. and Frances A.
*Census History of the 7 Bates Brothers, of
Hickman Co., Tennessee and Some of their
Descendants.* Greenbelt, MD, J.E. Bates,
c1990. 42p. 1. Bates family. 2. Tennessee-
Genealogy. [G39-2].

BATES -- Brown Harvey, Sr...et al. *South
Side Cousins, Batson Connection.* Clarksville,
TN, Hinton Haven Farm, 1988. iv, 873p. 1.
Bates family. 2. Tennessee-Genealogy. [G39-3].

BATTEY -- Battey, George Magruder, III.
*Batteys of England or Wales, Rhode Island and
Georgia. Bealls of Scotland and Maryland.
Carrs of England and Rhode Island. Deitrich
(Deaderichs) of Germany, Virginia and
Tennesse. Magruders of Scotland, Maryland and
Georgia. Nixons of Delaware, VanDykes of
Holland, Delaware and Tennessee. (Descent of
Francis Stewart Battey of Albany, Georgia).*
Washington, DC, 1940. 1p., 8 leaves.
[L1187; VV13].

BAUGH -- NAS. *Personal Genealogy, Containing
Data on Baugh, Blair, Crawford, Hammer,
Mitchell, Simpson.* Abingdon, [VA?], n.d. pni.
[VV13].

BAUGH -- Baugh, Minnie L. *Ancestors of Minnie
L. Baugh, including the Hammer, Crawford,*

McMahon, and Simpson Families of Tennessee and Virginia. Abingdon, [VA?] 1910. pni. [VV13].

BAUGHMAN -- Baughman, J. Ross. Harvest Time: Being Several Essays On The History of The Swiss, German & Dutch Folk in Early America named Baughman, Layman, Moyer, Huff, and Others Across New York, Pennsylvania, Virginia, Tennessee, Missouri, Arkansas, and Four Centuries. Edinburg, Va, Shenandoah History, c1994. 312 p.
    LC CALL NUMBER: CS71.B788 1994

BEAL -- Bales, Clarence A. Bales Family in East Tennessee. Jefferson City, TN, 1952. Various pagings. 70 leaves. [X66-FW].

BEAN -- Grady, Jamie Vineyard (Ault). William Bean, Pioneer of Tennessee and His Descendants. Knoxville, TN, 1973. 350p. [NG20; D835].

BEASLEY -- Sims, Hattie Schakelford. The Silas Mercer Beasley, Jr. Story. A Brief Family History, 1752-1978. Loretta, TN, Sims, 1978. 115 p. in various pagings. 9 leafs of plates. [C45].

BEATTY -- Beatty, Troy. Beatty, A Family History. Memphis, TN, 1952. 375p. Contributing families: Troy, Pearson, Mumford, etc. [X68-FW].

BEAUDOIN -- Beaudoin, Kenneth L. The Family of Napoleon Beaudoin I of Cadillac, Michigan, with a Brief Account of the Beaudoin Family on the North American Continent Since 1667... Memphis, TN, Priv. Print., 1949. 1 Pamphlet. [X69-FW,NY,SL].

BECKHAM -- Beckham, James Madison. Genealogy of the Beckham Family in Virginia and the Branches thereof in Kentucky, Tennessee, Pennsylvania and West Virginia with Family Sketches. Richmond, VA, Presses O. E. Flanhart Printing Company, 1910. 80p. [L1318; D870; VV14; VP16].

BEDWELL. -- King, Larry. *A Bedwell Family:* *Robert Bedwell Sr., Fourteen Generations of* *His Descendants from St. Giles Parish,* *Cripplegate, London, England in 1637 to All* *the Fifty United States of America and Many* *Foreign Countries in 1992.* Hendersonville, TN, L. King, 1982. vi, 377p. DC gives underscored part of title. [C47; DC250].

BEEMAN -- Beeman, Ray. *The Beeman, Beaman,* *Beemon Family of North Carolina and* *Mississippi. Especially the Ivy Beeman Line.* Memphis, TN, Beeman, Searcy, AK, Browning, 1977, 62 leaves. [D891].

BELL. -- Lewis, Leroy Carlisle. *Leander Bell* *of Henderson County, Tennessee: A Genealogical* *Survey and Historical Record of His Life, and* *the Lives of his Descendants and His* *Ancestors.* Searcy, AK, L.C. Lewis, 1990? 156p.
LC CALL NUMBER: CS71.B452 1990b.

BELL -- Pettem, Silvia. *The James Houston* *Bell Family: Past and Present.* Boulder, CO, H.J. Bell, Jr., c1985. v, 148p. 1. Bell family. 2. Bell, James Houston, 1844-1935. 3. Tennessee-Genealogy. [G46-3].

BELLAH -- Bellah, Lovick Pierce. *Register* *of the Bellah Family, Descendants of William* *Ballagh of Charles Town, S.C.* Nashville, TN, Bellah, 1945. 185p. [D931; X75-FW].

BENSON -- Benson, John T., Jr. *Bensons:* *Early Settlers from North Carolina to Middle* *Tennessee, 1796-1820: A Booking Showing the* *Ascendants and Descendants of John R. Benson,* *1796-1873, Nancy Wooten Benson, 1803-1872 -* *2nd rev. ed.* Gallatin, TN, J.T. Benson, Jr., 1980. 414p. DC gives underscored part of title. Cover title: Bensons, Middle Tennessee and the Carolinas. Spine Title: Bensons. [C54; DC280].

BERNARD -- Bernard, William Dallas, et al. *The John Bernard and Mary Abney Genealogy,*

*Fluvanna County, Virginia.* Lascassas, TN, Bernard, 1975. 261 leaves. [S211; D1000; VV15].

**BERNARD** -- Montoye, Betty A. *The Barnard Family, 1640-1976. Nantucket Island, Massachusetts to Carroll County, Indiana.* Knoxville, TN, Montoye, 1976. vii, 145p., 2 leaves of plates. [C56].

**BERRY** -- Berry, W. Ross. *"Our Berry Patch"; Some Descendants of Reddick Hunter Berry of Western Tennessee. Also Descendants of Robert A. Tucker, I, Asa D. Evans, and William B. Whitaker, etc.* Pontiac, MI, W.R. Berry, 1982. 535p. [C57; NG21].

**BERTRAM** -- Dalton, Myrtle B., Ed. *Bertram Book; A Picture Book... and Short Biographical Sketches of About 1300 Members of the Bertram Family in the Vicinity of Sunnybrook, KY.* Jonestown, TN, 1959. Pages unnumbered. [X83-FW].

**BEVELHEIMER** -- Bevelheimer, Edmond, Frederick. *From Whence We Came: The Descendants of Conrad Bevelheimer, 1764-1984.* Elmwood, TN, E.F> Bevelheimer, c1985. A-T, 152p, a-t p.126p. of plates. 1. Bevelheimer family. 2. Bevelheimer, Conrad-Family. 3. Pennsylvania-Genealogy. [G54-2].

**BEWLEY** -- Bewley, Shelby Jackson. *Bewley Roots in Tennessee.* Rineyville, KY, S.J. Bewley, 1985- v. <1 >. Contents: V. 1. Anthony Bewley. [C59].

**BILBREY** -- Eldridge, Charles S. *History, Tennessee, My People, and Me [Bilbrey Family].* [NGN19-3-93]

**BIBY** -- Hansen, Colleen Bibee. *Bibee Family Directory.* Salt Lake City, UT, Colleen Bibee Hansen, 1982. 64p. Published for the Biby Family Reunion, July 17, 1982, Knoxville, TN. [C60].

BIRD -- NAS. *The Byrd Family.* Chattanooga, TN, 1916. 3p. (Notable Southern Families). Detached from the Lookout. [L1617].

BISHOP -- Goggans, Helen Mitchell and Mavis P. Kelsey, R.. *The Mitchell Family of Tipton County, Tennessee: Their Antecedents in Southside Virginia, Including Jones and Bishop and Their Numerous Descendants.* Kingsland, AR, H.M. Goggans, c1990. x, 301p. 1. Mitchell family. 2. Jones family. 3. Bishop family. NGN gives underscored part of title. [G58-1; NGN17-6-91].

BLACK -- Black, Natalie K. *Pioneer Preacher: Descendants to 1980 of the Rev. Samuel Black (1700-1770) of Pennsylvania and Albermarle County, Virginia.* Madison, TN, N.K. Black, 1981. 346p. D gives underscored part of title. [C64; DS58].

BLACK -- West, North E. *William Black, Senior, Lineage Documents.* Compiled for Family History Students. Murfreesboro, TN, N.E. West, 1985. 205 leaves. [DC322].

BLACKBURN -- Challacombe, W. A. *The Benjamin Blackburn Family and Notes on Blackburns in America.* Maryville, TN, A.B. McSpadden, 1988. 120, 16p. 1. Blackburn family. 2. Blackbur, Benjamin, d. 1791- Family. [G59-2].

BLACKLEY -- Perry, Gregory M. *The Charles Blackley Family of Knox County, Tennessee.* Decorah, IA, Anundsen Pub. Co., 1991- v. <1- > [NGN18-6-92].
  LC CALL NUMBER: CS71.B64622 1991

BLACKWELL -- Blackwell, Nancy Neckers. *Ancestors, Descendants and Connections of Carle Gratz Blackwell and Goldie Blanche Hill; Virginia, North Carolina, Tennessee...* Zionsville, ?, Blackwell, 1985, 210p. [DC328].

BLACKWELL -- White, Paul Richard. [G60-1]. See above: AYERS. [G26-2].

**BLAIN** -- NAS. *The Blain Family of Albemarle County, Virginia and Tennessee.* Memphis, [TN], Tennessee, DAR, G.R.C. 1948. pni. [VV17].

**BLAIN** -- Hooker, Ruth N. *The Blain Family of Albemarle County, Virginia and Tennessee.* Memphis, [TN], 1948. 48, 1 leaves. D omits place of publication. [D1143; VV17].

**BLAIR** -- Charles R. *Some Descendants of John and Elizabeth ( Snider ) Blair of Miller's Cove, Blount County, Tennessee.* 1st ed. Knoxville, TN, C.R. Blair, 1990. 49p. 'Including a chapter on the brothers and sisters of John Blair, a compolation of census data related to the Blair's of Blount County, and an overview of some of the early Blair families of East Tennessee and southwestern Virginia.' 1. Blair family. 2. Blair, John, ca.1770 - ca.1850-Family. 3. Tennessee-Genealogy. [G60-2].

**BLAIR** -- Webb, Margaret Vance. *John Blair "The Miller" of Washington County, Tennessee.* Knoxville, TN, Tennessee Valley Pub., 1993. ix, 163 p. 93-60703:
   LC CALL NUMBER: CS71.B645 1993

**BLAND** -- Gottschalk, Katherine Cox. *Bland Family of Pitt County, North Carolina and of Shelby County, Tennessee.* NP, 1940. 52 leaves. [D1185].

**BLEVINS** -- Blevins, Laccie W. & Ray E. *Jonathan Blevins, Sr. of Virginia and His Descendants.* Powell, TN, L.W. Blevins, 1982. xii, 177p. [C67].

**BLEVINS** -- Privett, Harriett Kinnaird. *Glimpses of the Blevins Family ( Virginia - Tennessee - Alabama ).* NP, 1964, ca.285 leaves. [D1203; VV18].

**BOLEN** -- Nelson, Virginia Knight. *Rhea County Relatives: A History of the Bolen, Fisher, Goad, Jewell, Knight, Purser, Ryan,* and *Spence Families.* Knoxville, TN, V.K. Nelson, 1982. x, 158p. [C71].

BOLIN -- Boling, Marion. *Genealogy of the Boling Family of Sullivan County, Tennessee and Washington County, Virginia.* NP, 1982. pni. [VV19].

BOLRON -- Bowron, William M. *Historical Fragments Pertaining to the Cotherstone Branch of the Bolron Family.* Chattanooga, TN, 1891. 13, 3p. (X117-FW lists as BOWRON.) [X104-FW].

BOLTON -- Bolten, Charles Knowles. *The Chief Slave-Dealing Family of the Old South, the Boltens of Tennessee.* NP, 1937. pni. Collection of type-written and manuscript material, including wills, deeds, correspondence, and mounted photographs. [L1843].

BONDURANT -- Maxson, Margaret Evelyn Nelms. *Robert M. Bondurant.* Nashville, TN, Maxson, 1978. v, 340p. [D1291].

BONEY -- Bell, Emily Boney. *Boney Family.* Gatlinburg, TN, Bell; Bell, 1971. 12, 6 leaves. [D1295].

BONNER -- Bonner, Kathryn R. *The Bonner Family Records.* Marianna, AK, K.R. Bonner, 1979. 100p. This record is primarily of the Bonners of Surry and Sussex Counties, Virginia. Those that went to Wilson, Madison, and Shelby Counties, Tenn.; and those that went on to Phillips Co., Arkansas. [DC369].

BOONE -- Baer, Mabel Van Dyke. *Boone, Christian and Moore Families, Carroll and Madison Counties, Tennessee.* NP, 1959. 9, 11, 7, 7 leaves. [D1318].

BOONE -- Boone, Pat. *Together: 25 Years with the Boone Family.* Nashville, TN, T. Nelson, c1979. 128p. Summary: The well-known singer describes his career and family life from the

early days to the present. 1. Boone, Pat. 2.
Singers-United States-Biography. 3. Boone
family. 4. Christian biography.
[G69-1; C74].

BOONE -- Mayfield, R. N. ... *Boone Notes;
Family Records of Some of the Ancestors,
Descendants and Kindred of Col. Daniel Boone.*
Johnson City, TN, Mayfield, 1931-33. 27
leaves. [X108-NY].

BOONE -- Mayfield, R. N. *Boone Family
History and Boone Notes.* Johnson City, TN,
Mayfield, 1945. 10, 66, 5 leaves. X gives
underscored part of title and 66, 6 leaves.
[D1324; X109-SL].

BOOTH -- Booth, Robert Williams. *Samuel
Spurlock Booth (ca. 1854-1934) Who Married
Emily Wallman in 1873 and Descendants.*
Nashville, TN, Randell House Pubs., R.W.
Booth, 1981. 249p. [C74].

BORDOIN -- Beaudoin, Kenneth Lawrence. *The
Family of Napoleon Beaudoin I$^{er}$ of Cadillac,
Michigan; With a Brief Account of the Beaudoin
Family on the North American Continent Since
1667; 292 Years of Continued Residence.*
Memphis, TN, Priv. Print., 1949. 12, 6
leaves. X lists as BEAUDOIN & pagination as:
"1 Pamphlet". [L1992; X69-FW,NY,SL].

BORROWS -- Matthews, Wilbur L. *Borrows
Genealogy from North Carolina and Bedford
County, Tennessee, to Greene County, Missouri.*
Severn, MD, W.L. Matthews, 1979. 12 l. [C76].

BOTTOMS -- Burdick, Nancilu B. *Legacy: The
Story of Talula Gilbert Bottoms and Her
Quilts.* Nashville, TN, Rutledge Hill, c1988,
175p. 1. Bottoms, Talula Gilbert, 1862-1946.
2. Bottom Family. 3. Quiltmakers-Southern
States-Biography. 4. Quilts-Southern States-
History-20th Century. [G73-1].

BOURNE -- Katz, Gertrude P. *Old Letters, Old
Biographies, and Old Family Trees of the*

Bourne, Carr, Darden and Allied Families of
Virginia, Tennessee, and Other States. Valley
Stream, NY, 1973-74. 1 vol unpaged.
[X114-NY; VV21].

BOWEN — Fletcher, Virginia Billingsley.
Time and Tide: A Francisco Family History:
The Ancestors and Descendants of Christopher
Francisco and Halana Bower of Southwest
Virginia and Claiborne County, Tennessee.
Fort Lauderdale, FL, V.B. Fletcher, c1989.
xvii, 418p. 1. Francisco family. 2. Bower
family. 3. Francisco, Christopher, 1804-1884-
Family. 4. Bowen, Halana, 1818-1884-Family.
5. Virginia-Genealogy. 6. Tennessee-
Genealogy. [G77-1].

BOWEN — Grady, Jamie Ault. Bowens of
Virginia and Tennessee; Descendants of John
Bowen and Lilly McIlhaney. Knoxville, TN,
Grady, 1969. A leaves, viii, 178p. D omits
underscored part of title.
[L2017; NG23; D1395; VV21].

BOWEN — Grady, Jamie Ault. Bowens of
Virginia and Tennessee. Knoxville, TN, 1969-
76. 2 Vols. Fort Wayne Library has 30p.
supplement. [XFW,NY].

BOWEN — White, Mary Coghlan. In the Sweet
By and By: Stories and Records of Families
West, Bowen... Nashville, TN, Cokesbury,
c1987. 286p. [DC396].

BOWEN — See below: CAMPBELL. [L2939; D2108].

BOWMAN — Bowman, Roy L. The Bowman and
Related Families of Claiborn County,
Tennessee. Revised Edition. Clinton, TN,
R.L. Bowman, c1986. 414p. [DC401].

BOX — NAS. Box Book with McElroy and Floyd;
The Box Families of South Carolina and
Tennessee... and Other Parts of the
Southeastern, U.S.A., Including... Kin of
James Box, b. 1799, d. 1877. Bragg City, MO.,
1975. 241p. [X117-FW,SL].

**BOYD** -- Lambeth, Mary Weeks. [L2070]. See above: BAILEY: [L757].

**BOYT** -- Boyt, E. Blance. *Boyt Family.* Memphis, TN, The Family, 1915. 150p. [X119-FW].

**BRABSON** -- Brabson, Estalena Rogers. *John Brabson I, Patriot of the American Revolution.* Seymour, TN, Tri-County News, 1975. 137p. [D1462].

**BRACKIN** -- Brackin, Henry B. *The Brackin Family in the Southeastern United States.* Nashville, TN, Henry B. Brackin, 1979. [D1468; DS74].

**BRADEN** -- Braden, Harold J. *Bradens of Virginia, Tennessee, Utica, Missouri.* Lee's Summit, MO, H.J. Braden, 1988. x, 102p. 1. Braden family. 2. Campbell family. 3. Nelson family. [G81-1].

**BRADFORD** -- French, Marline R. *The Bradford and Kirkpatrick Ancestry of Virginia, Tennessee and Texas, and Some of Their Descendants.* NP, 1959, 27 leaves. [D1475; VV22].

**BRADFORD** -- Lorenzen, A. W. *An American Tree: Its Roots and Branches.* Nashville, TN, A.W. Lorenzen, 1979. 33 l. Photocopy. [DC418].

**BRADFORD** -- Saunders, Sara Bradford. *Salt of the Earth.* Madison, TN, S.B. Saunders, 1987. 181p. 1. Bradford family. 2. Weakley family. [G81-2].

**BRADLEY** -- Hankins, Edith Jackson. *Will and Edna Bradley.* Memphis, TN, E.J. Hankins, 1985. 26 leaves, 1 leaf of plates. 1. Bradley family. 2. Bradley, William Joshua, 1884-1967-Family. [G81-3].

**BREIT** -- Anderson, Beverly Bright Davis. *Breit / Bright - Seifert Genealogy: A Record*

of the Families of Adam Breit and Henry
Seifert, Who Came to America from Germany,
Adam in 1848, Henry about 1830.  Oak Ridge,
TN, B.B.D. Anderson, 1984.  389p.  [DC446].

BREWER   --   Brewer, Warren H.  *History of
Brewer Family of North Carolina, Tennessee,
Indiana, and Illinois*, and McKnight, Galyean
( Gallion ) Barr, Hutton, Bloxom, Lamb, Lewis,
and Related Families, also Woodworth, Newkirk,
Crossland, Finley, Hatch, Hubbard and Carter.
Terre Haute, IN, Brewer, 1935.  50p., 70 numb.
leaves.    D gives 69 l. and title as
underscored.  [L2244; D1564].

BREWER   ---   McConnell, Grace Conn.  *The
History of James S. Brewer and Nancy Elizabeth
Steele Brewer*.  Nashville, TN, G.C. McConnell,
1983.  iii, 36 l.  [C86].

BREWER   --   McConnell, Grace Conn.  *The Conn -
Rigsby and Brewer - Steele Families*.
Nashville, TN, Insty-Prints, 1988.  vi, 172p.
1. Conn family.  2. Rigby family.  3. Brewer
family.  [G87-3].

BREWSTER   --   NAS.  *William B. Brewster:
Virginia - Tennessee, 1793-1853 (Notes,
comments, observations)*.  Provo, UT, 1966.
124p.  [X126-FW; VV23].

BRIGANCE   --   Brigance, Albert H.  *Brigance
Genealogy*.    Maryville,  TN,   Brigance
Enterprises, 1982.  ii, 169p.  [C87].

BRIGHT   ---   Anderson, Beverly Bright Davis.
*Breit - Bright -- Seifert Genealogy:    A
Record of the Families of Adam Breit and Henry
Seifert, Who Came to America from Germany,
Adam in 1848, Henry about 1830*.  Oak Ridge,
TN, B.B.D. Anderson, 1984.  iii leaves, 398p.
[C87].

BRITTON   --   Jobe, Sybil Shipley.  *From Out Of
the Past Rode All of These Britons:    A
Genealogical History of the William Britton,
Sr. Family of Green County, TN*.  Neosho, MO,

S.S. Jobe, 1986. v, 131p. 15p. of plates.
1. Britton family. 2. Britton, William, d.
1840 or 1. 3. Tennessee Genealogy. [G89-3].

BROCK -- Brock, E. Ralph, Jr. *Brock: An Oral Family History.* United States. E.R. Brock, c1989. iv, 125p. 1. Brock family. 2. Tennessee-Biography. 3. Oral Biography. [G90-1].

BRODERS -- Broders, Martin A. & Robert J. *The Ancestry of Broder Christian Broders(en) of North Friesland and New York.* 1st ed. Knoxville, TN, M.A. Broders, Spring Valley, NY, R.J. Broders, 1987. 316 leaves. DC gives 316p. 1. Broders family. 2. Broders, Christian, 1843-1886-Family. 3. Denmark-Genealogy. [G90-2; DC467].

BROOKS -- NAS. *The Brooks Family.* Chattanooga, TN, 1916. 3p. (Notable Southern Families). Detached from the Lookout of February 3, 1917. [L2379].

BROOKS -- Edwards Bruce Montgomery. *The Brooks of Virginia.* Baltimore, MD, Gateway Press, Knoxville, TN, Montgomery Pub. Co., 1985. v, 342p. [C89].

BROWN -- NAS. *Brown and Related Families Records, Tennessee, North Carolina, South Carolina, Maryland.* NP, 1975. 40 leaves. [X137-LA].

BROWN -- Brown, Charles Sidney. *Our Family, The Descendants of Leonard Brown with Collateral Lines.* Nashville, TN, C.S. Brown, 1984. xx, 465p. [C91].

BROWN -- Fort, John. *Make Way for the Great.* Nashville, TN, Benson Printing Co., 1950. ix, 174p. [D1713].

BROWN -- Henderson, Rebecca Ann Davis. *Walter Walker Brown, Sr. of Virginia and Tennessee: With Allied Families Breece, DePriest, Hensley, Johnson.* Madison, AL,

R.D. Henderson, 1994. ix, 537 p.
LC CALL NUMBER: CS71.B38 1994b.

BROWN -- Johnson, Lillian Vesta Brown. *My Findings*. Smyrna, TN, L.B. Johnson, 1987-
v. <1 >. Contents: v. 1. Brown, Gunn, Harris, Rowland, Windrow, and others. 1. Brown family. 2. Gunn family. 3. Harris family. 4. Rowland family. 5. Tennessee-Genealogy. [G99-3].

BROWN -- Brown-Johnson, Lillian Vesta. *My Findings*. Smyrna, TN, L.B. Johnson, 1987-1991. 2 v.
LC CALL NUMBER: CS71.B88 1987

BROYLES -- Broyles, John Kenneth. *The Broyles Family Ties: Including Fisher, Jones, Rockwood, Corey, Richmond, Chamberlain, Edson, Hathaway, Newton, etc*. Rockwood, TN, Broyles, 1969. ?? v. DAR has vol. 1. [L2511; D1765].

BROYLES -- Broyles, John Kenneth. *The Broyles Family Ties*. Rockwood, TN, Broyles, 1969-78. 8 Vols. [X138-FW].

BRYAN -- Freeman, Julie. *A Heritage of Faith*. Memphis, TN, J. Freeman, 1985. 115p. [DC504].

BRYDEN -- Hudlow, James H. *Bryden Family History*. Chattanooga, TN, J.H. Hudlow, 1985. 63p. [DC508].

BRYDEN -- Hudlow, James H. *Bryden Family of Canada and the United States*. Chattanooga, TN, J.H. Hudlow, 1985. xi, 46p., 1 leaf of plates. 1. Bryden family. 2. Hudlow family. 3. Canada-Genealogy. [G103-2; C96].

BRYDEN -- Hudlow, James H. *The Bryden - Chase Connection*. Chattanooga, TN, J.H. Hudlow, 1987. 10, 18p. 1. Bryden family. 2. Chase family. [G103-2].

BRYDEN -- Hudlow, James H. *The Bryden - Chase Connection*. Chattanooga, TN, J.H. Hudlow, 1989. 18p. [DC509].

BUCHMAN -- Buchman, Calvin. *Buchman =
[ Bukham [romanized form]]; [Translated to the
Russian by Irene Zepelinsky].* Nashville, TN,
Buchman, 1977, iii, 175 [i.e. 209] leaves, 12
leaves of plates. [C97].

BUCKLEY -- Buckley, Shirley Gray. *The
Buckley Family Genealogy: A Genealogical
History of the Descendants of James Buckley.*
Bradford, TN, S.G. Buckley, 1987. iii, 232p.
1. Buckley family. 2. Buckley, James, ca.
1722-1787-Family. [G104-3; DC512].

BULLARD -- Kistler, Harletta Bullard.
*Bullard, Seven Generations ca. 1730-1987:
Tennessee, Missouri, and Texas.* West Chester,
?, H.B. Kistler, iii, 63p. [DC524].

BULLARD -- Krechniak, Helen Bullard. *A
Bullard Family: Including Fisher, Pond, Jones,
Rockwood, Corey, Richmond, Chamberlain, Edson,
Hathaway, Newton, etc.* Ozone, TN, Krechniak,
1966. 74, 4 leaves. D gives underscore part
of title. [L2632; D1843].

BUMPASS -- Bumpus, Anne Shirley. *The
Bumpass Family from Person County, North
Carolina.* Columbia, TN, Bumpus, Durham, NC,
Townsend, 1972. 157p. [D1857; X145-FW,IG,SL].

BURDEN -- Bowden, Martha Burden. *Mountain
of Dreams.* - 1st ed. - Sevierville, TN,
Nandel Pub. Co., c1988. 285p. 1. Burden
family. 2. Bowden, Martha Burden-Family. 3.
Sevier County (Tenn.) - Biography. [G106-3].

BURGER -- Burger, Eva Smith. *The Burger
Branch: A Genealogy of the Burger Family from
the Arrival of the Immigrant in Pennsylvania,
to the Shenandoah Valley of Virginia, to the
Eastanallee Valley of East Tennessee, and
Beyond.* Huntsville, AL, E.S. Burger, 1990.
iv, 217 p.
    LC CALL NUMBER: CS71.B9545 1990

BURNETT -- Burnete, Earl E. *Burnett -
Parsons Ancestral Line with Some Collateral*

Branches; Also... Newspaper Clippings,
Abstracts of Wills and Deeds in Virginia and
Tenn. Data on Kindred Families of Atchley,
Baker, Cameron, Clark, Evans, Franklin, and
Others. Sebastopol, CA 1964. 1 Vol.
[X149-FW,SL].

BURRESS -- Burress, Charles G. and Pamela
(Anderson) Jenson. The Family of William
Burress (ca. 1799-1850) of Tennessee. NP,
1971. 27 leaves. [NG26].

BYRD -- Skeen, A. T. Coveys of Birds.
Troutman, NC, A.T. Skeen, 1989. xiv, 447p.
1. Byrd family. 2. Tennessee Genealogy.
[G113-1].


# C


CAIN -- Cain, Fayette B. Caney Fork Kin.
Holladay, TN, Cain, 1981. 218p. [DS100].

CAIN -- Cain, Stith Malone. A History of our
Cain Family of Virginia, Alabama and
Tennessee. Whitewater, WI, 1970. 78 leaves.
[D2033; VV30].

CALLAWAY -- Carpenter, Sarah Mercer. The
Callaway Family. NP, n.d. 28 leaves. Copy
of reprint from Missouri historical society
collections, Vol. V, No., 1, 1927. [D2064].

CALLAWAY -- Hoffmeyer, Bessie Dee
(Callaway). The Callaway Clan. Collegedale,
TN, Priv. Print by College Press, 1948. 93p.
[L2890].

CALDWELL -- Faler, June. Caldwell Family
Newsletter for the Descendants of Andrew and
Martha Caldwell of Lancaster County, PA,
Descendants to North Carolina and Tennessee.
Fairhope, AL, Caldwell Family Committee of the
Caldwell Family Association, 1990. 169 p.
91-180863
  LC CALL NUMBER: CS71.C14 1990

CAMPBELL -- NAS. *Campbell Family of Knox County, Tennessee.* NP, 1947. 52 l. [D2116].

CAMPBELL -- Battey, George Magruder III. *The Campbell's of Virginia and E. Tennessee, with Special Reference to One of the Several David Campbell's of Revolutionary Days.* By the great-grandson of Judge David Campbell (1750-1812), of Washington, Rhea Co., Tenn. Washington, DC, 1940. 6 numb. leaves. [L2956; VV31].

CAMPBELL -- Braden, Harold J. [G117-1]. See above: BRADEN. [G81-1].

CAMPBELL -- Campbell, John F. *The Campbells of Drumaboden, on the River Lyennon, Near Rothmelon, County Donegal, North of Ireland.* Nashville, TN, Foster & Parkes, c1925. 147p. [L2947].

CAMPBELL -- Fassnacht, Grace Spencer. *Campbell Kith and Kin: Descendants of Archibald Campbell and Elizabeth Baker, Who Came from Campbell County, Virginia to Knox County, Tennessee, 1796.* Chattanooga, TN, G.S. Fassnacht, between 1983 and 1987. ii, 185p. 1. Campbell family. 2. Campbell, Archibald, ca. 1730-ca.1802-Family. [G118-1].

CAMPBELL -- Petty, Gerald M. *Index to Historical Sketches of the Campbell, Pilcher and Kindred Families.* Nashville, TN, 1911. Index by Gerald M. Petty, 1962. pni. [X167-LI].

CAMPBELL -- Pilcher, Margaret Campbell. *Historical Sketches of the Campbell, Pilcher, and Kindred Families,* Including the Bowen, Russell, Owen, Grant, Goodwin, Amis, Carothers, Hope, Taliaferro, and Powell Families. Nashville, TN, Marshall & Bruce Co., c1911. 444p. D gives underscored part of title. [L2939; D2108].

CAMPBELL -- Robertson, Robert Crawford. *Pioneer Families of Randolph and Perry*

Counties, Illinois; Notes on the Campbell, Crozier, Flack, Milligan, Steel, and Thompson Families; The Crawfords of Ballynease, Londonderry, Ireland with Descendants in the U.S.A. and Their Descendants in the Elsey, Garven, Matthews, and Robertson Families. Chattanooga, TN, 1960. 67p. [A113].

CANNON -- Fincannon, Al G. Fincannons, Cannons, Voncannons, Vuncannons, and Related Families. Chattanooga, TN, 1990. viii, 579p. 1. Fincannon family. 2. Cannon family. 3. Vuncannon family. [G118-3].

CANNON -- Stephens, Nadine Heatherly. Our Norris Lake Area Ancestry: _Heatherleys and Related Families_: Cannon, Childress, Craig, Ford, Hicks, Jackson, Reynolds, Spangler, Wilson and Others. DC gives title as underscored and lists under HEATHERLEY. Jacksboro, TN, Action Print., 1988. 250p. 1. Heatherley family. 2. Cannon family. 3. Childress family. 4. Tennessee-Genealogy. [G119-1; [DC1710].

CANTRELL -- Whitley, Edythe Rucker. Cantrell - Potter - Magness; Ancestry of Alvin Edward Potter, Sr. Nashville, TN, Whitley, 1938. 86, 14 leaves. [D2133].

CARDEN -- Katz, Gertrude Price (Mrs. Alexander Katz). Bible Records of Allen Dickinson Carden, B. 1792, D. 1859, and His Wife, Maria H. Hyde, B. 1807, D. 1858 and Their Descendants; Allied Families of Tennessee: Park, Bosler, Black, Seaton, Bowling, Lucas, Whitmore, and Others. NP, 1973. 16 leaves. [S413].

CARMACK -- NAS. Carmack Cousins Newsletter. Chattanooga, TN, The Cousins, 1984- . --v. See shelflist for DAR Library Holdings. [DC604].

CARPENTER -- Ross, Mattie B. Some Descendants of Edward Garrett, Thomas Johnson, Stephen Young, and Related Families: Solomon

*Barfield, Thomas Hamlin, Henry Rampy, N. G. Ross.* Cleveland, TN, 1974. 89p. [X167-FW].

CARPENTER -- Ross, Mattie Belle Carpenter. *My Ancestry: Some Ancestors of William and Elizabeth Arnold Carpenter... and Related Families.* Cleveland, TN, M.B.C. Ross, 1987. 113p. [DC611].

CARROLL -- NAS. *The Carroll Family.* Chattanooga, TN, 1917. 3p. (Notable Southern Families). Detached from Lookout. [L3069].

CARTER -- Bragg, Emma W. *Scrapbook: Some Reminiscences of a Native Nashville Septuagenarian.* Nashville, TN, E.W. Bragg, 1985. iv, 32p. 1. Afro-Americans-Tennessee-Nashville-Genealogy. 2. Afro-Americans-Tennessee-Nashville-Biography. 3. Nashville (Tenn.)-Genealogy. 4. Nashville (Tenn.)-Biography. 5. Richardson family. 6. White family. 7. Carter family. 8. Bragg, Emma W., 1911-     -Family. [G124-2; C581].

CARTER -- Brooks, Sylvia Layton. *Abraham Carter of Greene County, Tennessee: His Kith and Kin and the Collateral Lines of the Author.* Knoxville, TN, Tennessee Valley Pub., 1994. i, 352 p. 94-78235.
LC CALL NUMBER: CS71.C323  1994

CARTER -- Carter, David Wendel. <u>Notable Southern Families, Carter of Tennessee</u>, Including the Taylors; Descendants of Colonel John Carter of Tennessee. Chattanooga, TN, Pamphlet ed., The Lookout Publishing Co., c1927. 31p. DC gives underscored part of title. [L3098; D2204; DC623].

CARTER -- Carter, John Denton. <u>The Carters of Greene County, Tennessee:</u> An Early American Frontier Family. Biloxi, MS, Carter, 1981. 53 leaves. v. <1  > Contents: Pt. 1. From New Jersey to Tennessee. D gives underscored part of title. [C117; D2209].

CARTRIGHT -- Robinson, Amy Cartright. *The Descendants of William and Elizabeth (Shipley) Cartright of Sullivan County, Tennessee.* St. Petersburg, FL, A.C. Robinson, 1987. ca. 800p. Limited ed. of 100 copies. 1. Cartwright family. 2. Cartright, William, 1807-1876-Family. 3. Tennessee-Genealogy. [G126-1].

CATE -- Dawson, Amelia (Cate). *Our East Tennessee Kinsmen: Cate, Henry, and Related Families.* Seaford, DE. 1962. 69, 90p. [L3174; S453].
--- *Index.* d'Arand, Virginia, et al. Knoxville, TN, Tennessee Soc. of the Revolution, 1970. 24, 49p. [S453].

CATE -- Manly, Elizabeth Cate. *The Cates of Lower East Tennessee and Related Families.* Cleveland, TN, Manley, 1971. 71, 5 leaves. [D2264].

CAVE -- De View, Donna Harper. *Benjamin Cave, 1760-1842.* Knoxville, TN, 1960. 8 leaves. "Written to Supplement A Cave Genealogy Compiled and Privately Printed... in 1949 by Byron L. Cave of Lancaster, Ohio. Genealogy of the Cave family." [L3185; NG29].

CECIL -- Jourdan, Elise Greenup. *Greenup, Witten, Cecil.* Baltimore, MD, Gateway Press, Knoxville, TN: Orders to E.G. Jourdan, 1989. xvi, 336p. 1. Greenup family. 2. Witten family. 3. Cecil family. [G129-1].

CHAFFIN -- Peterson, Olive Chaffin. *Abner Chaffin of Jackson County, Tennessee and Sons Bailaam, Elias, Joseph, William.* An Account of Their Emigrations to Missouri, Illinois, and Montan. *Related Families:* Albert, Fox, Van Oss, Vaughn, Wilkerson, Young. NP, Peterson, 1966. v, 90p. D gives underscored part of title. L gives compilers as "Albert, Carl Bert (and others)"; shows Provo, Utah as place of publication and indicates Olive Chaffin Peterson signed the Preface. [L3219; D2298].

CHAMBERS -- Horlacher, Gary T. *Chambers and Moad Families*. Orem, UT, Horlacher, 1987. vi, 110p. 1. Chambers family. 2. Moad family. 3. North Carolina-Genealogy. 4. Tennessee-Genealogy. 5. Missouri-Genealogy. [G131-2].

CHANCE -- Chance, Hilda. *Chance of Ohio, Virginia, North Carolina, Georgia, Texas, Tennessee, Kentucky, Delaware, Maryland, Pennsylvania, Michigan, California, Indiana, New Jersey*. Liberty, PA, 1970. 19 leaves. [A122; VV36].

CHANCE -- Chance, Hilda. *Supplement to Chance of Ohio, Virginia, North Carolina, Georgia, Texas, Tennessee, Kentucky, Delaware, Maryland, Pennsylvania, Michigan, California, Indiana, New Jersey*. Liberty, PA, 1970. 19 leaves. [A122; VV36].

CHANDLER -- Chandler, Melvin Leon. *The William Chandler Descendants and Related Neighbors: the Coopers, the Pinkertons, and Cothams*. Rockwood, TN, M.L. Chandler, c1990. xv, 1038p. 1. Chandler family. 2. Chandler, William, ca. 1770-1845 or 6-Family. 3. Cooper family. 4. Pinkerton family. 5. Cotham family. 6. Tennessee-Genealogy. [G132-1].

CHASE -- Hudlow, James H. [G]. See above: BRYDEN. [G103-2].

CHILDRESS -- Stephens, Nadine Heatherly. [G136-1]. See above: CANNON. [G119-1].

CHITWOOD -- Chitwood, I. O. *Descendants of Matthias Chitwood*. Winfield, TN, H. Chitwood in cooperation with R. Chitwood, c1986. xii, 554p. 1. Chitwood family. 2. Chitwood, Mathias, 1681-1754-Family. [G136-3].

CHITWOOD -- Pope, Margaret C. *The Family of Squire and Mary Wray Chitwood*. Memphis, TN, Towers Press, 1983. viii, 246p. [C128].

CHOATE -- Williams, Irene Choate. *Choates of the South: Descendants of Christopher Choate of Maryland* Wartrace, TN, I.C. Williams, v.<1 >. [G136-3].

CHRISTIAN -- Bailey, Thomas B. *Christian - Skelton History and Genealogy.* Kingsport, TN, 1964. 297p. [X186-FW.SU].

CHRISTIAN -- Christian, H.C. *Record of the Families of Gilbert Christian and Moses Fisk.* Chattanooga, TN, 1969. 59p. [L3420].

CLABAUGH -- Harrell, Elizabeth J. *The Clabaughs: An Account of the Life and Times of Frederick Clabaugh of Maryland in 1742 and His Descendants Who Migrate to East Tennessee and Then On To Alabama and Texas: With a Special Chapter on Henry Haggard, 1746-1842, a Frontier Baptist Preacher of Virginia, East Tennessee and Alabama, and His Family.* Los Altos, CA, B. Harrell, c1982. v, 174p. 1. Clabaugh-family. 2. Clabaugh, Frederick, d. 1780 or 1-Family. 3. Haggart-Family. 4. Haggard, Henry, 1746-1842-Family. [G140-2].

CLAYBROOK -- Smith, Jonathan Kennon. *Our Claybrook Heritage (Madison County, Tennessee).* Jackson, TN, J.K.T. Smith, c1993. i, 64 leaves.
    LC CALL NUMBER: F444.C63 S65 1993

CLAGHORN -- Josserand, Gertrude Gleghorn (Mrs. Guy D.) *Robert Cleghorn His Descendants and Allied Families.* Memphis, TN, G.C. Josserant, 1980. v, 479p. 1. Claghorn family. 2. Cleghorn, Robert, b. ca. 1760-Family. [G140-3].

CLAIBORNE -- Bissell, Lolita Hannah. *Cliborn - Claiborne Records.* Nashville, TN, L.F. Bissell. 1986. 370p. [NG30; DC715].

CLARK -- NAS. *Because They Endured: A History of the Clark and Sanders Ancestors of Rutherford and Wilson Counties, TN. - 1st ed. -*

San Jose, CA, Gentrace Associates, c1986. 13, ii, 413p. 1. Clark family. 2. Saunders family. 3. Rutherford County (Tenn.)-Genealogy. 4. Wilson County (Tenn.)-Genealogy. 5. Afro-Americans-Genealogy. [G141-2].

CLARK -- Clark, Barbara Elaine. *Search for Myself: One Woman's Heritage.* McKenzie, TN, B.E. Clark, 1984. 92, xvii p., 24p. of plates. [C133].

CLARK -- Nagy, J. Emerick. *A Family Record of William Martin Clark (1826-1895) and Mary Elizabeth Blackman (1831-1875).* Nashville, TN, Nagy, 1960. 30 leaves. [D2499].

CLARK -- Shannon, Betty Biggers. *Our Clark Legacy.* Austin, TX, B.B. Shannon, c1990. 145p. Limited ed. of 50 copies. 1. Clark family. 2. Tennessee-Genealogy. [G142-2].

CLAUS -- Franklin, Della P. *A Book of Remembrance of the Clouse Family: Descendants of George Clouse I.* Cookeville, TN, P.C. Franklin, c1982. vi, 567, 136p. 1. Claus family. C gives: Prietta Clause Franklin as editor/compiler. [G142-3; C135].

CLAWSON -- Clawson, Virginia. *The Family Symphony.* Nashville, TN, Broadman Press, c1984. 160p. 1. Clawson family. 2. Clawson, Cynthia. 3. Christian biography-United States. 4. Church music-United States. 5. Gospel music-History and criticism. [G143-1].

CLAYTON -- Clayton, Claud Franklin. *Family Notes and Recollections.* Knoxville, TN, Clayton, 1959. vi, 1075 or 6p. [L3560; D2541].

CLAYTON -- James, Wanda Clayton. *Lemuel Clayton: Ancestors and Descendants.* Memphis, TN, W.C. James, 1984. 112, v, iii leaves. LC CALL NUMBER: CS71.C622 1984a

COATES -- Tucker, D. A. *Coats Kin: From North Carolina to Tennessee to Arkansas.*

Houston, TX, D.A. Tucker, 1987. 179p. 1.
Coates family. 2. Southern States-Genealogy.
[G146-1].

COBB -- Cobb, Bill. *Cobb: An American
Family*. Smithville, TN, B. Cobb, 1985. 97p.
Pages 86-97 blank. 1. Cobb family. 2.
Southern States-Genealogy. [G146-1].

COBB -- Cobb, Joe H. *Nicholas Cobb:
Descendants and Relatives, 1613-1983*.
Nashville, TN, M.L.W. Pub., Co., 1984. vi,
583p. Spine Title: Nicholas Cobb
Descendants. [C138].

COBB -- Cobb, Rodney Dale. *Our Cobb Family:
A History of Our Origins in the Royal Colony
of North Carolina, Robertson County,
Tennessee, and Cass County, Texas*.
Sacramento, CA, Cobb, 1975. 88p.
[S520].

COBB -- Edwards, Bruce M. *The Cobbs of
Tidewater*. Knoxville, TN, The Montgomery Pub.
Co., 1976. 128p. [X197-FW,NY].

COBB -- Turner, Virginia (McKenney). *The
Cobb Family of "Rocky Mount". Piney Flats,
Tennessee, 1613-1972*. Dallas, TX, Pauline
Massengill DeFriece, 1973. 142p.
[S518].

COBB -- Weddington, Andrew S. and Cully A.
Cobb. *The Cobbs of Tennessee. Descendants of
John Cobb of Cobbs Court, County Kent,
England, 1324-1968*. Atlanta, GA, Printed by
Ruralist Press, 1968. xvii, 120p.
[X-DP/FW/IG/NY/PH/SP].

COFFEY -- Coffey, Laurence H. *Thomas Coffey
and His Descendants, with a Brief Sketch of
the Life of Thomas Coffey, a Pioneer in North
Carolina from Virginia, and of Reuben Coffey,
a Pioneer in Indiana from North Carolina, and
Others*. Chattanooga, TN, N. Sander, 1931. 3,
102p. [L3680; D2623; VV40].

COFFIN -- Coffin, Margaret. *List of the Descendants of Charles Coffin and Susan Woodbridge Ayer Coffin.* Knoxville, TN, 1937. 22 numb. leaves. Mimeographed and additional corrections in manuscript. [L3689].

COKER -- Hill, Euel Ray. *The Hills of Tennessee and Texas.* El Paso, TX, E.R. Hill, 1982. 138p. 7 leaves of plates. Cover title: "Hill, Coker, Gibson, & Sharp Family Histories". 1. Hill family. 2. Coker family. 3. Gibson family. 4. Sharp family. 5. Tennessee-Genealogy. 6. Texas-Genealogy. [G148-3].

COLE -- Cole, Charles Evans. *Ordinary Americans from Kohl to Cole, 1790-1980; with Pertinent Information and Related Families.* Nashville, TN, Coleoptera Press, 1981. 77p., 18p. of plates. C indicates errata slip inserted. [C140; NG31].

COLEHAN -- Ratledge, Ernest Stephen & Sandra Nipper Ratledge. *Appalachian Ancestors.* Cleveland, TN, E.S. Ratledge, 1983. xii, 336p. [C141].

COLEMAN -- Dickson, Roy S, Jr. <u>The Descendants of James A. Dickson, ca. 1820-1864, of Tennessee and Texas:</u> *Allied Families, Coleman, Fulbright, Harkey, Nail, Tippen.* Bartlesville, OK, R. S. Dickson, c1987. 232p. DC gives underscored portion of title and lists under DICKSON 1. Dixon family. 2. Dickson, James., ca. 1820-1864-Family. 3. Coleman family. 4. Fulbright family. [G149-3; DC1039].

COLEMAN -- Seaman, Catherine Hawes Coleman. *Letters from Migrating Southern Families of the 19th Century: the Letters of Coleman, Harris, and Hawes Families as the Migrate from Virginia to Kentucky, Tennessee, Mississippi, and Arkansas, 1810-1900.* Sweet Briar, VA, Sweet Briar College Printing Press, 1987- v. <1-2 >. 1. Coleman family-Correspondence. 2. Harris family-Correspondence. 3. Hayes family-Correspondence. [G150-1].

COLLAR -- Brown, Christine R. *Ancestors and Descendants of Joshua Williams and John Collar with Additions, Corrections, & Revisions.* Knoxville, TN, Campbell, 1984. xii, 289p. DC gives underscored portion of title. 1. Williams family. 2. Williams, Joshua, ca. 1747-ca. 1833-Family. 3. Collar family. 4. Collar, John, b. ca. 1632-Family. 5. Massachusetts Genealogy. 6. Maine-Genealogy. [G150-1; DC3958].

COLLIER -- Collier, William Miller. *A Letter and a Memorandum as to Colliers in Tennessee.* Auburn, NY, 1949. 4 leaves. Typewritten (Carbon Copy). [L3796].

COLLINS -- Markland, Ruby Collins. *The Jonathan Collins Family and Descendants of Penn., Va., Ky., Tenn., Mo., and Points West.* Provo, UT, J. G. Stevenson, 1969/1970. xii, 236p. [A137].

COLLINS -- Markland, Ruby Collins. *Supplement to The Jonathan Collins Family and Descendants of Penn., Va., (Ky.), Tenn., Mo., and Points West.* Pleasant Grove, UT, R. C. Markland, 1985. 134, xxxiv p., 1 leaf of plates. 1. Collins family. 2. Colins, Jonathan-Family. [G151].

COLVETT -- Stanfill, Latayne Colvett. *Colvett Family Chronicles: The History of the Colvett Family of Tennessee, 1630-1990.* Glendale, CA, Heirloom Press, 1991. xxiii, 635p.
LC CALL NUMBER: CS71.C728 1991

COMEGYS -- Moss, Ernestine Park. *Cornelius Comegys of Kent County, Maryland.* Memphis, TN, Ernestine Parke Moss, 1982. 186p. 3 leaves of plates. 1. Comegys family. [G152-3; C144; DC801].

COMPTON -- Blalock, Delton D. *British and American Comptons from the Colonial Era to the Modern Day in New York, New Jersey, Virginia, Tennessee, Alabama, and Texas, 1634-1984.*

Hanceville, AL, 1984. 257p., 2p. of plates. [C144; VV41].

CONLEY -- Johnson, Mrs. Ross B. *A Conley / Condley Family of Virginia, Tennessee, Missouri and Arkansas.* Lakewood, CO, Johnson, 1981. 30 leaves. [D2754].

CONN -- McConnell, Grace Conn. [G154-1]. See above: BREWER. [G87-3].

COOK -- Cook, Jerry W. *The Cook Family in America: A Family History of Thomas and Milly ( Marcum ) Cook and Their Descendants of Bedford County, Tennessee (c.1770-1973).* Normandy, TN, Cook, 1773. 343p. [X209-FW,NY].

COOK -- Grimes, Jay Cook. *Grimes, Cook, and Related Families of Wayne County, Tennessee: A Genealogy: Related Families, Johnson, Morris, Montague, 1800-1960.* Auburn, AL, J.C. Grimes, 1960. 123p. D lists under GRIMES and gives no place of publication. 1. Grimes family. 2. Cook family. 3. Johnson family. 4. Morris family. 5. Wayne County(Tenn.)-Genealogy. 6. Tennessee-Genealogy. [G155-1; D5326].

COOK -- Kelsey, Mary Wilson. *Robert Wilson, 1750-1826 of Blount County, Tennessee: Some of His Descendants and Related Families Including Gould, Cook, Brooks, Huson, Shearer, Stribling.* - 1st ed. Houston, TX, M.W. Kelsey, c1987. xii, 299p. NGS lists under WILSON, gives no place of publication and omits cover title. Cover Title: Robert Wilson, 1750-1826, Scotch-Irish immigrant of Blount County, Tennessee. 1. Wilson family. 2. Wilson, Robert, 1750-1826-Family. 3. Gould family. 4. Cook family. 5. Blount County (Tenn). [G155-1; NGS12].

COOPER -- Chandler, Melvin Leon. [G156-1]. See above: CHANDLER. [G132-1].

COOPER -- Cooper, Homer C. *Cooper, McKenny, Ferrell/Farrell, Woddell, Gothard, Wilson &*

*Patton Families of Augusta & Rockbridge Counties, Virginia; York & Adams Counties, Pennsylvania; Blount, Knox, & Roane Counties, Tennessee; Pocahontas, Gilmer & Ritchie Counties, West Virginia; Wayne County, Kentucky; Vigo & Sullivan Counties, Indiana; York County, South Carolina.* Athens, GA, 1963. 7 leaves. [L3990; VV43].

COOPER -- Cooper, Noah W. *Sketch of Noah B. Cooper and Wife Lucinda Jenrette, with Family Records.* Nashville, TN, Cooper, 1947. 163p. [D2830].

COOPER -- Young, Asher Leon. *William Armstrong Cooper: Seventy-Three Years a Baptist Preacher.* Nashville, TN, A.L. Young, 1980. ii, 184p. [C148].

COPE -- Parish, Joan Bartholomew. *Coping with the Copes.* Brentwood, TN, Parrish, 1979. xiii, 94, x leaves, 58 l. of plates. [C148].

CORLEY -- McCarthy, Lynette Nolen. *William Corley and David Nolen Descendants of Tennessee and Illinois, 1730-1982.* Normal, IL, L.N. McCarthy, 1982. v, 47 leaves. [C150].

CORLEY -- McMaster, Phyllis Olewine & Gerald B. Corley. *The Descendants of John W. Corley of Hardeman County, Tennessee: Including Allied Family Lines of Carl, Dick, Hudson, McMaster, and Thompson.* Albany, OR, P.O. McMaster, G.B. Corley, Huntington Beach, CA, 1989. v. 1 (various pagings). 1. Corley family. 2. Corley, John W., 1814-1858-Family. 3. Tennessee-Genealogy. [G158-2].

COROTHERS -- See above: CAMPBELL. [L2939; D2108].

COTHAM -- Chandler, Melvin Leon. [G160-1]. See above: CHANDLER. [G132-1].

COTTRELL -- Cottrell, Ellen Rowland. *Descendants of Nicholas Cottrell of Rhode*

*Island.* Knoxville, TN, W.M. Cottrell, 1988. 161p.

COURTNEY -- Ritchie, Ruth. *Genealogy of Some East Tennessee Families of the Early Nineteenth Century.* Charlottesville, VA, 1945. 96p. [X-217-FW; VV44].

COWDEN -- Cowden, John B. *The Southern Cowdens.* West Nashville, TN, Cowden, c1933. 3, 112p. [L4140; D2955].

CRANDALL -- Crandall, Arorestus P. *Genealogy of a Branch of the Crandall Family.* Chattanooga, TN, W. I. Crandall, 1888. 62p. [X22-LI,MH].

CRAWFORD -- NAS (Various Crawford Family Members). *Edward Crawford's Family: With Special Emphasis on Those Descendants Who Lived In or Passed Through Macoupin County, Illinois, with Eventual Concentration in Illinois, Missouri, Oregon, Texas, Tennessee.* - 1st ed. Illinois, Crawford Family Book Committee, 1988. 372p. 1. Crawford family. 2. Crawford, Edward, ca. 1762-1826-Family. [G164-3].

CRAWFORD -- Crawford, Charles Travis. *The Crawford Family (North Carolina and Tennessee)... with Interesting Notes of the Origin and History of the "Crawford Clan".* Laurenceburg, TN, Priv. Print, Crawford, 44p. "The Leake Family Genealogy"; 6 p. at end. [L4215].

CRAWFORD -- Holland, Cornelia Burns. *Lazarus Crawford, A Glimpse of His Life and His Descendants.* Franklin, TN, C.B. Holland, 1989. 1 volume in various paginations. [DC873].

CRESAP -- Cresap, Joseph Ord and Bernarr Cresap. *The History of the Cresaps.* - *Rev. ed.* Gallatin, TN, Cresap Society, 1987. 803p., 16 p. of plates. 1. Cresap family. 2.

Cresap, Thomas-Family    3. Cresap, Michael,
1742-1775-Family.      4.  Maryland-Genealogy.
[G165-1].

CRESWELL -- Creswell, John Olin. *Creswell,
History and Genealogy, 1744-1967*. Maryville,
TN. Printed by Marion R. Mangrum.  D gives:
Knoxville,  TN.  Creswell.  c1967.     256p.
[L4239; D3057]

CROCKETT -- French, J. C. P. *Davy Crockett
and the Crockett Family*.  Chattanooga, TN,
Lookout Pub., 1951.  25p.  [X227-FW].

CROCKETT -- French, Janie Preston Collup.
*The Crockett Family and Connecting Lines*.
Spartanburg, SC, 1974 (1928), 611p.  Reprint
of the ed. pub. by King Print Co., Bristol,
TN.  [L4268; S589].

CROCKETT -- Simmons, June Pitts. *Nathan
Crockett, the Eldest Brother of 'Davey'.
Genealogy of His Son*. Sharon, TN, Simmons,
c1928.  40 l. [D3079].

CROCKETT -- Simmons, June Pitts. *Nathan
Crockett, the Eldest Brother of 'Davey',
Genealogy of His Son, John*.  Sharon, TN,
Simmons, 1975.  40 l.  [S590]

CROW -- Smiley, Howard Crosby. *Some of the
Descendants of Revolutionary Veteran, John
Crow, 1740-1830. (Ruth Holland, Elizabeth
Clark, 1752-1800)* Memphis, TN, Smiley, 1975.
15 leaves.  1. Crowe family.  Only S gives the
names in parentheses.  [G167-3; S594].

CRUMLEY -- Crumley, Jeff. *Harmon H. Crumley
Family: Descendants of George Crumley, Sr.,
Sullivan County, Tennessee*. Gaithersburg, MD,
J. Crumley, 1982.  105p., 1 leaf of plates.
Updated  ed.  of  George  Crumley  Family  of
Sullivan County, Tennessee compiled by Hugh H.
Mottern, et al, 1964. [See below].  [C161].

CRUMLEY -- Haunschild, Ormal Crumley. *The
Crumleys of Frederick Co., Va., and Green Co.,*

*Tenn., and Their Descendants.* Ada, OK, 1975. pni. [VV48].

CRUMLEY -- Mottern, Hugh H. *George Crumley Family of Sullivan County, Tennessee.* Glenview, IL, Mottern, 1964. 230p. [D3123; X231-FW].

CRUTCHER -- Merritt, Robert K. *Larkin Crutcher of Robertson Co., Tenn.* Wichita, KS, Merritt, 1957. 38 leaves. [D3125].

CURNUTT -- Greenwood, Mary Maxine. *The Descendants of Calloway Curnutt: Anderson County, Tennessee.* Terre Haute, IN, 1986. 30p. [NGS4].

CURTIS -- King, Mable L., Robert Warren King & Adele Moore Muller. *Descendants of Michael Curtis, Elisha Felton, Virginia and North Carolina to Lawrence County, Alabama.* Memphis, TN, M.L. King, 1982. 2 v. ( v leaves, 355p., 27 leaves of plates). [C164].

CUSTER -- Custer, Chester E. *The Descendants of Jacob and Sarah Custer.* Nashville, TN, C.E. Custer, c1973. 89 leaves. [L612; DC923].

# D

DALE -- Dale, W. Andrew. *My Tennesseans.* Nashville, TN, T. Tyler, 1989 vi, 251p., 2p. of plates. 88-90421
   LC CALL NUMBER: CS71 .D139 1989

DALTON -- Horton, Lucy H. *Daltons of Virginia.* Franklin, TN, n.d. 45 leaves. Typed. [X238-FW; VV50].

DAMRON -- Allen, Delilah Catherine (Nelms). *Dr. George Damron, Born Tennesse, 1796, Eary [sic] Day Settler Bonham and Ector, Fannon County, 1829. Also Nelms Family.* NP, 1973. 19 leaves. [NG35].

DANNER -- Getzendanner, D. Thomas
*Getzendanner of Md. and S.C., His Descendants.*
*The Getson and Danner Families of Ark., Ala.,*
*Miss., Tenn., Texas .* [NGN MAY/JUN 95].

DANTZLER -- Taylor, Isaac Lemuel. *The*
*Lemuel Dantzler Family.* Ooltewah, TN, I.L.
Taylor, 1982. 52 leaves in various
foliations. [C169].

DARDEN -- Darden, Newton Jasper. *Darden*
*Family History with Notes on Ancestry of*
*Allied Families: Washington, Lanier, Burch,*
*Strozier, Dodson, Pyles, McNair, Barnett: A*
*Memorial of Dearden - Durden - Dardens of the*
*United States of America, Particularly in*
*Virginia, Georgia, Tennessee, Alabama,*
*Mississippi, and Texas.* Edited, rev., and
enl. by Leroy W. Tilton. Washington, DC,
1957. 190p. [L4530; VV51].

DARNELL -- Twain, Mark. *The Grainger -*
*Sheperdson Feud. Facsimile of That Episode's*
*First Publication prior to Adventures of*
*Huckleberry Finn, with An Account of Mark*
*Twain's Use of the Bloody Encounters at*
*Compromise, Kentucky by Edgar Marquess Branch*
*& Robert H. Hirst.* Berkeley, CA, Friends of
The Bancroft Library, University of
California, 1985. 91p. (No. 33 in the series
of keepsakes by the Friends of the Bancroft
Library for its members). 1. Twain, Mark,
1835-1910. Adventures of Huckleberry Finn.
2. Darnell Family. 3. Watson family. 4.
Vendetta in literature. 5. Vendetta-
Tennessee. 6. Vendetta-Kentucky. [G175-1].

DAVANT -- Hanahan, Hardin Davant. *A Place*
*in History: The Davant Family.* Knoxville,
TN, H. D. Hanahan. 1972. 224p. 1. Davant
family. 2. Georgia-Genealogy. 3. South
Carolina-Genealogy. 4. Southern States-
Genealogy. [G175-3; NG35; D3286].

DAVIDSON -- Dixon, Elizabeth Williamson.
*The Davidson and Allied Families Originating*
*in North Carolina.* NP, 1956. 2 v. (495 l.).

Supplement: The Davidson Family of North Carolina and Tennessee, 1959 bound separately. Includes a copy of Alexander - Davidson reunion, Swannanoa, N.C., August 26, 1911: addresses by F. S. Sondley and Theo. F. Davidson. [D3298].

DAVIDSON -- Hand, Robert Stephens. *Those Members of the Davison / Davidson Family Who Descended from William and Elizabeth Davison of County Armagh, Ireland, and Settled in North Carolina and Tennessee, and Late in Mississippi, Texas, and Elsewhere.* Chadds Ford, PA, R.S. Hand, 1990. iv, 206p. 1. Davison family. 2. Davidson family. 3. Davison, William, ca 1684-ca. 1723-Family. 4. Ireland-Genealogy. [G176-2].

DAVIES -- McNamara, Billie R. *From The Rhondda Valley to the Clinch River Valley and Beyond; A Genealogy of the Descendants of John Davies.* Knoxville, TN, 1962. 151p. [NG35].

DAVIS -- Anderson, Beverly Davis. *Davis: Ancestors and Descendants of Elihu and Caroline Lightbody Davis.* Oak Ridge, TN, B.D. Anderson, 1989. 514p., 1 leaf of plates. 1. Davis family. 2. Lightbody family. 3. Davis, Elihu, 1839-1887-Family. 4. Davis, Caroline Lightbody, 1841-1918-Family. [G177-1; DC953].

DAVIS -- Beyl, Larry C. *Descendants of James Davis, 1761-1831, White County, Tennessee Pioneer.* McMinnville, TN, 1973. 79, 2p. [X245-LA].

DAVIS -- Boyd, Larry Craig. *Descendants of James Davis, 1762-1831, White County, Tennessee Pioneer.* McMinnville, TN, Boyd, 1973. a-e, 79p. [D3308].

DAVIS -- Davies-Rodgers, Ellen. *Turns Again Home: Life on an Old Tennessee Plantation Trespassed by Progress.* Brunswick, TN, Plantation Press, c1992. 384p.
LC CALL NUMBER: F444.B85 D39 1992

DAVIS -- Davis, Charles P. *Scribbles and Arrows: The Search for Uriah (Hugh) Davis, Weakley Co., Tenn., Pioneer.* [NGN MAR/APR 95].

DAVIS -- Davis, David Ragland. *Davis Families of American Descent, 300 Years in America; Especially Showing the Interrelations of the Davis - Bowe - Ragland Families and Emphasizing the Families That Settled in Limestone County, Alabama, and DeSoto County, Mississippi.* Memphis, TN, D.R. Davis, 1989. x, 386p. 1. Davis family. 2. Rowe family. 3. Ragland family. 4. Alabama-Genealogy. 5. Mississippi-Genealogy. [G177-2].

DAVIS -- Heck, Arch Oliver. *Descendants of Hezekiah Davis I, A Settler in Northeastern Tennessee in the Latter Part of the 1700's.* Columbus, OH, 1965. 4 v. (xii, 467p). [L4643].

DAVIS -- Lambeth, Mary (Weeks). *Memories and Records of Eastern North Carolina.* Nashville, TN, 1957. 252p. [L4638].

DAVIS -- McNamara, Billie R. *From the Rhodda Valley to the Clinch River Valley and Beyond: A Genealogy of the Descendants of John Davies.* Knoxville, TN, B.R. McNamara, 1982. xii, 152p. [C172].

DAVIS -- Pickens, Flossie Henry. *Davis - Reese and Related Families.* Maryville, Tennessee, Pickens, 1963. xii, 165p. [L4645; D3349].

DAVISON -- Hand, Robert Stephens. [G178-3]. See above: DAVIDSON. [G176-2].

DAY -- Seivers, Edna Wallace. *The Ancestors and Descendants of Volney Lionel Day.* Knoxville, TN, E.W. Seivers, 1989. iv, 180p. 1. Day family. 2. Day, Volney Lionel, 1848-1926-Family. 3. Tennessee-Genealogy. [G179-3].

**DAYTON** -- Henning, Elma. *The Ulrich Rinehart Family and Descendants, 1704-1985.* Dayton, TN, E.A. Henning, 1986. x, 432p.
LC CALL NUMBER: CS71.R574 1986

**DEADERICK** -- Battey, George Magruder III. *... The Pioneering Deadericks of Virginia & Tennessee. From Data in the Possession of Lyon Childress of Nashville and John Williams Childress of Washington.* Washington, DC, 1940. pni. [VV54].

**DEAL** -- Deal, Fern W. *The Deal Family.* Knoxville, TN, Mannis Printing Co., 1975. ii, 153, 40p. [D3402].

**DeARMOND** -- D'Armand, Roscoe Carlisle. *DeArmond Families of America; d'Armond, D'Armand, D'Armond, DeArman, DeArment, DeArmon, DeArmond, Dearmont, Deyarmon, DeYarmon, Deyarmond and Related Families.* 1st ed. Knoxville, TN, Family Record Society, 1954. X gives date as 1965. xv, 699p. [D3416; X249-CH,DP,FW,IG,LA,MH,NY,OS,PH,SP].

**DeARMOND** -- D'Armand, Roscoe Carlisle. *DeArmond Families of America and Related Families* - 2nd ed.. Knoxville, TN, c1986. xv, 732p., 7 leaves of plates. Reprint. Originally published: Limited ed. Knoxville, TN, Family Record Society, 1954. With new appendix. 1. DeArmond family. [G182-2].

**DELOZIER** -- Edwards, Richard Laurence. *Ancestors and Descendants of the Edwards - Mathias, Delozier, and Related Families that Pioneered through Virginia, Carolinas, Tennessee, Kentucky, Illinois, Missouri, Kansas, and Spread to Descendants in Thirty-Seven States and Two Provinces in Canada.* Coffeyville, KS, R.L. Edwards, 1985. xvi, 597p. 1. Edwards family. 2. Mathis family. 3. Delozier family.
[G184-3; C205; VV60].

**DE LAND** -- Leete, Frederick DeLand. *The DeLand Family in America, A Biographical*

Genealogy. DeLand, FL, (Nashville, TN, Parthenon Press). 1943. 414p. [L4773].

DENTON -- Whitley, Edythe. *Some of the Descendants of Rev. Richard Denton.* McMinnville, TN, Womack Printing Co., 1959. 94p. [L4834; D3514].

DERBY -- Elam, Charlotte Adee Edmondson. *The Descendants of Perry Lewis Derby, 1804-1877.* Memphis, TN, Elam, 1965. 1 v. unpaged. D gives 36 leaves. [L4851; D3520].

DERRYBERRY -- Wilkinson, A. Mims. *The Derryberry Family of Tennessee: the Long and Hardison Connections and the Westmoreland, Dickerson, and Royall Families of Giles County; the Royall Genealogy (Virginia) 1623-1935.* Stone Mountain, GA, A. M Wilkinson, 1989. 1 v. various foliations. 1. Derryberry family. 2. Hardison family. 3. Long family. 4. Royal family. 5. Tennessee-Genealogy. 6. Virginia-Genealogy. [G187-1].

DeSHA -- DeSha, Wallace Eugene. *Sprays of Oak Leaves and Acorns.* Chattanooga, TN, DeSha, 1969. 135p. Bound with Twigs and leaves to oak leaves and acorns. [D3528].

DEW -- White, Ernestine Dew. *Genealogy of Some of the Descendants of Thomas Dew, Colonial Virginia Pioneer Immigrant, Together with Genealogical Records and Biographical Sketches of Families in Virginia, Maryland, North Carolina, South Carolina, West Virginia and Tennessee...* Greenville, SC, White, 1937. 349p. D gives underscored title. [L4891; D3544; VV55].

DICKSON -- Smith, Austin Wheeler. *The Dickson McEwan and Allied Families Genealogy.* Cookeville, TN, Smith, 1975. 512, 58, 93p. On Spine: The Revised Dickson -- McEwen and Allied Families Genealogy. [S689].

DILLINGHAM -- Kelley, Sarah Foster. *The Dillingham Family of Middle Tennessee.*

Nashville, TN, 1979. ii, 75p. NG gives 74p. [C185; NG37].

DIXON -- Dickson, Roy S, Jr. [G192-2]. See above: COLEMAN. [G149-3; DC1039].

DIXON -- Dixon, Thomas Edward. *The Descendants of Thomas Dixon, Planter.* Columbia, TN, c1950. 82p. [L5005].

DIXON -- Smith, Austin Wheeler. *The Dickson - McEwen and Allied Families Genealogies.* Cookeville, TN, 1945. 512p. [L5004].

DOAK -- Calhoun, William Gunn. *Samuel Doak, 1749-1830.* NP, Calhoun, Washington College Tenn., Pioneer Printers, 1966. vii, 51p. [D3645].

DOAK -- French, Janie Preston Collup (Mrs. J. Stewart French). *The Doak Family.* Spartanburg, SC, The Reprint Co., 1974 (1933). 98p. Armstrong, Zella, Norable southern families. S gives: Reprint of ed. publ. by the Lookout Pub. Co., Chattanooga, TN. [L5010; S700].

DOBBIN -- Barekman, June B. *Some Dobbin - Skiles Kin from Pennsylvania to North Carolina and Tennessee. Additional Lines: Coker, Cowan, Dailey, Graham, Hess, Palmer, Barekman. Ed. 2 Rev. and enl.* Chicago, IL, 1968. 44p. [X265-FW].

DODSON -- Callahan, Mary Lee Dodson. *Genealogy of Charles Dodson of Southwest Virginia and Watkins H. Dodson and His Wife, Jerusha Ann Blakemore of West Tennessee.* NP, 1953. 124, xvi leaves. [D3665; VV56].

DODSON -- Lynn, Catherine Gaffin. *The Dodson Family of Warren County, Tennessee, and Allied Families.* Centerville, TN, Lynn, c1974. 286p. [S703; D3670].

DODSON -- Sloan, Emma T. *Charles Dodson of Richmond County, Va.* Nashville, TN, 1940. 74p, 35 leaves. [X266-FW; VV56].

DOGGETT -- Lynch, Pauline Jones. *The Doggett Family: Generations of Miller Doggett (1789-1841) from Virginia to Tennessee, 1809.* Lewisburg, TN, P.J. Lynch, 19789. 94p. [C187].

DONALDSON -- Edwards, Christine Williams. *The Donaldson Family of Caswell County, North Carolina and Wilson County, Tennessee.* Athens, AL, Mrs. Thomas E. Edwards, 1972. 62 leaves. Cover title: The Donaldson family of middle Tennessee. [C189-1; D3681].

DONALDSON -- Warren Lillian C. & Robert C. Williams. *The Donaldson Odyssey: Footsteps to Freedom.* - 1st ed. Seattle, WA, L.C. Warren & R.C. Williams, 1991. 352p. 1. Donaldson family. 2. Washington(State)-Genealogy. 3. Alabama-Genealogy. 4. Tennessee-Genealogy. 5. Afro-American Genealogy. [G196-1].

DONNELLY -- Neal, Carl B. *The Donnelly - Barry - Butler Families and Their Kinfolk of Johnson Co., Tenn.* Olympia, WA, Neal, 1958. 158 leaves. [D3688].

DONELSON -- Burke, Pauline Wilcox. *Emily Donelson of Tennessee. Also, Coffee Family.* Richmond, VA, 1941. 2 v. [NG37].

DORN -- Martin, Ethel Dorn. *The Life of Peter and Katherine Dorn.* Maryville, TN, Brazos, 1968. 144p. [L5094].

DOUGLAS -- Harris, Ruth Eleanor Poole. *Ruth Eleanor Douglas Journal: with Genealogies of Douglas, Noell, Callaway, Clemens, Moorman, and Other Related Bedford County, Virginia Families: Also Genealogies of Douglas Families of Tennessee, Kentucky, Missouri.* Nashville, TN, Douglas Family Publishers, 1979 - v. [C191; VV57].

DOWNS -- Hamilton, James Edward. *1000 Descendants of the Downs Families of Early Trigg County, Kentucky and Stewart County,*

*Tennessee.* Aberdeen, SD, J.E. Hamilton, 1993.
v, 58 leaves.
LC CALL NUMBER: CS71.D7515 1993

DULANY -- Hecathorn, Ann Austin. *Preston
and Susan Hutson Dulany, 1800-1993: Tennessee,
Illinois, and Beyond.* Knoxville, TN,
Tennessee Valley Pub., 1993. iii, II, 251p.
LC CALL NUMBER: CS71.D3369 1993

DRAKE -- Drake, Robert. *The Home Place: A
Memory and Collaboration.* Memphis, TN,
Memphis State University Press, 1980. xiii,
161p. [C192].

DRAPER -- Anderson, Ethel Nichols. *Draper
Families in America.* Nashville, TN, Parthenon
Press, c1964. 514p. [D3753].

DROKE -- NAS. *Special Report.* Droke Family
Assn., Blountville, TN. n.d. pni. [X274-NY].

DROKE -- NAS. *Some of the Seven Generations
of the Family of Jacob Droke; an Old Tennessee
Family Along Reedy Creek in Historic Sullivan
County.* Los Angeles, CA, The Droke Family
Assoc. 1961. 9p. [X274-PH,SU].

DRUMRIGHT -- Dowland, Gracie Drumright.
*The 'Drumright' Family Tree.* NP, Dowland
Nashville, TN, Eveready Press, 1974. 254p.
[D3775; X275-NY].

DUGGAN -- Butler, E. Dean. *History of the
Duggin and Related Families of Cameron County,
Tennessee.* Memphis, TN, E.D. Butler, 1979.
98 l. [C196].

DUNCAN -- Crawford, John C. *John Duncan of
Blountsville, Tennessee and His Descendants.*
Maryville, TN, 1959. 29p. [L5283].

DUNCAN -- McRaven, William H. *Duncan Family
of Glasgow, New York, New Orleans (and)
Mississippi. Alexander Duncan, 1773-1849,
Mary (nee McFarland) Duncan, 1779-1863.*
Nashville, TN, 1959. 171 leaves. [X278-NY].

**DUNLAP** -- Dunlap, Marian Ray. *A Family History and Descendants of Adam Dunlap, Sr., With Roots in Blount County, Tennessee.* Effingham, IL, M.R. Dunlap, 1989. vii, 82, xxi p.
LC CALL NUMBER: CS71.D918 1989

**DYKES** -- Dykes, John M., Jr. *The Dykes Line of East Tennessee -- Rev.* Charlotte, NC, Dykes, 1980. ca. 400p. [C201].


# E


**EAGER** -- Trotter, Susie (Eager). *History of the Eager Family, from the Coming of the First Immigrant, William Eager in 1630, to date, 1952.* Nashville, TN, 1952. 251p. [L5389].

**EAKER** -- Eaker, Lorena Shell. *The Shoe Cobbler's Kin: Genealogy of the Peter (Ecker) Eaker, Sr. Family.* Baltimore, MD, Gateway Press, 1976 - c1985. 2 v, Vol. 2 published Church Hill, TN, SCK Publications. Contents: v. 1. 1701-1976 -- v. 2. 1985. [G206-3].

**EASLEY** -- Easley, Jim. *Stephen and Mary Ann ( David ) Easley in Sullivan County Tennessee.* (NGN18-3-92).

**ECKEL** -- Eckel, Alexander. *History of the Eckel - Moser Families.* Sevierville, TN, 1920. 10p. [X288-LI].

**ECKEL** -- Rubicam, Milton. *The Eckel Family of Maryland, Pennsylvania, Tennessee, North Carolina and Delaware.* Hyattsville, MD, 1955. v, 70 leaves. [NG 39; D3951; VP65].

**EDMISTON** -- Edmiston, Prentess P. *A Branch of the Edmiston Family Tree from Ireland to North Carolina to Pennsylvania to Virginia to Tennessee to Arkansas and to Texas, A. D. 1700-1964.* Harlingen, TX, 1964. 14 leaves. Typescript (Carbon copy). [L5485; VV59].

EDMONDS -- Yadon, Lawrence J. II. *The Newton J. Edmonds Family of Rhea County, Tennessee and Greene, Laclede, and Webster Counties, Missouri.* Tulsa, OK, L.J. Yadon, 1980. vii, 21 l., 5 l. of plates. [C205].

EDMONDSON -- Elam, Charlette Adee Edmondson. *The Descendants of Lt. Robert Edmondson, 1753-1816.* Memphis, TN, Elam, 1966. 1 v. (unpaged). D gives: 60 leaves. [L5486; D3977].

EDMONDSON -- Edmondson, Charles. *Colonists and Pioneers: The Edmondsons, Tinkles, Wades, Wards, Pattons, Hattons, Bealls, Calverts, and Some Others.* Memphis, TN, C. Edmondson, 1981. 121p., 1 leaf of plates. [C205].

EDWARDS -- Edwards, Bruce Montgomery. *The Edwards of Northhampton.* Knoxville, TN, Montgomery Pub. Co., 1973. viii, 293p. [D3993].

EDWARDS -- Edwards, Richard Laurence. [G208]. See above: DE LOZIER. [G184-3; C205; VV60].

ELDER -- Nelson, Virginia Knight. *Families Named Elder in East Tennessee.* Knoxville, TN, V.K. Nelson, 1986. xiv, 133p. [DC].

ELDRIDGE -- Donnelly, Polly Watkins. *A Branch of the Eldridge Family: Descendants of Jefferson and Rachel Blair Eldridge.* Cleveland, TN, P.W. Donnelly, 1987. 32, 13p. [DC1166].

ELDRIDGE -- Eldridge, Charles S. *History, Tennessee, My People, and Me.* Dayton, OH, C.S. Eldridge, c1991. 4, 491 p.
    LC CALL NUMBER: CS71.B6253 1991

ELLENBERGER -- Sauls, Blance Ellenburg and Diana Smith Chesser. *An Ellenburg Family History.* Johnson City, TN, B.E. Sauls and D.S. Chesser, c1988. 223p. 1. Ellenberger family. 2. Tennessee-Genealogy. [G211-2].

ELKINS -- Turner, Mayme Gertrude Yager.
*The Elkins family from Virginia to Middle
Tennessee and Texas.* United States. M.G.Y.
Turner, 1989. ii, 169p.
LC CALL NUMBER: CS71.E4372 1989

EMISON -- Emison, James Wade. ... *Emison
Family* ... Vincennes, IN, 1941. 6 numb.
leaves. Typed. [L5656].

EMISON -- Emison, James Wade. *The Emison
Families, Revised; Origin and History of the
American Emisons, with Partial Genealogical
Notes on the Following Collateral Families:
Baird, Clark, Holmes, Posey, Allen, Dunning,
Rabb, Sinclair, Scott, Campbell - McClellan -
Patterson - Cullop - Mantle - Brevoort;
Simpson, McCord - Hogue; Reiley.* Vincennes,
IN, 1947, x 243p. [L5657].
        -- *Supplement.* NP, 1950. 4 v.
Contents: (1) James Family - (2) Sinclair,
Blackburn, and Buckley Families - (3) Reiley
Family - (4) Randall, Chew, Porter, Shipley,
Mansell, and Gassaway Families. [L5657].

EMISON -- Emison, James Wade. *The Emison
Families, Revised; Origin and History of the
Kentucky Emisons, with Partial Genealogies and
Notes on Emisions (sic) of Virginia,
Tennessee, Long Island and Massachusetts.
Also the following Collateral Families:
Baird, Holmes, Clark, Love, Posey - Wade.*
Vincennes, IN, 1954. x, 360. [L5658; VV61].
        -- *Supplement.* Vincennes, IN, 1962.
vii, 399p. [L5658].
        -- *Final Supplement.* Vincennes, IN,
1969. vii, 329p. [A217].

ENGLISH -- Collier, Leroy. *Thomas English
and Descendants and Some of Their Kin.* Bowling
Green, KY, L. and M. Collier, 1986. 165p. 1.
English family. 2. English, Thomas, d.
1664-Family. 3. Tennessee-Genealogy.
[G215-2].

EPPES -- Johnson, Mary Lou (Shoemaker) and
Mae L. Treadwell. *The Family of Edward Eppes*

*of Knox County, Tennessee.* NP, 1951. 68 leaves. [L5701].

EVANS  --  Albert, Ethel Evans. *Southwest Virginia Kin: A Genealogical and Historical Account of the Evans, Ferrell, Kelly, Counts, Stinson and Related Families.* Kingsport, TN, Albert, 1977-  v.  [C216].

EVANS  --  Bonfield, Hortense. *Evans and Related Families.* __, TN, H. Bonfield, c1993. x, 766 p.
      LC CALL NUMBER: CS71.E92  1993

EVANS  --  Duckworth, Reda Thornton, transcriber. *Collection of Letters (1867-1886).* Germantown, TN, R.T. Duckworth, c1984. 38 leaves.  1. Evans family-Correspondence. 2. Wood family-Correspondence.  3. Southern States-Biography.  4. Southern States-Genealogy. [G219-1].

EVANS  --  Whitley, Edythe. *Evans Family, Maryland & Tennessee.* NP, 1971, 100 leaves. [D4187].


F


FANCHER  --  Fancher, Pearl Bufford. *The Johnson Fancher Family of Sevier County, Tennessee.* Atlanta, GA, Fancher, 1977. ii, 51 leaves.  1. Fancher family.  2. Sevier County, (Tenn.)-Genealogy. [G222-1; C219].

FANNIN  --  Fort, Kate Hynes. *Memoirs of the Fort and Fannin Families.* Chattanooga, TN, Press of the McGowan & Cooke Co., 1903. 232p. Contents:  Memoirs of Martha Low Fort - Memoirs of Kate Haynes Fort - Death of Dr. Tomlinson Fort, 1859. (From Altanta medical and surgical journal, June (1859) - Sketch of Dr. Fort, by Judge J. Hellyer. (From Atlanta medical & surgical journal, May 1885). Battle of Twelve Mile Swamp of Davis Creed, by J.P. Fort - Public Life of Dr. Tomlinson Fort, by

G.F. Milton - Last campaign First Georgia
regulars by J.P. Fort. - "Uncle Joe" a Family
Portrait by Fannie F. Brown - A war wedding in
1865 by Sarah F. Milton - A story of Arthur
Ford by Sarah F. Milton - A story of Neddy
Pace by Sarah F. Milton - Fannin and His Men.
Genealogies of Families of Tomlinson and
Martha Low Fort. [A223].

FARIS -- Phillips, Wm. H. Farises in
Virginia. Nashville, TN, Farris, 1952. 59,
10, 26p. [X311-FW].

FARIS -- Reynolds, Katherine. The Faris
Family, Virginia, Tennessee and Texas (1607-
1950). NP, 1957. 129, 99 l. [D4249; VV64].

FAULK -- Harrell, Elizabeth J. The Osbornes
and Related Families: Jones, Fowlkes,
Robertson & Gayle: An Account of Thomas
Osborne, Who Arrived in Virginia in 1619, and
His Descendants, Who for Five Generations
Lived in Henrico (now Chesterfield) County,
Virginia, then Moved First to Amelia (now
Price Edward) County, Virginia, then to
Charlotte County Virginia, and Later to Middle
Tennessee. Los Altos, CA, E.J. Harrell,
c1983. x, 213p., 1 folded leaf of plates. 1.
Osborne family. 2. Faulk family. 3.
Robertson family. [G223-2].

FAULKENBERRY -- Tumlinson, Rebecca L.
Tennessee to Texas: It Happened Like This:
Stories of Research and Remembrance. Limited
1st ed. Channelview, TX, Tumlinson, 1979. 65
leaves. [C221].

FAW -- NAS. Walter Wagner Faw Papers.
Manuscript Division, Tennessee State Library
and Archives, Nashville, TN, 1961. 34p.
[X314-FW].

FENNER -- Barrett, Ruth Leslie. The Fenner
Forebears of Samuel Fenner Leslie, 1877-1969:
Their Lives, Their Descendants, Their Kin in
North Carolina, Virginia, Tennessee, Alabama,
Mississippi, Arkansas, and Texas. Windom, TX,

R.L. Barrett, 1987. 357p. 1. Fenner family.
2. Leslie, Samuel Fenner, 1877-1949.
[G225-3].

**FERGUSON** -- Ferguson, William Otto.
*Descendants of James and Elizabeth Fleming*
*Ferguson, Bedford County (now Marshall)*
*Tennessee.* Rocky Mount, NC, H.W. Ferguson,
1988. 135, 8p. 1. Ferguson family. 2.
Ferguson, James, 1757-1816-family. 3.
Tennessee-Genealogy. [G226-3].

**FERGUSON** -- Ferguson, William Otto. *We*
*Fergusons and Related Families.* Monroe, LA,
W. O. Ferguson, 1985. xxix, 418p. 1.
Ferguson family. 2. Ferguson, Samuel Maley,
b.1778-Family. 3. Southern States-Genealogy.
Lineage beginning with Samuel Maley Ferguson,
born in 1778 in South Carolina, later moving
to Georgia and Mississippi and including
descendants in forty other states.
[G226-3; C225].

**FESMIRE** -- Khalid, Alice Ann Fesmire.
*Fesmire, A Family History and Genealogy:*
*Martin Fesmire and His Descendants in North*
*Carolina and Tennessee with Branches in*
*Indiana, Ohio, Mississippi, Texas, and*
*Oklahoma.* Baton Rouge, LA, Land and Land
Printers, 1982. 218p. [C226].

**FESSLER** -- Fessler, William T. *Fessler*
*Ancestories: Foreign Origins and Family*
*Summaries and Briefs in Pennsylvania: Also*
*Briefs in California, Illinois, Indiana, Iowa,*
*Kansas, Kentucky, North Carolina, Missouri,*
*Ohio, Virginia: Plus Hundreds of Other*
*Surnames.* Haddonfield, NJ, 1980. [VV65].

**FIELDEN** -- Fielden, Marvel L. *The Fielden*
*Stream: A Family History of the Fieldens of*
*East Tennessee.* Knoxville, TN, Tennessee
Valley Pub., Glen Allen, VA, 1991. x, 640 p.
LC CALL NUMBER: CS71.F455 1991

**FINCANNON** -- Fincannon, Al G. [G228-3].
See above: CANNON. [G118-3].

FINN -- Hunter, Patricia Finn. *A Finn Genealogy, 1750-1985: Some Ancestors and Descendants of Colman Finn, 1823-1916, Grandson of Rickard Finn, 1750-1833 of Adair County, Kentucky*. Knoxville, TN, P.F. Hunter, 1986. 206p. DC gives underscored part of title. 1. Finn family. 2. Finn, Colman, 1823-1916-Family. 3. Kentucky-Genealogy. [G229-1; DC1256].

FINNEY -- Buchanan, Jane Gray. *Thomas Thompson and Ann Finney of Colonial Pennsylvania and North Carolina: Lawrence Closs, and John Thompson: Allied Lines of Finney, McAlister, Buchanan, and Hart*. Oak Ridge, TN, J.B. Buchanan, 1987. 402p. 1. Thompson family. 2. Thompson, Thomas, D. ca. 1795-Family. 3. Finney family. 4. McAlister family. NGS & DC list as THOMPSON. DC gives underscored title. [G229-3; NGS11; DC3630].

FISK -- See above: CHRISTIAN. [L3420].

FISK -- Fisk, Moses. *The Life and Writing of Moses Fisk*. (compiled and edited by Tim Barlow) Crossville, TN, Barlow, 1980. 234p. Contents: Barlow, T: The Life of Moses Fisk -- Fisk, M. Historical Sketch of Tennessee -- Fisk, M. Tyrannical Libertymen -- Fisk, M. Conjectures Respecting the Ancient Inhabitants of North America -- Michaux, F.A. A Journey Through Middle Tennessee with Moses Fisk. -- Survey of the Line between Tennessee and Virginia -- Moses Fisk's Correspondence. -- Moriarty, G.A. The Fisk Family of Laxfield, Suffolk County, England. -- Bond, H. The New England Ancestors of Moses Fisk. -- Christian, H.C. The Days of Moses Fisk. [C230].

FISHER -- Jones, William L. *The Fisher Scrapbook, 1730-1972*. Milan, TN, Jones, 1968. x, 350p. D gives underscored part of title. [S860; D4421].

FITCH -- Lewis, Ailene Fitch. *Fitch, Crawford, Davis, McFarland Francis, Holderman* and *Allied Lines from Pennsylvania, Tennessee, Kentucky, North Carolina, Illinois to Johnson County, Missouri; 1722-1971.* Holden, MO, Lewis, 1971. 42 leaves. [X323-NY].

FITCH -- Lewis, Ailene Fitch. *Fitch, Crawford, Davis, Holderman, Francis, McFarland and Allied Lines from Pennsylvania, Tennessee, Kentucky, North Carolina, Illinois to Johnson County, Missouri; 1722-1976.* Holden, MO, Lewis, 1976. 130p. [D4438; VP73].

FLAGG -- Flagg, Charles Allcott. *Descendants of Josiah Flagg of Berkeley County, W.Va.; with Sketches of Flagg, Keyes, Foss, Shively, Hughes, Slemons, and Campbell Ancestries; A Memorial to Henry Gaither Flagg of Tennessee, by His Son, Joseph Walker Flagg.* Boston, MA, T. R. Marvin & Son, 1920. pni. [VV67].

FLOURNOY -- Cheek, Menifee Reed. *Flournoys of France from England to America.* Nashville, TN, The Society (of the DAR), 1957, 32 leaves. [D4503].

FLOWERS -- Flowers, Jarrott Val. *Some Descendants of Ralph Flowers of Buckingham County, Virginia and Smith County, Tennessee.* Scottsdale, AZ, Paragon Printing, 1991. xxiv, 183p.
LC CALL NUMBER: CS71.F629 1991

FORCE -- NAS. *Force - Foree - Ford Records.* ?, TN, 1944. 26 leaves. [D4548].

FORD -- NAS. *Ford History and Genealogy, Including Allied Families; One Line of Descendants of William Ford, Who Landed in Plymouth, Massachusetts, November 21, 1621.* Oak Ridge, TN, 1956. 235 leaves. [L6249].
-- *Errata and Addenda.* Also Index to Names of Descendants of William Ford of the Fortune, Their Material [sic] Ancestors and Spouses. Oak Ridge, TN 1963. 30p. [L6249].

FORD -- Cain, Stith Malone. *A History of Our Ford Family of Virginia, Kentucky, Indiana,*

Mississippi, Missouri, and Tennessee.
Whitewater, WI, Cain, 1971. 82 leaves.
[S886; D4550; VV68].

FORD -- Ford, Frederick W. *Ford History and
Genealogy, Including Allied Families; One Line
of Descendants of William Ford, Who Landed at
Plymouth, Massachusetts...1921 [sic]*. Oak
Ridge, TN, 1960, x 253p. Also, errata,
addenda and index of names to descendants of
William Ford of the Fortune, etc. Oak Ridge,
TN, 1963. 30p. [X330-FW,MH].

FORT -- Fort, Kate Haynes. *Memoirs of the
Fort and Fannin Families*. Chattanooga, TN,
Macgowan & Cook Co., 1903. 232p. [D4586].

FORT -- Fort, Robert C. *Forts of the Old
Seventh and Fourteenth District, Robertson
County*. Cookeville, TN, R.C. Fort, c1985.
163p., 2 leaves of plates. 1. Fort family.
2. Robertson County, (Tenn.)-Genealogy. C
gives: "Cover Title: Forts". [G236-1; C235].

FOUCHE -- Howell, Mrs. J. G. *Genealogy of
Fouche, Penrod, Eshelman and Allied Families;
American Revolutionary Soldiers of
Pennsylvania, Massachusetts, Tennessee*.
Kansas City, MO, D.A.R., 1948. 147 leaves.
[X333-FW,SP; VP76].

FOWLER -- Arthur, Glenn Dora Fowler (Mrs.
James Joyce Arthur). *Annals of the Fowler
Family with Branches in Virginia, North
Carolina, South Carolina, Tennessee, Kentucky,
Alabama, Mississippi, California and Texas*.
Austin, TX, Arthur, Ben C. Jones & Co., 1901.
xvi, 327p. Index inserted after publication.
[L6339; D4611; VV69].

FOWLER -- Fowler, Grover Parsons. *The House
of Fowler; A History of the Fowler Families of
the South, Embracing Descendants of John
Fowler of Virginia and Branches in North
Carolina, Georgia, Tennessee, Kentucky,
Alabama, Texas; Also Records of Allied
Families*. Hickory, NC, 1940. 754, 2p. D

gives underscored title and note: "Index by Mrs. Frank Cline bound separately." [L6343; D4615; VV69].
-- *Index* by Mrs. Frank Cline, Hot Springs, AR, 1962. 69 l. [L6343].

FOWLER -- Traver, Jerome D. *Fowler Family Facts: Virginia, North Carolina, Tennessee, Illinois, Iowa, and Wisconsin.* Williamsburg, VA, J.D. Traver, [1991] 36 leaves. [NGN18-3-92 & Nov/Dec 94 & May/Jun 95]. LC CALL NUMBER: CS71.F788 1991

FOX -- McCain, William D. *Eight Generations of the Family of Henry Fox (1768-1852) and His Wife Sarah Harrell Fox (1772-1848), of South Carolina, Tennessee, Alabama, and Mississippi.* Hattiesburg, MS, McCain, 1975. 4 v. X gives 2 v. [D4637; X335; NGN SEP/OCT 95].

FRANCIS -- Coalston, Eula De Ree Francis. *Our Francis Family and Relatives.* Humboldt, TN, E.D.F. Coalston, ix, 103p. [G238-3].

FRANCISCO -- Fletcher, Virginia Billingsley. [G239-1]. See above: BOWEN. [G77-1].

FRASER -- Nelson, Virginia Knight. *Samuel Frazier, A Whig of 1776, One of the Framers of Tennessee's Constitution, 1796, the First State Senator from Greene County, Tennessee, 1796, His Wife Rebecca Julian and Their Descendants.* Knoxville, TN, Nelson, 1978, 203p. 1 leaf of plates. D lists under FRAZIER and shows title as: Samuel Frazier of Tennessee and His Family.
[C239-2; D4673].

FRIERSON -- Stephenson, Theodore Frierson. *The Friersons of Zion Church and Their Descendants.* Nashville, TN, Parthenon Press, 1938. 235p. X omits date.
[D4701; X341-FW].

FRIZZELL -- Frizzell, Myra. *A Frizzell Family Record.* Johnson City, TN, M. Frizzell, 1982. iv, 86 leaves. Paperback. [C242].

FROST -- Frost, Wright Wilson. *The Frosts and Related Families of Bedford County, Tennessee* - 1st ed. Knoxville, TN, Frost, 1962. 342p. D does not give author. [L6491; S931; D4720].
-- *A Supplement to the Frosts and Related Families of Bedford County, Tennessee*. Knoxville, TN, 1972. 343-375p. [S931].

FUDGE -- Tyler, Maudie Fudge. *The Descendants of Jacob Fudge, Senior, 1723-1980*. Memphis, TN, Tyler, 1981. 137p. [D4733].

FULBRIGHT -- Dickson, Roy S, Jr. [G244-3]. See above: COLEMAN. [G149-3].

# G

GAFFIN -- Lynn, Catherine Gaffin. *Gaffin Family*. Centerville, TN, Lynn, 1969. 79p. [D4779].

GAINES -- NAS. *Members of the Gaines Family Organize Prepare to Erect Monument to Members Who Fought in the Revolutionary War*. Clippings from the Nashville, Tennessean, July 31, 1916. Mounted and Bound. 3 1. [X350-NY].

GALBRAITH -- Moran, Clara Galbreath Royse and Marie Galbreath Good. *Galbraith*. Collinwood, TN, 25, [1] leaves of plates. Compiled in 1943. Collinwood, TN, J.W. Galbreath, Sr., 198_. 25 [1] leaves. 1. Galbraith family. [G248-2].

GALLAGHER -- Gallagher, Joy Quandt. *The Gallaghers of the Pelham Valley of Middle Tennessee and Beyond: 1840s-1992*. Winchester, TN, J.Q. Gallagher, c1992. 600 p. 92-90014:
LC CALL NUMBER: CS71.G157 1992

GALLIMORE -- Gallimore, Russell N. *The Gallimore Family Tree*. Memphis, TN, R.N. Gallimore, 1990. 69, 3 leaves.
LC CALL NUMBER: IN PROCESS (UTILITY LOAD) [SIC]

GAMBLE — Brown, Louise G. & Jane C. Luna. *The Descendants of Bradley Gambill*. Columbia, TN, The Authors, 1979. 238 p., 4 leaves of plats. DC lists as GAMBILL and gives 238 leaves. [C248; DC1375].

GARDNER — Myers, Nella Smith. *The Gardner Family of East Tennessee. - 1st ed.* Knoxville, TN, St. Clair Enterprises, 1986. 383p. 1. Gardiner family. 2. Tennessee, East-Genealogy. [G250-3].

GARDNER — Myers, Nella Smith & Lawrence St. Clair Myers. *Supplement to The Gardner Family of East Tennessee.* Knoxville, TN, St. Clair Enterprises, 1986. 60p. 1. Gardiner family. 2. Tennessee, East-Genealogy. [GS250-3].

GARDNER — Myers, Nella Smith. *The Gardner Family of East Tennessee.* Knoxville, TN, St. Clair Enterprises, 1986. 383, 60p. [DC1383].

GARRISON — Garrison, Lloyd Russell. *The Descendants of John Garrison of Sumner County, Tennessee.* Denton, TX, Terrill Wheeler Printing Company, 1961. 53p. [L6682; D4876].

GEORGE — Brumley, Francis G. *The George History, 1752-1979.* Rogersville, TN, East Tennessee Printing Co., 1980. vi, 251p. [C254].

GEORGE — Smith, Austin Wheeler. *The George - Lacy Genealogy.* Cookeville, TN, Smith, 1940. 1p., 77 numb. l. [L6737; D4936].

GIBBS — NAS. *Nicholas Gibbs and His Descendants, 1733-1977.* Knoxville, TN, Nicholas Gibbs Historical Society, 1977. 102, 253p. [C256; NG45; D4963].

GIBBS — NAS. *Ancestry of Nicholas Gibbs.* Knoxville, TN, Nicholas Gibbs Historical Society, 1984. 24p. [C256].

GIBBS — Rutledge, Fred A. *Some Descendants of Theodore H. Gibbs, 1806 News York-1886*

Tennessee. Baltimore, MD, F. A. Rutledge,
1986. iii, 18, 197p. 1. Gibbs family. 2.
Gibbs, Theodore H., 1806-1886.
[G257-1].

GIBBS -- Rutledge, Fred A. *Some Descendants
of Theodore H. Gibbs, 1806 New York-1886
Tennessee*, 4th ed. Baltimore, MD, F.A.
Rutledge, 1994. xv, 80p.
   LC CALL NUMBER: CS71.G443 1994

GIBBS -- Smith, Jonathan Kennon. *The Gibbs
Place in Madison County, Tennessee*. Jackson,
TN, J.K.T. Smith, c1993. 10 leaves.
   LC CALL NUMBER: F444.J2 S62 1993

GIBSON -- Hill, Euel Ray. [G257-2]. See
above: COKER. [G148-3].

GIFFORD -- Brown, Christine R. *The
Genealogy of the Gifford Family from
Massachusetts to Maine*. Knoxville, TN,
Campbell Printing, 1981, c1980. v, 451p.
[DS267].

GILBERT -- Gilbert, Eliza Howe. *A Record of
the Benjamin Gilbert Branch of the Gilbert
Family in America (1620-1920). Also the
Genealogy of the Falconer Family of
Nairnshire, Scotland (1720-1920) to Which
Belonged Benjamin Gilbert's Wife, Mary
Falconer*. Johnson City, TN, Johnson City
Publ. Co., 1920. 64p., 1 leaf.
[L6803].

GILL -- Simms, Vivian York. *The Descendants
of Thomas & Sarah ( Bennett ) Gill and Related
Families. Including English Emigrants,
Palatines, Puritans, Mayflower Immigrants, and
Royal Lineages*. Murfreesboro, TN, V.Y.
Simms, 1988. ix, 217, 35p.
   LC CALL NUMBER: CS71.G474 1988

GILLILAND -- Webb, Matilda Jenkins. *These
Are My Roots: Genealogy and Jenkins
Genealogy*. Newport, TN, M.J. Webb, 1984. iv,
93p. [C259].

GIST -- Anderson, Frank Gist. *The Gist Family of White County, Tennessee.* NP, 1937. 17 leaves. [D5031].

GLENN -- Glenn, Wayne. *The Glenn Family of Lancaster County, Pa. Lincoln County, N.C. White County, TN, Marshall County, TN and Christian County, Mo...* Nixa, MO, W. Glenn 1985. 13 leaves. [DC1436].

GOODPASTURE -- Goodpasture, A. V. & W.H. *Life of Jefferson Dillard Goodpasture, To Which is Appended a Genealogy of the Family of James Goodpasture.* Nashville, TN, Cumberland Presbyterian Publishing House, 1897. 3, (5) - 308p. D gives underscored part of title and 308, 15p. [L6980; D5124].

GOODPASTURE -- Goodpasture, Robert A. *Captain James Goodpasture, Tennessee Pioneer, Son of Abraham and Martha ( Hamilton ) Goodpasture, with Some Descendants.* Sunnvale, CA, 1972. 9 leaves. [S1020].

GOODPASTURE -- Goodpasture, Robert Abraham. *Early Goodpaster (Goodpasture) Families in America.* Sunnyvale, CA, 1972- 1 v. 5 parts. Pt. 1. Virginia, Tennessee, Kentucky, Ohio 1st ed; rev. - Pt. 2 Kentucky, Ohio, Indiana, Illinois, Iowa Records: military, census, marriage, cemetery, deeds & wills, births. 1 v. - Pt. 3 Addendum. Some Descendants, bits and pieces. - Pt. 4 Compendium: additional records, more descendants, "Spots", "Blacks" - Pt. 5 Appendix: More additional descendants. [S1022].

GOODPASTURE -- Goodpasture, Robert Abraham. *Early Goodpaster (Goodpasture) Families in America.* Salt Lake City, UT, Heritage Research Institute, 19__ v. Contents: Pt. 3 Addendum. Some descendants. Bits and pieces. [S1023].

GOODWIN -- See above: CAMPBELL. [L2939; D2108].

GOODWIN -- Grady, Jamie Ault. *Goodwin*. Knoxville, TN, J.A. Grady, 1981. A-B, viii, 253p., 1 leaf of plates. [C267-1].

GORDON -- Gordon, Thomas Gilbert. *The John Hilton Gordon Family, Rutherford County, Tennessee*. Tampa, FL, T.G. Gordon, 1988 (Decorah, Iowa. Anundesn Pub. Co.) 512p. 1. Gordon family. 2. Gordon, John Hilton, 1811-1884-Family. 3. Tennessee-Genealogy. [G267-1].

GOULD -- Kelsey, Mary Wilson. [G268-3]. See above: COOK. [G155-1; NGS12].

GOURLEY -- Gourley, Sam. *Gourley Generations: Tenn., N.C., & Ky.* Cunningham, KY, S. Gourley, 1992. 623p.
LC CALL NUMBER: CS71.G98 1992

GRAHAM -- Graham, Joe C. *The Gallant Grahams of America - Tennesse ed.* Quinton, AL, J.C. Graham, 1989. x, 344p. 1. Graham family. 2. Tennessee-Genealogy. [G269-2].

GRAHAM -- Graham, John M. *The Grahams of Pinewood.* - 1st ed. - Sharpsburg, GA, WHW Associates, 1986. x, 97p. 1. Graham family. 2. Tennessee-Genealogy. [G269-2].

GRANT -- See above: CAMPBELL. [L2939; D2108].

GRAVES -- NAS. *The Graves Newsletter.* Chattanooga, TN, Graves Family Assoc. NY has vol. 1-3 no. 3, June, 1969 to Winter, 1971. Quarterly. [X383-NY].

GRAVES -- Graves, Aubrey E. *Pioneer Settlers of Blount and DeKalb Counties, Alabama; John Graves, Pioneer and Allied Graves Families of Alabama and North Carolina.* Chattanooga, TN, Graves, 1968. 186p. D gives underscored part of title. [L7185; D5224].

GRAVES -- Graves, Jessie Wagner. *Branching Out From Stephen Graves (1759-1828).*

Knoxville, TN, Tennessee Valley Pub., 1991.
199p. LC CALL NUMBER: CS71.G7742 1991

GRAVES -- Neal, Thomas Howe Rowe. *Harbison, Graveston, Know County, Tennessee and the Graves Genealogy.* Knoxville, TN, 1973. 141p. [NG47; X383-FW].

GRAY -- Marlar, Ruth Gray & Ollie May Gray O'Connor. *The Grays - Relatively Speaking.* Memphis, TN, R. Gray Marlar, 1983. 63 leaves, 2 leaves of plates. [C273].

GREENFIELD -- Vick, James Andrew. *Greenfield, Colonel Thomas, Immigrant to Maryland: Some of His Ancestors and Descendants.* Waco, TX, J.A. Vick, 1989. vi, 511p. 1. Greenfield family. 2. Greenfield, Thomas, 1648-1715-Family. 3. Maryland-Genealogy. 4. Tennessee-Genealogy. [G272-2].

GREENUP -- Jourdan, Elise Greenup. [G272-3]. See above: CECIL. [G129-1].

GRIDER -- Jacobs, Josephine Grider. *Marse John Goes to War.* Memphis, TN, Davis Printing Co., c1933. 111p. [D5303].

GRIFFITH -- NAS. *Genealogy of the Edward Griffiths Family (Born October, 1833, Mold, Northeastern Wales, Died November 10, 1910, Wooldridge, Tennessee) and His Descendants.* NP, 198_. 13 leaves. [C277].

GRIFFITH -- Cunningham, Eileen F. R. *Griffith Family.* Nashville, TN, 1975. 19p. [X390-FW].

GRIMES -- Grimes, Jay Cook. [G275-1]. See above: COOK. [G155-1; D5326].

GRIMMETT -- Price, David, Jr. *Grimmett, Grimmitt, Grimmitte & Lane.* Brentwood, TN, 1977. 88p. [C277; NG48].

GRIMMETT -- Price, David. *The Grimmetts of Virginia of the Revolutionary War Era and*

*Their Descendants.* Brentwood, TN, Price, c1989. 150p. [C277; D5329].

GROOVER -- Lovell, Eloise Groover & Nettie Lewis Groover Manly. *The Peter Groover Family, 1762-1981: A History of Some Generations of Peter and Sarah Groover, Nine Generations.* Hermitage, TN, E.G. Lovell, 1981. vi, 191p., 2p. of plates. Cover Title: Groover Family History. "1982 supplementary bulletin to the Groover Family History." [C279].

GRUBB -- Wanger, F. P. *The Grubb Families of America; John Grubb of Tennessee.* Pottstown, PA, 1910. Genealogical Table. [L7371; VP89].

GUNN -- Johnson, Lillian Vesta Brown. [G280-3]. See above: BROWN. [G99-3].

GUSS -- Anderson, Beverly D. *Guss: Ancestors and Descendants of Abraham L. and Susan Maria Sophia Rindlaub Guss.* [Note: DC gives Rindbannt for Rindlaub] Oak Ridge, TN, B.D. Anderson, 1988. vii, 430p. 1. Guss family. 2. Guss, Abraham L., 1834-1887- Family. 3. Guss, Susan Maria Sophia Rindlaub, 1836-1936. [G282-2; DC1539].

GWIN -- Hornback, Joyce Gwin. *The Gwins of North Carolina and Tennessee.* Pearl, MS, Hornback, 1986. 96p. [DS292].

# H

HAGGART -- Harrell, Elizabeth J. [G288-3]. See above: CLABAUGH. [G140-2].

HAGEY -- Hagey, King Albert. *The Hagey Families in American and the Dulaney Family.* Bristol, TN, - VA King Printing Co., 1951. 714p. [D5415].

HALCOMB -- Giulvezan, Isabel Stebbins. *Notes on Hiram H. Halcomb (1789-1869) of*

*Caswell County, North Carolina, Robertson County, Tennessee, Logan and Simpson Counties, Kentucky and His 16 Children.* St. Louis, MO, Giulvezan, 1961. 55 l. FW gives no date. [D5436; X-FW].

**HALE** -- Lynch, Muriel Nadine Hale. *Spanning the Centuries with Hale Family.* __, MO, Arrow Print Co., Independence, MO, M.N.H. Lynch distributor, 1990. ii, 398p. 1. Hale family. 2. Tennessee-Genealogy. [G289-3].

**HALE** -- Whitley, Edythe Rucker. *Hale Family...* Nashville, TN, 1934, 1, 38, 7p. Mimeographed. [L7519].

**HALE** -- Whitley, Edythe Rucker. *Lineage of Mrs. E. P. McKellar, Through the Hale Family of Virginia and Tennessee.* Nashville, TN, Whitely, 1945. 33 l. [D5446; X400-LA; VV83].

**HALE** -- Wood, Melba. *My Maternal Ancestry, Dean, Matlock, Hale, Gahr Families in Tennessee and Missouri.* Godfrey, IL, 1969. 21 leaves. X lists as DEAN & gives date of 1968. [L7527; X248-NY,SP].

**HALE** -- Wood, Melba. *My Maternal Ancestry, Dean, Matlock, Hale, Gahr Families in Tennessee and Missouri.* Godfrey, IL, [1968]-1987. 2 v. Vol. 2 has subtitle: Dean, Matlock, Haile, Gahr, Binkley, Ellis, Vick, Woolsey, East Tennessee pioneer Matlock families. Vol. 2 published in Chesterfiled, IL. 1. Hale family. [G289-3].

**HALL** -- Hall, Marvin F. *History of the Hall - Ayers - Holland Family. Virginia, North Carolina, Georgia, Tennessee, Texas.* Scarsdale, NY, Hall, 1976. 100 leaves. [D5466; VV83].

**HALL** -- Whitley, Edythe Rucker. *Lineage Through Several Lines of Descent of Martha Lucille Hall,[sic] Marshall, Nashville, Tennessee; Whitson, Families of Hall, Nunnally, Stephenson, Cade, Daughtery*

*[Daugherty ?], McCray and Other Connections.*
*NP, 1969. 1 v. Typescript. [D5474].*

HALL. -- Wood, Melba. *My Maternal Ancestry:*
*Dean, Matlock, Gahr Families (in Tennessee and*
*Missouri).* Godfrey, IL, M. Wood. 1968-1987.
2 v. Vol. 2 has subtitle: Dean, Matlock,
Haile, Gahr. Binkley, Ellis. Vick, Woolsey,
East Tennessee pioneer Matlock families. 1.
Hale family. [G289-3].

HAMBLEN -- NAS. *The Hamblen and Allied*
*Families.* Kingsport, TN. D.W. Hamblen, 1991.
83p.
LC CALL NUMBER: CS71.H223 1991

HAMBRIGHT -- Wooten, John Morgan. *The*
*Hambrights of Tennesse.* Cleveland, TN,
Wooten, 1937. 20p. [D5495].

HAMEL. -- Hemphill Family History Committee,
Margaret Hemphill Anthony, Chairman.
*Hemphills in North Carolina.* Collegdale, TN,
College Press, xii, 246p. [C290].

HAMILTON -- Parrish, Verle Hamilton.
*Hamilton, Mullins, Fleming, and Related Lines.*
*of Ky., W.Va., No. Car., and Tenn.* Stamping
Ground, KY, Parrish, 1975. 80p. [S1100].

HAMILTON -- Tatum, Margaret E. Hamilton.
*All These Years: Biography and Family History.*
Cleveland, TN, M.E.H. Tatum, 1982. 232p.
[C291].

HAMNER -- Hooker, Ruth N. *The Hamner Family*
*of Albemarle County, Virginia and Tennessee*
Memphis, TN, 1949. pni. [VV84].

HANCOCK -- Hancock, Richard R. *John Hancock*
*of Virginia and His Descendants.* Chattanooga,
TN, Mrs. G.O. Kreiger, 1957. 103, xii leaves.
[X407-FW,MH].

HANCOCK -- Hancock, Richard Ramsey & Walter.
*Some Descendants of John Hancock (1733-1802)*
*of Goochland, Fluvanna and Patrick Counties,*

*Virginia.* Woodbury, TN, 1938. 91 leaves.
Typed. [L7675].

HANCOCK -- Ward, Maureen Hancock. *The
Hancock Brothers from Virginia : William
Hancock, 1738-1818, Stephen Hancock,
1744-1827.* Richfield, ID, Distributed by the
Hancock Family Organization, c1992. ix,
308p. LC CALL NUMBER: CS71.H2410 1992

HANKINS -- NAS. *The Hankins Workshop.*
Knoxville, TN, P.H. Skaggs, 1983- . --v.
Numbering irregular. See shelflist for DAR
Library holdings. [DC1595].

HANNA -- NAS. *Second Reunion of the
Descendants of James and Susan Bryson Hanna,
Held at Bethpage, Sumner County, Tennessee...
1891, with a Genealogical Record.* Nashville,
TN, 1892. 30p. [X408-LI].

HANNA -- Montoye, Betty A. (B). *Hanna
Family: 1774-1974; Laurens District, S.C. to
Carroll County, Indiana.* Knoxville, TN, 1974.
78p. [X409-FW/LA/NY].

HANNAWALT -- Hannawalt, Dwight Moody. *The
Hannawalt Family in America, c1750-1972.* Old
Hickory, TN, 1973. vi, 362p. [S1106].

HANSARD -- Burns, Annie Walker. *Hansard -
Christian Family History Records.* Knoxville,
TN, Hansard Family Register, 1978. xiv, 124
leaves. Reprint with new index of the 1951
ed. published by A.W. Burns, Washington.
[C294].

HANSARD -- Burns, Annie Walker. *Hansard
Military Records of the Civil War: Also, Some
Cherokee Records of the Hansard Name.*
Knoxville, TN, Hansard Family Register, 1978.
xxiv, 38 leaves. Reprint of the 1964 ed,
published by A.W. Burns, Washington with a new
index. [C294].

HANSARD -- Garrett, Winnie H. *The Hansard -
Hansford Family History: Comprising the*

Surnames of Hanford- - Handford - Hanford - Hansard - Hanserd - Hansird - Hansford and the Variant Forms from A.D. _15 to A.D. 1984. . Baltimore, MD, Gateway Press, 2 v. (xxxii, 1109p.) 1 leaf of plates. [C294].

**HANSARD** -- Hansard, Sam L. *Descendants of John Hansard of Amherst County, Virginia, 1766-1976.* Knoxville, TN, Hansard, 1977. xviii, 444p. [C294; VV85].

**HARBISON** -- Neal, Thomas H. *Harbison, Graveston, Knox County, Tennessee, and the Graves Family.* Knoxville, TN, 1973. 121p. [X411-IG].

**HARDEMAN** -- Hardeman, Nicholas Perkins. *Wilderness Calling: The Hardeman Family in the American Westward Movement, 1750-1900.* Knoxville, TN, University of Tennessee Press, c1977. xiv, 357p. D gives underscored part of title. X gives date of 1976. [C296; DC1606; D5584; X411-LA].

**HARDING** -- Bivins, Willie Hardin. *East Tennessee Letters: Nineteenth Century: with Illustrations and Genealogical Notes.* Oklahoma City, OK, W.R.H. Bivins, c1984. xi, 203p. 1. Reeves family-Correspondence. 2. Harding family-Correspondence. 3. Tennessee-Biography. 4. Tennessee-Social life and customs-19th century. 5. Tennessee-Genealogy. [G297-3].

**HARDISON** -- Wilkinson, A Mims. [G297-3]. See above: DERRYBERRY. [G187-1].

**HARLLEE** -- Harlee, William Curry. *Kinfolks, a Genealogical and Biographical Record of Thomas and Elizabeth ( Stuart ) Harlee, Andrew and Agnes ( Cade ) Fulmore, Benjamin and Mary Curry, Samuel and Amelia ( Russell ) Kemp, John and Hannah ( Walker ) Bethea, Sterling Clack and Frances ( King ) Robertson, Samuel and Sophia Ann ( Parker ) Dickey, Their Antecedents, Descendants, and Collateral Relatives, with Chapter Concerning State and*

*County Records and the Derivation of Counties of Alabama, Florida, Georgia, Mississippi, North Carolina, Pennsylvania, South Carolina, Tennessee, Texas, and Virginia.* New Orleans, LA, 1934-37. Searcy & Pfaff, Ltd. 4 V. Contents: v. 1. Harllee Section. - v. 2. Fulmore Section. Curry Section. Kemp Section. - v. 3. Bethea Section, Robertson Section, Dickery Section. v. 4. General Indexes. [L7764; VP93].

**HARRELL.** -- Simpson, Virginia Harrell. *Our Harrells of South Carolina.* Chattanooga, TN, V.H. Simpson, n.d. 2 v. Part 2. Descendants of Jacob Harrell. [DC1632].

**HARRIS** -- Johnson, Lillian Vesta Brown. [G301-2]. See above: BROWN. [G99-3].

**HARRIS** -- Roberson, Erma Harris. *Harris Tree and Branches: Descendants of John Taylor Harris, North Carolina and Tennessee.* Cullman, AL, Printed by Brook Litho c. 19__? ?p. [L7831].

**HARRIS** -- Roberson, Erma Harris. *Harris Tree and Branches: Descendants of John Taylor Harris, North Carolina and Tennessee.* Cullman, AL, Gregath Pub. Co., c. 1990. 145p. 1. Harris family. 2. Harris, John Taylor, 1775-1868 or 9-Family. 3 North Carolina-Genealogy. 4. Tennessee-Genealogy. [G301-2].

**HARRIS** -- Seaman, Catherine Hawes Coleman. [G301-3]. See above: COLEMAN. [G150-1].

**HARRISON** -- Harrison, George Edgar. *Some of the Descendants of James Mason Harrison.* Crossville, TN, Harrison, 1966. 52 leaves. [D5700].

**HARRISON** -- Kerr, Marguerite Harrison. *Laurels of Big Ivy.* Columbia, TN, P-Vine Press. 1981. vii, 332p. [C301].

**HATHCOCK** -- Hathcock, Douglas W. *Hathcock Family History.* Huntsville, AL, D. W.

Hathcock, 1967-<1984 > v. <1, 3, 6-8, 10
> v. 1. Hathcock families in Monroe County,
Mississippi, 1847-1900. v. 3. Hathcock
families in early American history, 1730-1790.
v. 6. Hathcock families of Alabama and other
southern states. v. 7. No special title. v.
8. Hathcock families of Tennessee, 1812-1880.
v. 10. Hathcock families of Georgia, 1795-
1880. [G304].

HAWORTH -- Hatchett, Mrs. Jerry L. *Haworth
Family of England and America.* Knoxville, TN,
1973. 59p. [X427-FW].

HAWES -- Hudgins, Helen Hawes. *The Richard
Hawes Family of Kentucky.* Franklin, TN, H.H.
Hudgins, 1986. iv leaves, 271p.
   LC CALL NUMBER: CS71.H418 1986

HAYES -- Hays, Maude Calloway. *Hays Records
and Roberts and Allied Families.* Chattanooga,
TN, 1951. 1 v. (various pagings). [L8051].

HAYES -- Price, David. *A Short Genealogy of
Anderson Sharp Hayes.* Brentwood, TN, 1977.
66p. [C307; NC51].

HAYES -- Seaman, Catherine Hawes Coleman.
[G307-1]. See above: COLEMAN. [G150-1].

HAYNES -- Haynes, Grace. *The Daddy Haynes
Story.* Morristown, TN, Morrison Printing Co.,
1968. 319p. [D5861].

HAYWARD -- Heyward, James Barnwell. *The
Colonial History of the Heyward Family of
South Carolina, 1760-1770, Together with an
Abbreviated Genealogy, 1770-1870.* Nashville,
TN, McQuiddy Pr. Co., 1907. 38p. [L8086].

HEATHERLEY -- Stephens, Nadine Heatherley.
[G309-1] See above: CANNON.
[G119-1; DC1710].

HENDERSON -- NAS. *Henderson Research -
Virginia, Georgia, Ky., Tenn.* Cincinnati, OH,
NP, n.d. [VV91].

HENDERSON -- Mitchell, Reba Henderson. *The Family of Samuel Henderson, 1786-1867, of Monroe County, Tennessee*: A Genealogical and Historical Record of Samuel Henderson and His Wife, Nancy Blair, Their Twelve Children, and Their Descendants to the Present Generations. NP, 1980. 85p. in various paginations. NG gives underscored part of title and 99p. [C313; NG51].

HENDERSON -- Roberts, H. D. Henderson Family Research; (Virginia, Kentucky, Tennessee, Georgia, Indiana, etc.) Orange, CA, Author, 1967. 15p. [X436-FW; VV92].

HENDRIBKS -- Hendrix, Violet Hendricks, Ed. The Hendrix Family of Carter County, Tennessee: Descendants of John Hendrix, 1756-1846, as known to the editor in 1975. Compiled from County, Census, War, & Family Records and Other Sources. Kingsport, TN, Hendrix, 1976. 280p. [C314].

HENDRIX -- Hendrix, Violet. The Hendrix Family of Carter County, Tennessee. Kingsport, TN, Hendrix, 1976. 280p. [D5956].

HENRY -- NAS. Descendants of James and Samuel Henry, Revolutionary War Soldiers. Knoxville, TN, Padd Letter Service, 1962. 310p. [D5967].

HENRY -- Dawson, Aurelia Cate. Our Tennessee Kinsmen. Seaford, DE, Dawson, 1962. 90p. [D5966].

HENRY -- Henry, Jeanne Hand. My Henry Family: Pennsylvania, Virginia, Tennessee, Alabama, Mississippi and incidentally Oklahoma. New Market, AL, Southern Genealogical Services, 1973. 69p. [D5973; VP101].

HENRY -- Sharp, Eron M. The Henry Family: Descendants of Samuel Henry and His Son John M. Henry. Memphis, TN, E.M. Sharp, 1978. 84 leaves. [DC1740].

HENRY -- See above: CATE. [L1174].

HENSON -- Duggins, Lydia A. *Cousins (of) Tennessee*. Bridgeport, CT, 1965. Unpaged. [X439-NY].

HERNDON -- Elliott, Rita Jones. *The Herndon and Connor Families*. Chattanooga, TN. Elliott, 1961. 151p. [D6002; X440-FW].

HICKLE -- Moss, Ernestine Parke. *Hickle Heritage*. Memphis, TN, Moss, 1979. 134p. [C318; DS339].

HICKMAN -- Hilton, Hope A. *Edwin and Elender Webber Chiles Hickman; Some Progenitors and Descendants. Early Pioneers of Virginia, North Carolina, Kentucky, Missouri, and Utah*. Salt Lake City, UT, 1967. iv, 167p. [L8315; VV93].

HICKS -- Brigance, Pat Hicks. *Descendants of William C. Hicks: A Genealogy of William C. Hicks*. Maryville, TN, Brigance Enterprises, 1983. iv, 124p. [C318].

HILDEBRAND -- Bell, Annie Walker (B.). *Hildebrand and Hilderbrand Families. Records of Eastern Cherokee to Honor Nancy Ward, the Famous Indian Woman of Tennessee*. Washington, DC, 1958. 1X-3X, 43 l. [X446-FW,NY].

HILDEBRAND -- Clemmer, Sudie. *Nancy Ward and the Hildebrand Family of Polk County, Tennessee; Reprinted Newspaper Clippings from the J.D. Clemmer Scrapbooks*. Bemton, TN, Polk County News, 1962. 12 leaves. [L8348].

HILL -- Hill, Euel Ray. [G319-1]. See above: COKER. [G148-3].

HILL -- King, Larry. *Blue Ridge Mountain Kinfolks: A Record of Ancestors, Descendants and Relatives of the Author and Wife Including Fisher, Gilbert, Hall, King, Kirby, Lawson Families*. Hendersonville, TN, L. King, c1976. 335p. [DC1785].

**HILLIS** -- Hillis, Russell W. *Hillis Family History: The Life and Times of Florence & Russell W. Hillis...* Knoxville, TN, Tennessee Valley, 1990. 67p. [DC1787].

**HILLSMAN** -- Hillsman, Thomas Wingo. *The Hillsman / Hilsman Family.* Nashville, TN, McQuiddy Printing Co., 1977. xi, 504p. [DS347].

**HINES** -- Williams, Martha White. *William Hines and Martha Bright of Knox County, Tennessee.* Bean Station, TN, 1970. 45 (i.e.50) leaves.

**HIXSON** -- Armstrong, Zella. *Notable Southern Families: Hixson of Tennessee...* Chattanooga, TN, The Lookout Pub. Co. 193_, 12 leaves. [X450-NY].

**HIXSON** -- Hixson, James Ephraim. *Hixson oe [sic] Tennessee.* Pamphlet ed. Chattanooga, TN, Lookout Publ. Co., 1940. 20p. [L8446].

**HIXSON** -- Hixson, James E. & Zella Armstrong. *Hixson - Hixon of Tennessee.* 2nd ed. Chattanooga, TN, Hudson Printing Co., c1955. 94p. D omits edition. Noticeable Southern Families. First ed. published in 1940 under title: Hixson of Tennessee. [See just above]. [L8447; D6158].

**HOBDY** -- Absher, Lee Alton. *Some Early Settlers of Upper Sumner County, Tennessee.* Knoxville, TN, Absher, 1966. 73, 3-25p. [D6173].

**HOCKER** -- Chenault, Dora Hocker & Elizabeth Frances Ludeman. *The Hocker Family and Some Related Families.* Chattanooga, TN, Ludeman, 1937. 98 leaves. [D6177].

**HOCUTT** -- Hocutt, Paul McKinley, Sr. *Alabama Holcutts from Early 1700 to 1972.* Clarksville, TN, Tostens American Yearbook Co., 1972. xviii, 173p. [S1220; NG53; DC1800].

HODGES -- Bruce, Thomas Allen. *The Hodge / Hodges Book: Focus on Virginia-Tennessee-Arkansas Descendants of William Riley Hodge, M.C.* Little Rock, AR, T.A. Bruce, 1982. 3 v. (256p.) Vol. 2 has special title: Reference Source Book for Hodge/Hodges Research, Virginia, Tennessee, Arkansas. [C324; NG53].

HODGES -- Patton, Juanita M. *The Family of Isham and Betsy Hodges from Virginia to Tennessee.* Nashville, TN, J.M. Patton, c1990. xiii, 117p.
   LC CALL NUMBER: CS71.H688 1990

HODGES -- Whitley, Edythe Rucker. *Lineage of Judith Gene Harris Doss (Mrs. L. W. Doss, Jr.). Nashville, Tennessee; Includes Hodges, Randle, Hearn, Parker, Turner, Truitt, and Smith.* NP, 1968. 1 v. Typescript. [D6185].

HOLMES -- Bruce, Eileen Diggles. *Our Holmes Ancestors.* Memphis, TN, Bruce, 1949. 81 leaves. X gives: iv, 82 l. [D6252; X459-NY].

HOLLIDAY -- Holliday, Alvis Milton, Sr. *The Holliday Family.* Brentwood, TN, A.M. Holliday, 1983. v, 602p., 1 leaf of plates. [C328].

HOLT -- Cooper, Albert L. *Ancestors and Descendants of John and Isable Holt, Williamson County, Tennessee.* Shelbyville, TN, Cooper, c1971. 486p. [A319; D6263].

HOLT -- Holt, Thomas. *6173 descendants of Ambrose Holt (1773-1866) - 1st ed.* Cypress Inn, TN, T. Holt, 1991. xi, 774 p.
   LC CALL NUMBER: CS71.H7575 1991

HOLT -- McMillion, Virginia. *The History of the Irby Bennett Holt Family of Tennessee and Texas.* Austin, TX, V. McMillion, 1989. 184p.
   LC CALL NUMBER: CS71.H7575 1989

HOLT -- Rainey, Buck. *The Fabulous Holts: A Tribute to a Favorite Movie Family.*

Nashville, TN, Western Film Collector Press, 1976. 215p. [C330].

HOLT -- Tatum, V. Holt (from notes provided by Madie Holt Black & others). *The Holt Family in Europe and American, 1248-1971; A Brief Account of the Genealogy, History, and Armory in England and Germany in Europe: Also in the State of Massachusetts, Connecticut, Virginia, North Carolina, Tennessee, Mississippi and Utah in America.* Cincinnati, OH, 1971. 16p. [S1236; VV96].

HOOKER -- Maes, Virginia I. *The Descendants of Samuel Hooker of the Carolinas, Tennessee, Indiana and Illinois.* Rushville, IL, 1942. 8p, 12 numb. leaves. X gives just 8p. Reproduced from typed copy. [L8600; X462-OH].

HOPE -- See above: CAMPBELL. [L2939; D2108].

HOPKINS -- Bruhn, Reva Hopkins. *Hopkins Forever: James Hopkins, Revolutionary Soldier, Virginia, North Carolina, Kentucky, Tennessee, Illinois, and Missouri.* Visalia, CA, R. H. Bruhn, 1984. ii, 74p. 110 pages of plates. [C332; VV96].

HOSKINS -- Hackworth, Kenneth Onan. *Jesse Hoskins, Tennessee Pioneer and His Descendants.* Oak Ridge, TN, [DC gives: Clinton, TN, Duvall & Davis] 1986. 278p. [NGS7; DC1853].

HOUGH -- Hough, Granville W. *Some Hought Families and Individuals of Mississippi and Tennessee Through 1920.* [NGN19-5-93].

HOWSE -- Mitchell, Mary Ann. *The House of Howses -- 1st ed.* Jackson, TN, M.A. Mitchell, c1988. 151 leaves.
LC CALL NUMBER: CS71.H8398 1988

HUBBS -- Hubbs, Ferol Violet (Frost). *Hubbs - Frost and Allied Families.* Greenville, TN, 1946. 1 v. (various pagings). [L8826].

HUBBS -- Hubbs, Ferol F. *Hubbs - Frost and Allied Families.* Greenville, TN, 1958. Unpaged. [X474-NY].

HUDDLESTON -- Huddleston, Tim. *Jarriott Morgan Huddleston Family, 1775 -*. Ooltewah, TN, Huddleston, 198-? iii, 199.4p. [D6468].

HUDLOW -- Hudlow, James H. [G335-3]. See above: BRYDEN. [G103-2].

HUDLOW -- Robinson, Marguerite E. *Hudlows in America.* Nashville, TN, 1969. 141p. [X474-FW,NY].

HUFF -- Waterhouse, Carmack. *Certain Topics on the Huff, Sharp, and Allied Families, Including Askew....* Oak Ridge, TN, C. Waterhouse. 1983. 139p., 1 leaf of plates. [C339].

HUGHES -- Horton, Lucy Henderson. *Family History.* Franklin, TN, Press of the News, 1922. 5, 289p. Cover title: Family history including Hughes, Dalton, Martin, Henderson, all originally of Virginia, and many kindred branches. [L8859; D6493; VV98].

HULL -- Taylor, Robert Hull. *Hulls in 1850: A Directory of Persons Surnamed Hull in the U.S. in 1850.* Baltimore, MD, Gateway Press, 1983. ix, 163p. [C340].

HUNT -- Brown, Mrs. Herbet (Imogene Hannan Brown). *Hunt - Denton Families of Va., Tenn., Ky., Ind., and Western States.* Alexandria, IN, 1969. 719 1. VV lists as: HUNT-DENTON. [S678 & S1286; VV54].

HUNT -- Little, T. Vance. *The Hunt's [sic] of Tennesse.* Nashville, TN, Vee El Ancestral Studies, 1969. 61 leaves. [A339; D6544].

HURT -- Hurt, Oscar H. *The Early Hurt Family of Virginia.* Memphis, TN, Hurt, 1958. 102 leaves. [D6585].

**HUSBAND** — NAS. *Harmon Husband.* NP, Tennessee DAR, G.R.C., 1971. 44P. [D6587].

**HUTCHINS** — Low, Mary Elizabeth. *Hutchings, Powell, Moore, Theweatt, Critchlow. Sutherland, Cattles, Edenton, etc.* Nashville, TN, 1940. 37 leaves. Photostat (positive) copies of records of certain Dinwiddie County, Virginia families, chiefly family letters from 1816-1877, on file in the Division of library and archives of the Department of Education of Tennessee. [L9001].

**HYDER** — Hardwick, Aline Hyder. *The Genealogy of Benjamin Hyder.* Bristol, TN, Hardwick, 1967. 43 leaves. [L9056; D6628].

## I

**INGHAM** — Waterhouse, Carmack. *Certain Topics on the Ingham, Waterhouse, and Allied Families, Including Abel, Arendt, Bailey, Barcroft, Bartolette, Beaumont, Bell, Bewley, Bye, Campbell, Colville, Craigmiles, Drummond, Eliot, Emerson, Emmons, Ferguson, Fisher, Fuller, Green, Hartpence, Hoff, Hoppock, Johnson, Kinsey, Knorr, Larison, Lequear, Mills, Murphy, O'Brien, Preston, Rudebock, Runk, Runkle, Sergeant, Smartt, Stevens, Stokes, Stone, Stryker, Talmadge, Taylor, Thompson, Tipton, Watson, Wilson, Wood, Woodruff, Wolverton.* Oak Ridge, TN, 1974. 272p. [X488-PH; S2669].

**INGHAM** — Waterhouse, Carmack. *A Supplement to Certain Topics on the Ingham, etc, Families.* Oak Ridge, TN, 1976. 89p. See immediately above. [X488-PH; C347].

## J

**JACKSON** — Hankins, Edith Jackson. *Bob and Pansy Jackson Family.* Memphis, TN, E.J. Hankins, 1986. 26 leaves, 1 folded leaf of plates. LC CALL NUMBER: CS71.J13 1986

JACKSON -- Hankins Robert Lee & Edith Jackson Haskins and Florence Jackson Haskins. Daniel Begat. Memphis, TN, The Authors, 1989. 138p. [DC1969].

JACKSON -- Jackson, Harry L. Some Descendants of John and Elizabeth Cummins Jackson in Kentucky: Kentucky Relatives of Stonewall Jackson. Cleveland, OH, Jackson, Clarksville, TN, Jostens Publications, 1976. 154p. [C350; D6703; X492-FW/LA/OH].

JACKSON - Sandel, Mary Eleanor. The Jacksons. NP, c1984. 92p. [NGS7].

JACOBS -- Symmonds, Dorothy. A History and Genealogy of the Pritchett, Rimmer, Jacobs, Hamilton, Eldridge, Etheridge, Smith, Brown, and Davidson Families from North Carolina, Tennessee, Illinois, Missouri, and Kansas in the Early 1800s to 1900s. Bellaire, TX, D. Symonds, c1985-<c1989 >. v. <1-2 >. Vol. 2 has title: A history of the genealogy of the families of Howland, Brown, Follett, Van Dyke, Lamb, Spaulding, and Davidson with related lines of Tret, Botsford, Parker, Burwell, Clark, Andrews, Symmonds, Burnaman, Ashbaugh, and Smith from Holland, England, Scotland, and France to Massachusetts, Connecticut, New York, New Jersey, Ohio, Iowa, Indiana, Nebraska, Kansas, and Texas from "The Mayflower" pilgrims in 1620 to the 1980s. 1. Pritchard family. 2. Rimmer family. 3. Jacobs family. DC lists as: PRITCHETT and shows title as: A history and genealogy of the Pritchett... and Davidson families. DC indicates the DAR Library holdings as: v. 1. [G345-1; DC2965].

JAMES -- James, Larry A. The James Family of Wilson County, Tennessee. Neosho, MO, L.A. James, 1980. 21 leaves. [C352].

JAMESON -- Jamison, Henry Downs. The Jamison Family. Nashville, TN, Jamison, McTigue, 1960. 113, 29 leaves. D lists under Jamison. [L9200; D6735].

JAMISON -- Jamison, Henry Downs. *Letters and Recollections of a Confederate Soldier, 1860-1865.* Nashville, TN, Jamison, McTigue, 1964. 190 leaves. [D6736].

JARNIGAN -- Jarnigan, Thomas Leeper. *Captain Thomas Jarnigan, 1746-1802: The Story of One of Tennessee's Early Pioneers and His Wife, Mary Witt Jarnigan, 1753-1829.* Enlarged and current ed., Lake Lure, NC, Powers, 1978. x, 209p. [C354-1]. See below: JERNIGAN. [G349-2].

JARRARD -- Jarrard, C. C. *Jarrards in America.* Oak Ridge, TN, 1974. A1 - 25p. [X495-FW].

JARRETT -- Patterson, Richard E. *West Saxony, 452 -- America, 1982: 1,529 Years of Family History.* Virginia Beach, VA, R. Patterson, 1982 -< 1983? >; v. <1- 3 >. Vols 2-3 consist chiefly on the Smith - Jarrett Genealogy, by Austin Wheeler Smith, originally published in 1941, with corrections as of 1958. Vol. 3 includes addendum: The Gooch Family in Williams County, Tennessee by Mrs. George F. Watson and the Williamson County Historical Society. Publications. [C354].

JEAN -- Jean, Arthur Glenn. *The Jean Family of North Carolina and Tennessee.* Boulder, CO, A.G. Jean, c1991. 1 v. (various pagings). LC CALL NUMBER: CS71 .J33 1991

JERNIGAN -- Powers, Lee Leeper. *Captain Thomas Jarnagin, 1746-1802: The Story of One of Tennessee's Early Pioneers and His Wife Mary Witt Jarnagin, 1753-1829.* Enl. and corr. ed. Lake Lure, NC, Powers, 1985. x, 326p. 1. Jarnagin, Thomas, 1746-1802-Family. 2. Jarnagin, Mary Witt, 1752-1829-Family. 3. Hamblen County (Tenn.)-Biography. 4. Pioneers-Tennessee-Hamblem County-Biography. 5. Jernigan family. 6. Witt family. [G349-2].
See above: JARNIGAN [C354].

JERNIGAN -- Jarnigan, William Spencer. *Genealogical Charts of the Jernigan Family.* Concord, MA, Walden Press, 1976. 4 Genealogical Tables. Contents: [1] Jernegans of England. 2d. and corr. ed. -- [2] Jarnigan's of TN, OH, TX. -- [3] Jernegans of VA, MA, & Early Jernigans of VA, NC, SC and Early Jarnigans/Jarnigans[sic] of VA, TN. -- [4] Jernigans of NC, SC. [C357].

JERNIGAN -- Jernigan, Verna (Thomas). *Leaves of the Jernigan Tree.* Manchester, TN, 1969. 63p. [NG57; X499-FW,NY,SP].

JEWELL -- James, Larry A. *The Jewell and Thomas Families of Frederick County, Maryland and Wilson County, Tennessee.* Neosho, MO, L.A. James, 1987. 24 leaves. 1. Jewell family. 2. Thomas family. 3. Maryland-Genealogy. 4. Tennesse-Genealogy. [G350-1].

JEWETT -- Moore, Joanne Cullom. *Some History and Genealogy of the Jouett Family.* Frenchman's Bayou, AK, J.C. Moore, 1988. 33 leaves. 1. Jewett family. 2. Virginia-Genealogy. 3. North Carolina-Genealogy. 4. Tennessee-Genealogy. [G350-1].

JOBE -- McGuire, (Mrs.) Fannie. *[Jobe or Job - Brooks Line: The Jobe Family being of the First in Penna. and Tenn.]* NP, F. McGuire, 1921-22. 260, 7 leaves. My childrens' ancestors and their descendants and allied families; v. 3. [DC1995].

JOHNSON -- Allen, Penelope Johnson. *Genealogy of a Branch of the Johnson Family and Connections.* Chattanooga, TN, Helen Betts Miller, 1967. viii, 447p. [D6803].

JOHNSON -- Grimes, Jay Cook. [G351-2]. See above: COOK. [G155-1; D5326].

JOHNSON -- Johnson, Abraham Malone. *Genealogy of a Branch of the Johnson Family.* Chattanooga, TN, W. I. Crendall, 1893. 154p. [D6819].

JOHNSON -- Johnson, Albert Lee & W. W. Helton. *Patrick Henry Jackson [?] 1843-1927: A Family History.* Kingsport, TN, Helton, c1976. iv, 65p. 1 folded leaf of plates. 1. Johnson family. 2. United States-Genealogy. [G351-3].

JOHNSON -- Johnson, Katherine Baker. *Family of Rev. William Jonson of Virginia and Tennessee.* NP, 1940. 54 leaves. [D6829].

JOHNSON -- Johnson, Katherine Baker. *Family of Rev. William Johnson of Virginia and Knox County, Tennessee.* NP, 1945, 42 leaves. [D6830; VV105].

JOHNSON -- Johnson, Sussannah (B.). *Recollections of the Rev. John Johnson and His Home.* Nashville, TN, Southern Methodist Pub. 1869. 348p. [X501-FW].

JOHNSON -- Johnson, William Cumming II, Ed. *John Cummings Johnson and Family of Ohio and Tennessee: Journals, Photos, Genealogy, Correspondence, etc.* Hiram, OH, Johnson, 1975. 179p. in various pagings. Covers years 1847-54. [X503-FW/NY/OH].

JOHNSON -- Massat, Theresa Fickling. *History and Genealogy of John Johnson of Wayne County, Tennessee and His Descendants, 1777-1990.* NP, 1990. 217p. [DC2012].

JOHNSON -- Walden, Kenneth E. *Facsimiles and Transcipts of Pages from an Old Record Book Relating Chiefly to the Johnson and Walling ( Wallen, Walden ) Families in Tennessee, Missouri, and Arkansas, 1745-1864 and Genealogical Tables.* Busch, AR, 1973. 36 leaves. "Fifty copies". 1. Walden family. 2. Johnson family. S lists as WALDEN. [G352-3; S2646].

JOHNSON -- Whitley, Edythe Johns Rucker. *Kith and Kin of Our President.* Nashville, TN, Whitley, 1967. 119p. [D6864].

JOHNSTON -- Johnston, Aaron Montgomery.
*Ancestors and Descendants of James and Althea
( Loose ) Johnston and Allied Families
Bennett, Criss, Gay, Loose, Maitland,
Montgomery, Palm, and Round.* Knoxville, TN,
c1983. ix, 408p. [C361; NG58].

JOHNSTON -- Sherrill, Charles A. *Johnston
Family Papers, 1824-1922: Including Tucker
Family Papers, Tucker Springs Hotel Company
papers, Herriford family papers.* Cleveland,
TN, C.A. Sherrill, 1987. 74p.
LC CALL NUMBER: CS71.J73 1987

JONES -- NAS. *Jones Family Papers.*
Nashville, TN, Tennessee State Library and
Archives, 1967. 37p. [D6941; X507-FW].

JONES -- Goggans, Helen Mitchell and Mavis
P. Kelsey, Sr. [G353-2]. See above: BISHOP.
[G58-1].

JONES -- Hall, Evelyn Cook & William C. *The
Jefferson Thomas Jones Genealogy; Being a
History of Jefferson Thomas Jones, Born 14
Aug., 1828 near Madisonville, Monroe Co.,
Tennessee and Later Living in Park, Green
County, Ind. and His Descendants of Tennessee,
Indiana, Iowa, etc. Also, Allied Families.*
Nevada, IA, E.C. Hall, 1985. vii, 276p.
[C363].

JONES -- Hooker, Ruth N. *Jones of Albermarle
in Carolina.* Memphis, TN, 1948. 24 leaves.
[X506-MH].

JONES -- Nixon, Anna M. <u>Genealogical
Gleanings</u> *Relating to Robert Jones ( Gulf ) of
Merion, and John Jacobs of Perkiomen, with
Many Connecting Lines.* Chattanooga, TN,
Lookout Pub. Co., 1924. 38p. D gives
underscored part of title.
[D6934: X506-LI,NY].

JONES -- Risdahl, Sarah Jones. *The Family of
Amasa and Jane Canine Jones of Delaware
County, Ohio and DeKalb County, Tennessee.*

Morristown, TN, S.J. Risdahl, 1994.   350 p.
   LC CALL NUMBER: CS71.J76   1994e

**JULIANS**   --   Manly, Elizabeth Cate.   *The Julians and Allied Families; Descendants of George and Rebecca Julian... Descendants of Rene de St. Julien.*   Cleveland, TN, 1972. 119p.   D and X show family as Julian. [NG58; D6965; X511-FW].

## K

**KECK**   --   Fletcher, Virginia Billingsley. *"Down in the Barnes": The Kecks of Claiborne County, Tennessee; The Ancestors and Descendants of John "Guider" Keck and His Wife Rebecca A. Yadon.*   Baltimore, MD, 1983. xxiii, 407p.   [C371; NG58].

**KECK**   --   Fletcher, Virginia Billingsley. *More Kecks of Claiborne County, Tennessee: William, Henry, and Matthew Keck ...* Chelsa, MI, Bookcrafters, c1992.   xv, 303 p.
   LC CALL NUMBER: CS71.K255   1992

**KECK**   --   Fletcher, Virginia B.   *More Kecks of Claiborne County, Tennessee: William, Henry, and Matthew Keck...*   [NGN19-5-93].

**KEITH**   --   King, Larry.   *Keith Kinfolks: Descendants of James Keith, Sr., from 1720 to 1979.*   Hendersonville, TN, xvi, 363p.   [C372].

**KELLER**   --   Keller, Klyne Jack.   *History of the Keller Family.* Madison, TN, Keller, 1956, 332p.   [D7017].

**KELLEY**   --   Moore, Elizabeth.   *The Kelley Family of Virginia; Also Sublett - Turner.* Knoxville, TN, E. Moore, 1972.   55p. [DC2066].

**KELSO** -- Smith, Virginia Naylor. *Kelso Kin.* Nashville, TN, Mrs. Roy Campbell Smith, 1979. 386p.   [D7045].

KENNAMER -- Kennamer, John Robert and Lorrie Garfield Kennamer. *The Kennamer Family.* Nashville, TN, McQuiddy Printing Co., 1924. 375p. [L9598; D7068].

KENNEDY -- Kennedy, J. P. *The Name and Family of Kennedy and Powers.* South Pittsburg, TN, Kennedy, 1941. 74 i.e. 75p. [D7077].

KENNEDY -- McKennon S. Tom & Deane Kennedy Hendrix. *The John Kennedy Ancestors of Maury County.* Mt. Pleasant, TN, S.T. McKennon, 1982. 108p. 9 leaves. C gives "Ltd. ed. of 200 copies. [G364-3; C376].

KEYES -- Keyes, William Shelton. *Keese Family History: Southern Branch.* Chattanooga, TN, 1950. 26p. Bound with Keese, W.R. Keese family history and genealogy, Cardington, OH, 1911. [L9671].

KILLEBREW -- Killebrew, Mary K. *Recollections of a Lifetime: Diary of a Journey from London to Adair County, Kentucky.* Franklin, TN, Mrs. C. Lynch. 153p. Written in 1902. [X524-FW].

KILPATRICK -- Kilpatrick, Arnett E. *One Branch of the Kilpatrick Family: Balis J. and Mary Kilpatrick and Descendants.* Riceville, TN, A.E. Kilpatrick, 1987. 1 v. (various pagings). 1. Kilpatrick family. 2. Kilpatrick, Balis J., 1796-ca. 1877-Family. 3. Southern States-Genealogy. [G368-3].

KINDRED -- Henrick, Ruby Rigor. *Thomas Kindred Family History: Albermarle County, Virginia to Morgan County, Tennessee, 1776-1986.* St. Louis, MO, R.R. Henrick, 1986. 48 leaves, 10 leaves of plates. 1. Kindred family. 2. Kindred, Thomas, ca. 1760-ca. 1840-Family. [G369-3].

KING -- King, Larry. *Blue Ridge Mountain Kinfolks: A Record of the Ancestors, Descendants, and Relatives of the Author and*

*His Wife, Including Fisher - Gilbert - Hall - Hartley - Hill - King - Kirby - Lawson Families.* Manchester, TN, King, 1976. v, 335p. [C381; X528-FW,LA,NY,PH].

**KING** -- Van Reekum, Hallie Virginia King. *A Partial History of Edward King (17-- to 1790) (Lancaster County, Pa. - Sullivan County, Tenn.)* NP, 1954. 88, 8 leaves. [D7193].

**KING** -- Wilson, Reba S. *Lees and Kings of Virginia and North Carolina, 1636-1976.* Ridgely, TN, Wilson and Glover Pub. Co., 1975. 185p. NG gives: "also by Betty S. Glover". D lists under LEE. X indicates 2 leaves of plates. [NG62; D7572; X527-FW/SL; VV110].

**KING** -- Womack, Don Lee. *Kings and Descendants of Izard County, Arkansas.* Memphis, TN, Revival Times, c1988. 100p. 22 leaves. [DC2109].

**KIRBY** -- Tyler, Maudie Fudge. *My Mom's Lines; My Kirby Klan.* Memphis, TN, M.F. Tyler, 1986. ca. 120 leaves. [DC2117].

**KIRKPATRICK** -- McCollough, E. Spears. *John Kirkpatrick of East Tennessee.* In The Lookout, Zella Armstrong Publisher, Chattanooga, TN, 1938. Vol. 1v, No. 10. [L9813].

**KIRKPATRICK** -- McCollough, E. Spears. *J David Kirkpatrick of Missouri.* Knoxville, TN, 1938. 4 numb. leaves. Typed. [L9814].

**KIRKPATRICK** -- McCollough, E. Spears. *The Kirkpatrick Family.* Knoxville, TN, 1971. Unpaged. [X531-SU].

**KITCHEL** -- Clem, Doris Kitchel & Dwain L. Kitchel. *Kitchell Family History.* Cullman, AL, Gregath Co., Knoxville, TN, Orders, D.L. Kitchell, 1989. xv, 881p. 1. Kitchel family. 2. Kitchel, Dwain L(orne), 1933-   . [G372-1].

KITTRELL. -- Whitley, Edythe Rucker.
*Kittrell Family*. Nashville, TN, 1938. 12
numb. leaves. [L9830].

KNIGHT -- Garrett, Jill K. *Knight Cousins*.
Columbia, TN, Author, 1967. 214p.
[X535-FW,IG,MY].

KNIGHT -- Nelson, Goarden S. & Virginia
Knight Nelson. *Knights in East Tennessee,
1789-1866: An Abstract of Public Records and
Other Materials for all Knight Families in
East Tennessee*. Knoxville, TN, G.S. & V.K.
Nelson, 1984. x, 97p. [C386-2].

KNOTT -- Caldwell, Willie Mae. *The Genealogy
of the Knott Family, 1617-1989: Founders of
Knott's Berry Farm, Buena Park, California*.
Buena Park, CA, Knott's Berry Farm. ii, 213p.
1. Knott family. 2. Tennessee-Genealogy.
[G374-3].

KUYKENDALL. -- Fullerton, Jane Hardin.
*Genealogical Notes on the Kuykendall and
Hardin Families*. Nashville, TN, Fullerton,
1964. 59 leaves. [D7346].

# L

LA FORGE -- La Forge, Robert M. [G381-3].
See above: BARNES. [G35-2].

LAIN -- Patterson, Edna Earle Fleming. *The
Lains of Wilson County, Tennessee and Some of
Their Descendants*. NP, Patterson, 1981. 49
leaves. [D7371].

LAMB -- Hooker, Ruth N. *Thomas Lamb, 1609-
1646 of Wintrop's Massachusetts Bay Colony and
Some of His Descendants in America. The
Albermarle and New England Ancestry of Josiah
Francis Earle of Crittendon County, Arkansas*.
Memphis, TN, 1947, 3p., 84 l. [X547-LA,MH].

LANGFORD -- Edwards, Bruce Montgomery. *The
Lankfords and Langfords of Virginia*.

Baltimore, MD, Gateway Press, Knoxville, TN, Montgomery Publ. Co., 1987. 492p. 1. Langford family. 2. Virginia-Genealogy. [G386-3].

**LANGFORD** -- Mabrey, Virginia Ann Hawkins. *The Langford Family, Their Life and Times from 1800-1978: Bound with Alfred Bennett Family & Samuel Dillon Family.* Cookeville, TN, Mabrey, 1979. a-c, xxix, 341p. [C399].

**LANHAM** -- Lanham, Megan Gabriel. *Snatched From the Dragon.* Nashville, TN, T. Nelson Publishers, c1990. 284p. 1. Lanham, Megan Gabriel-Journeys-China. 2. Lanham, Megan Gabriel-Family. 3. Lanham family. 4. China-Description and travel--1976- . 5. China-History-Tiananmen Square Incident, 1989. [G387-2].

**LAPP** -- Cast, Marion Lopp. *Lopp - Lapp Genealogy: North Carolina - Rowan - Davidson Counties... Tennessee, Missouri...* Belton, MO, Cast, 1988. 99 leaves. [DC2178].

**LAY** -- Lay, A. M. *Family History Records.* Huntsville, TN, Scott County Historical Society, 1985. 153, 24p. Cover title: Lay Family History. [C404].

**LEAR** -- Richey, James. *Richey - Hampson - Kimes - Lear - Lindsay Families of Scotland-PA-IL-KS-TN with Some Related Lines: Brindle, Britanick, Carrington, Campbell, Coe...* Decorah, Iowa, c1988. iv, 334p. 1. Ritchie family. 2. Lindsay family. 3. Lear family. [G392-2].

**LEE** -- NAS. *Some of the Descendants of Capt. Thomas Lee of Hawkins Co., Tenn and John Lee, Esq. of Johnston Co., North Carolina.* NP, 1972-1975. 1 v. in various foliations. [DS427].

**LEE** -- Johnston, Weldon. *Some Descendants of Captain Thomas Lee of Hawkins Co., Tennessee.* Madisonville, TN, Robert T. Lee, Jr., 1972. 63, xv p. [DS424].

LEE -- Johnston, Weldon. *John Lee, Esq. of Johnston Co., North Carolina & Some of His Descendants.* Madisonville, TN, Robert T. Lee, Jr., 1975. 72, viii leaves. [DS423].

LEE -- Lee, Thomas Lafayette. *A History of the Lee and Graves Families.* Sparta, TN, Lee, 1940. 32p. [D7561].

LEE -- Wilson, Reba Shropshire. *The Lees and Kings of Virginia and North Carolina.* Ridgely, TN, Wilson and Glover Pub. Co., 1975. 185, 1p. [D7572].

LESLIE -- Murphy, Marion Emerson. *Early Leslies in York County, South Carolina: Their Migration to Tennessee, Missouri, and Arkansas, Their Ancestry and Descendants* - 1st ed. San Diego, CA, 1972. xvi, 210p. "Sequel to Tennessee Murphys - Murpheys and Allied Families. Vol. 1.". [S1560].

LESLIE -- Murphy, Marion Emerson. *Early Leslies in York County, South Carolina: Their Migration to Tennessee, Missouri, and Arkansas, Their Ancestry and Descendants* - 3rd ed. San Diego, CA, 1976. xvi, 210p., 1 leaf of plates. [X567-NY].

LEWIS -- Burkett, Kathryn Lewis. *The Descendants of Thomas and Ann Lee Lewis, A Quaker family of Blount Co., Tennessee.* Carthage, Il, K.L. Burkett, 1989. 448p. 91-209336
    LC CALL NUMBER: CS71.L675 1989a

LEWIS -- Lewis, William G. *Lewis Family Pioneers of East Tennessee; Being an Account of the Revolutionary Records of Nathan Lewis of Wales, Some of His Descendants, and the Lewis Family History.* Marion, IN, Arnold-Barr Printing Co., 1928. 55, 1p. [L10460].

LEWIS -- McBride, Robert Martin. *A Footnote to a History of the Lewis Family, Being a Partial List of the Descendants of William Henry Lewis (1799-1879) of Jackson County,*

*Alabama.* Nashville, TN, 1954. 57 leaves. [L10469].

**LIGHTBODY** -- Anderson, Beverly Davis. [G401-1]. See above: DAVIS. [G177-1; DC953].

**LINCOLN** -- McMurtry, Robert G. *Kentucky Lincolns of Mill Creek.* Harrogate, TN, Lincoln Memorial Univ., 1939. 78p. [X572-FW].

**LINCOLN** -- Williams, Samuel C. *The Lincolns and Tennessee.* Harrogate, TN, Lincoln Memorial University, 1942. 33p. Revised edition of articles appearing in Lincoln Herald, vol. 43, no. 3-4, 1941 and vol. 44 no. 1, 1942. Johnson City, TN, The Watauga Press, 1942. 33p. Issued by the Department of Lincolnia, Lincoln memorial university. [L10563; D7712].

**LINDEMAN** -- Boswell, Imogene May. *The Ancestors and Descendants of Henry D. Lendermon: Randolph County, North Carolina, Greenville County, South Carolina, Maury County, Tennessee, Carroll County, Tennessee, Marshall County, Mississippi.* Wolfe City, TX, Henington Pub. Co., 1988. 337p. 1. Lindeman family. 2. Lendermon, Henry D., 1788-1845-Family. 3. Southern States-Genealogy. [G402-2].

**LINDSAY** -- Richey, James. [G403-1]. See above: LEAR. [G392-2].

**LINTON** -- Kelley, Sarah Foster. *The Linton Family of Linton, Tennessee.* Nashville, TN, S.F. Kelley, 1981. ii, 144p. [C417].

**LITTLE** -- Simmons, Dessie Little. *The Little Family.* Johnson City, TN, Simmons, 1975. 182p. [D7760].

**LIVELY** -- Louden, Claire Humphfres. *Second Supplement to Livelys of America 1982, to Livelys of America, 1690-1968, and Supplement of Lively of America, 1972.* McMinnville, TN,

National Association of Lively Families;
Ashland, KY. Gallahers, 1986. p. 1071-1993.
1. Lively family. [G405-1].

LIVELY -- Vallentine, John F. *The Livelys
of America*. McMinnville, TN, National
Association of Lively Families, 1971. xii,
892p. [D7767].

LIVELY -- Vallentine, John F. *The Livelys
of America. 1690-1968*. McMinnville, TN,
National Association of Lively Families, 1971-
73. 2 v. (1069, xxiv p. Vol 2 has title:
Supplement to Livelys of America 1972. Errata
slip inserted in v. 1. S indicates date of
1973 and Supplement pagination as 893-1069.
xxiv p. [G405-1; S1593].

LOFTIS -- Loftis, Jimmie R. *Loftis and the
Descendants of Laban Loftis*. Nashville, TN,
Cousins by the Dozens, c1993. xiv, 547p.
LC CALL NUMBER: CS71.L8186 1993

LOGUE -- Buchanan, Jane Gray. *John Logue of
North Carolina: History and Hypothesis: Logue
and Related Families of Delaware, Maryland,
Pennsylvania, Virginia, and Tennessee*. Oak
Ridge, TN. Buchanan, 1980. iv, 47 l. D gives
underscored title. [D7814; VV119; VP139].

LOGUE -- Watson, Virginia Gooch. *History of
the Logue Homes in West Wilson County, Tenn*.
NP, Watson, 1986. 37 leaves.
[C421; DC2284].

LONG -- Brannan, Caroline Grantlow Candler.
*John Long and Tennessee, Sketch of a Pioneer
and His Progeny*. New Orleans, LA, 1930. 2,
101, xiii p. [L10867].

LONG -- Atchley, Paul L. & Mary Ann Morris
Thompson. *Maud Horn's Atchley Family History,
Including Long, Maples, Scoggin, and Griffith
Families*. 2nd ed. Knoxville, TN, 1965, xiii,
530p. A reprint of the original e published
under title Family History: Atchley, Griffith,
Long, Maples, Scoggins, etc. [L10701].

LONG — Wilkinson, A Mims. [G408-1].
See above: DERRYBERRY. [G187-1].

LOONEY — Luna, Jane C and Leslie R.
Waltman. *The Descendants of Peter Luna (1759-1851)*. Columbia, TN, J.C. Luna, c1989. 501p.
1. Luna family. 2. Luna, Peter, 1759-1851-Family. 3. Looney family. 4. Tennessee-Genealogy. [G408-3].

LOVE — Love, Albert Gallatin. *Our Ancestors, The Love Family of Trezevant, Carroll County, Tennessee.* Washington, DC, 1953. 130 leaves. [L10769].

LOVE — Love, Jolee. *Love's Valley.* Nashville, TN, Ambrose Printing Co., 1954. 556p. [L10770; D7867].

LOVE — Love, Jolee. *Love's Letters.* Nashville, TN, Ambrose Printing Co., 1979. 2 v. (1198p.) Contents: Love's Valley. [See above]. [C424].

LOVE — Love, Miriam. *Family of James and Elspeth ( Thompson ) Love, Clayton and Hancock Counties, Iowa.* Chattanooga, TN, 1965. 44p. [X583-FW].

LOVE — Love, Robert A. *General Thomas Love of Western North Carolina and Western Tennessee and His Brothers Robert and James*, 2nd ed. *with additions and corrections.* St. Petersburg, FL, Love, 1955. 43, 2 leaves. D gives underscored title; no notice of edition. [L10766; D7868].

LOVELL — Lovell, Gordon Aubrey. *The Lovells Come to Tennessee.* Nashville, TN, Lovell, 1967. xi, 164p. [D7875].

LOVELL — Lovell, Marshall Wilson. *The Genealogy of the Family of the James W. Lovell Family, 1765-1981: Giving up to Nine Generations of Descendants and Biographical Sketches of Many of Them.* Heritage, TN, M.W. Lovell, 1981. 281p. Cover title: James W.

Lovell of Allen County, Kentucky, and
descendants. [C404].

LOWE -- McDuffie, Eva Loe. *The Lowe - Loe -
Low Family in Virginia, North Carolina,
Mississippi, Tennessee, Kentucky, and
Missouri.* NP, 1955. 109 leaves.
[D7888; VV120].

LUCEY -- Lucy, George Ramsey. *The Lucy
Millenium.* Hendersonville, TN, Lucy, 1978,
1979. 235p. [C426].

LUCKEY -- Luckey, Ann Colvin. *The Luckey
Family of Tennessee: A Genealogical History of
John Henry Luckey, William Franklin Luckey,
and Samuel Joseph Luckey of Gibson/Madison
Counties, Tennessee, Their Ancestors and
Descendants, 1732-1987.* Cullman, AL, Gregath
Co., 1987. v, 187 p.
LC CALL NUMBER: CS71.L938 1987

LUDDINGTON -- Green, Margaret Luddington.
*Samuel Ludington, Ancestors and Descendants.*
Smyrna, TN, Green, 1968. a-h, 25 leaves. D
gives underscored part of title; X shows 25
pages. [D7907; X586-FW].

LUMPKIN -- Lumpkin, Ben Gray and Martha
Neville Lumpkin. *The Lumpkin Family of
Virginia, Georgia, and Mississippi.*
Clarksville, TN, 1973. v, 139p. [S1625].

LUMPKIN -- NAS. *Minor, Scales, Cottrell,
and Gray Families of Virginia, North Carolina,
and Mississippi.* Clarksville, TN, 1974. vii,
133p. [S1626].

LUNA -- Luna, Jane C and Leslie R. Waltman.
[G412-1]. See above: LOONEY. [G408-3].

LUTON -- Boxley, Thaylia Pearson. *Family
Record of William Daniel Luton and Martha
Frances Meadors Luton.* Amarillo, TX, William
Dale Pearson, 1982. 60p. Cover title:
Meadors-Luton family history from 1836-1982,
Tennessee to Texas. [DC2318].

**LYLE** -- Bracy, Gladys Elizabeth Odil. *Lyle, Murrell, Nance, Morton Genealogy.* Nashville, TN, Bracy, 1965. 67 leaves. X gives 67p. [D7948; X589-FW].

**LYTLE** --- Lytle, Andrew Nelson. *A Wake for the Living: A Family Chronicle.* Nashville, TN, J.S. Sanders & Co.; Lanham, MD. Distributed to the trade by National Book Network, 1992, c1975. xxvi, 270p.
LC CALL NUMBER: PS3523.Y88 Z475 1992

M

**MACKEYS** -- Hoskinson, Josie V. H. & Bishop, Julia R. *Mackeys and Eberleys of Texas and Allied Families of McIlwaine, Elgin, Harrison, Adams, Smallwood, Stone, Troope, and Perry of KY., TENN., MD., and VA.* Norman, OK, 1965. xii, 172p. X libraries list under MACKEY. [NG67; X608-FW/GF/NY].

**MACLIN** -- Bond, Octavia Zollicoffer. *The Family Chronicle and Kinship Book of Maclin, Clack, Cocke, Carter, Taylor, Cross, Gordon, and Other Related American Lineages.* Nashville, TN, McDaniel Printing Co., 1928. 7, 663, 10p. [L11219; D8000; VV121].

**MACON** -- Whitley, Edythe Rucker. *One Branch of the Macon Family in America.* Nashville, TN, Whitley, 1981. 140 leaves. [DS447].

**MANDRELL** -- Mandrell, Louise & Ace Collins. *The Mandrell Family Album.* Nashville, TN, T. Nelson, 1983. 192p + 1 Sound Disc (33 1/3 rpm) in Pocket. Discography: p. 188-192. [C435].

**MANGUM** -- Palmer, John T. *The Mangums of Virginia, North Carolina, South Carolina, Georgia, Alabama, Mississippi, Tennessee, Arkansas, Texas, Utah, and Adjoining States --* Rev. ed. Santa Rosa, CA J.T. Palmer, [1992] x, 269p. LC CALL NUMBER: CS71.M266 1992

MANLY -- Manly, Elizabeth Cate. *My Husband's Folks: The Manlys and Galloways and Allied Families.* Cleveland, TN, E.C. Manley, 1972. 74p. Submitted by the Tennessee DAR, G.R.C. as vol. 10 of their American Bicentennial commemoration 1773-1976. [DC2354; X620-FW].

MARION -- Marion, Jessie A. *Marion, Bass, Shrite, Loudy, and Dick Families.* Blountville, TN, 1964. 61 l. [X622-NY].

MARKS -- Rhine, Nannetta Raines & Mary Sue R. Moseley. *The Saga of the Little Red Chair* - 2nd ed. - El Paso, TX, M.S.R. Moseley, 1983. 87p. Summary: Relates incidents in the early history of the Raines and Marks families in Tennessee, beginning in the days following the Civil War and coming forward to 1918. 1. Raines family-Juvenile literature. 2. Marks family-Juvenile literature. 3. Rhein family-Juvenile literature. 4. Tennessee-Biography-Juvenile literature. [G424-1].

MARSHALL -- Marshall, William C. *The Marshall Family of Southside Virginia and West Tennessee.* NP, 1989. 129p. [DC2370].

MARTIAU -- Smith, Jonathan Kennon. *Captain Nicholas Martiau, 1591-1657.* Memphis, TN, J. Edge Co., 1969. 43 leaves. [D8143; X625-LA].

MARTIN -- Francis, Frankie Passons. *The Charles Caffery Martin Family (ca. 1765-ca. 1854).* Sulphur Springs, TX, F.P. Francis, 198_. 148p. Cover Title: "On behalf of the Van Buren County [TN] Historical Society." 1. Martin family. 2. Martin, Charles Caffery, ca. 1765-ca. 1854-Family. 3. Southern States-Genealogy. [G426-1].

MARTIN -- Polk, Cynthia Martin. *Some Old Colonial Families of Virginia.* Memphis, TN, Paul & Douglass Co., 1915. 147p. Contents: Genealogies: Martin, Payne - Pillow, Payne - Fleming, Payne of Virginia, Fleming Family, Steptoe Family, Cro'Martin of Ireland, Payne of England, Americans of royal descent. Col.

William and Gideon Pillow, Sr.
[L11483; VV123].

MASHBURN -- Simpson, Edna Grant. *The
Mashburn Family of North Carolina and Georgia.*
Knoxville, TN, Simpson, 1975. 425 l. [DC2380].

MASON -- Gable, Bertha L. *Tenn. - Ark. -
Mo.: Windsor Mason Trail, 1787-1987.*
Clarksville, TN, B.L. Gable, 1987. 177p. 1.
Mason family. 2. Mason, Windsor, b. 1787-
Family. [G428-1].

MASSENGILL -- Massengill, Samuel Evans.
*The Massengills, Massengales, and Variants.*
Bristol, TN, King Printing Co., 1931. 908p.
Appendix A. - The Cobbs, B. - The Tiptons,
C. - The Jobes, including Fain, Ensor and
McMahon connections. D. - The Dysarts and
Brodens, including the Rhea connection. E. -
The Evanses, including the Vance and Colville
connections. F. - The Smiths including the
Humphrey connection. [L11544; D8198].

MASSENGILL. -- Massengill, Samuel Evans.
*Records of the Henry Massengill Memorial and
Directory Near Johnson City, Tennessee.*
Bristol. TN, 1940. 10 leaves. [L11545].

MASSENGILL. -- Massengill, Samuel Evans,
M.D. *A Sketch of Medicine and Pharmacy and
View of Its Progress by the Massengill Family
from the Fifteenth to the Twentieth Century.*
Bristol, TN-VA, The S.E. Massengill Co., 1940.
144p. 3 plates. [L11546].

MASSENGILL -- Massengill, Samuel Evans,
M.D. *A Sketch of Medicine and Pharmacy and
View of Its Progress by the Massengill Family
from the Fifteenth to the Twentieth Century.*
Bristol, TN-VA, The S.E. Massengill Co., 1942.
6, 445, 3p. "Second edition".
[L11547].

MASTERS -- Masters, Jack. *Masters Family
History, 1691-1989.* Gallatin, TN, 1989.
584p. 1. Masters family. [G429-1].

MATHIS -- Edwards, Richard Laurence.
   [G429-3]. See above: DELOZIER:
   [GS184-3: C205; VV60].

MAXEY -- NAS. *Miscellaneous Maxey Records*.
   NP, Tennessee DAR, G.R.C., 1944. 22 leaves.
   [D8269].

MAXWELL -- Maxwell, Robert O. *Thomas
   Jefferson Maxwell. His Ancestors and
   Descendants with The Changing Times*.
   Collegdale, TN, College Press, 1966. 148p.
   [X634-FW,NY].

MAY -- Mays, Rayford Glynn. *Mays and Pullen
   Pioneers: Tideland Virginia to Tennessee and
   North Alabama:   Across Four Centuries*.
   Franklin, NC, 1983. pni. [VV126].

MAY -- Woodruff, Audrey L. W. *Descendants of
   John May, Sr. and Sarah Jane ( Phillips ) May,
   1760-1967 of Virginia, Tenn., Kentucky... and
   Allied Families of Hanson, Wall, Rook,
   Mundell*. Kansas City, MO, 1967. 62p.   DC
   gives underscored part of title and 61p.
   [DC2405; X634-FW; VV126].

McADOO -- Lemons, Nova A. *John McAdoo of
   Virginia, North Carolina, Tennessee, and
   Kentucky*. Dallas, N.A. Lemons, 1991. iv,
   52p. [DC2424].

McALPIN -- Hazelton, Trica Willey. *Some
   Descendants of Alexander McAlpin, Sr., of
   Abbeville District, SC, and Wilkes Co., GA,
   and Alexander McAlpin, Jr., of Green Co., TN
   and Henry McAlpin of Greene County., TN. and
   Daniel McAlpin of Johnson Co., IN*.   Las
   Cruces, NM, 1987. 11p. [NG65].

McALLISTER -- Buchanan, Jane Gray.
   [G432-3]. See above: FINNEY:
   [G229-3; NGS11; DC3630].

McANALLY -- McAnally, James L. *The McAnally
   Family in America*. Columbia, TN, 1976. iii,
   86 leaves, 3 leaves of plates. [C448].

McANALLY -- McAnally, Thomas S. *The McAnallys, Descendants of Hamilton and Winifred.* Nashville, TN, T.S. McAnnally, c1988. 330p. 1. McAnally family. [G433-1].

McBRIDE -- McBride, Robert M. *McBride Family of Rutherford County, Tennessee.* Nashville, TN, 1963. 89p. [X594-FW].

McCALLIE -- McCallie, Thomas H. *The McCallie Family in Tennessee; An Early Family Record; An Autobiographical Sketch and a Genealogy.* Laguna Beach, CA, K.M. Johnson, 1960. 47, 5 leaves. [X595-LA].

McCALLUM -- Farrell, Louis & Flora Janie Homer Hooker. *McCallums; Daniel McCallum, Isabel Sellers, Their Antecedents, Descendants and Collateral Relatives.* Nashville, TN, Farrell and Hamer, S.C.: Hooker, 1946. 234p. [L10930; D3825].

McCAMMON -- McCammon, Samuel. *Diary of Samuel McCammon... 1846-1854.* Knoxville, TN, n.d. 191p. Mimeo. [X595-DP].

McCAMPBELL -- McCampbell, Nellie Pearl. *Samuel Shannon McCampbell, Sarah Prudence Smith McCampbell, Ancestry and Descendants.* Knoxville, TN, 1965. 166 leaves. D gives underscored part of title. [L10931; S1634; D8329].

McCONNELL -- Martin, John G. *The McConnell Family: Descendants of George McConnell and Susannah Snavely: Genealogy.* Kingsport, TN, J.G. Martin, 1980. iv, 121p. [C452].

McCLANAHAN -- Willliams, Katharine Kearsley. *The McClanahans of Augusta and Roanoke Counties with Addendum of Related Families Walton, Poage, Griffin, Tosh, Brechinbridge, Leftwich.* Chattanooga, TN, 1983. 48 leaves. [NG65].

McCLAREN -- Greenway, Carol Forrest. *Alexander McClaren with excursis[sic] on*

Related Families of Va., N.C., S.C., and Tenn.
1977. 306 leaves. [D8145; VV127].

McCORMICK -- McCormick, Andrew Phillip.
Scotch-Irish in Ireland and America, as Shown
in Sketches of the Pioneer Scotch-Irish
Families McCormick, Stevenson, McKenzie and
Bell in North Carolina, Kentucky, Missouri and
Texas. New Orleans, LA. 1897. 1 v. various
pagings. [L10983].

McDONALD -- Grant, Isabel F. Genealogy of
the McDonald Family. Knoxville, TN, White
Stores, 1967. 123p. [X602-FW].

McELHANEY -- Hall, William K. Descendants
of George McElhany, Who Died September 2,
1893, Grainger County, Tennessee and of Joel
Phillips, Born March 3, 1806 in Tennessee,
Died February 14, 1893, Greene County,
Missouri. NP, 1979. 104 leaves. [D8449].

McFARLAND -- McFarland, Louis B. Memoirs
and Addresses of L. B. McFarland. Memphis,
TN, Author, 1921. 221p. [X603-FW].

McGAUGH -- James, Larry A. The McGaugh
Family of Tennessee and Missouri. Neosho, MO,
James, 1978. 62p. [D8471].

McGAVOCK -- NAS. McGavock Federal Cemetery,
Franklin, Tennessee. Franklin, TN, Franklin
Chapter #14, United Daughters of the
Confederacy, c1989. 42p. 1. Franklin(Tenn),
Battle of, 1864-Registers. 2. McGavock
Confederate Cemetery (Franklin, Tenn.) 3.
United States-History-Civil War, 1861-1865-
Registers. 4. Confederates States of America.
Army-Registers. 5. McGavock family.
[G440-1].

McGAVOCK -- Aiken, Leona Taylor. The
McGavocks of Two Rivers. Kingsport, TN,Aiken,
1975. v, 51p. [S1661].

McGAVOCK -- Aiken, Leona Taylor. The
Descendants of James McGavock, Sr., and the

*McGavock Mansions, Fort Chiswell, Va. and Carnton, Tn.* Kingsport, TN, L.T. Aiken, c1986. vi, 34p. 1. McGavock family. 2. McGavock, James, 1728-1812-Family. 3. Fort Chiswell Mansion (Max Meadows, Va.) 4. Canton Mansion ( Franklin, Tenn. ) [G440-1].

McGAVOCK -- Rudy, Jeannette C. *Historic Rivers.* Nashville, TN, Blue & Gray Press, c1973. 127p. [D8474].

McINTURFF -- Montgomery, Johnnie Esther. *McInturff Families: Travel from Blount County, Tennessee.* Maryville, TN, Montgomery, 1977. vi, 224p. [C459].

McIVER -- NAS. *McIver Collection.* Tennessee State Library and Archives, Nashville, Ms Division, Registers No. 4. 1962. 9p. [X606-FW].

McKEE -- Whitley, Edythe Rucker. *Lineage of Mildred McKee (Mrs.) Newberry through the Wilson, McKee, Carr, Donnell, Marshall, etc. Families to Join the DAR.* Nashville, TN, E.D. Whitley, 1985. 129p. [DC2490].

McKIBBEN -- Simms, Vivian York. *The Descendants of William & Marry Simms: England to Illinois and Beyond: Related Families of McKibben, Oakley, and Others.* Murfreesboro, TN, V.Y. Simms, 1989. x, 216p. 1. Simms family. 2. Simms, William-Family. 3. McKibben family. 4. Oakley family. 5. Great Brittain-Genealogy. [G443-1].

McMATH -- McMath, Frank Mortimer. *Collections For a History of the Ancient Family of McMath.* Memphis, TN, C.A. Davis Printing Co., 1937. 272p. [D8550].

McMEANS -- McMeans, Heath Leigh. *The McMeans of Alabama, Texas, and Tennessee: A Genealogical Record.* Birmingham, AL, H.L. McMeans, 1992. 168p.
LC CALL NUMBER: CS71.M475665 1992

McMURRAY -- McMurray, Rhuy K. *The Tennessee Colony*. Greensburg, KS, 1966. pni. [X612-SG].

McMURTRY -- McMurtry, David C. *Report to the National Societies of the Daughters of the American Revolution and the Sons of the American Revolution on the Inaccuracies in the Family and Revolutionary War Service Records of John McMurtrie of Philadelphia, John McMurtrie of New Jersey and Tennessee, Captain John McMurtrie of Kentucky as Recorded by Frederick James McMurtrie*. Lexington, KY, McMurtry, 1983. 1 v. in various pagings. [DS463].

McNAIRY -- Whitley, Edythe. *McNairy Family*. NP, 1955. 50 leaves. [D8567].

McPHEE -- Albert, Mary Elizabeth Mayche McFee and Linsy D. *Genealogy of the John Ervin McFee Family of Buncombe County, North Carolina, and Related Families of Trice, Whited, Morrow, and Strube*. Memphis, TN, M.E.M. Albert, 1985. 89 l. [C463].

McQUEEN -- Neal, Carl B. *The McQueen Family of Johnson County, Tennessee*. Olympia, WA, 1958. 147 l. [X614-NY,SP].

McQUITTY -- Day, Ednw Kay Herbst & David Newton McQuitty. *The Mcquitty, McQuiddy, McQuady Family*. Baton Rouge, Oracle Press; Sweetwater, TN, D.M. McQuiddy, 1984. iii, 490p., 27p. of plates. [C464].

McSPADDEN -- McSpadden, Anna B. *Way Back When --- Happenings We Remember and Genealogies*. Maryville, TN, A.B. McSpadden, 1980. 160p. [C464].

MEADOR -- Meador, Victor Paul. *The Meador Families of North Central Tennessee*. Kansas City, MO, Meador, 1971. 231p. [D8624; X636-FW].

MERRILL -- Robinson, Winifred M. (M.). *Some Descendants of Nathaniel Merrill, Who Was In*

*Newbury, Mass., 1635.* Kingsport, TN, 33p. [X643-FW].

MILLER -- Nicklin John Bailey Calvert. *The Millers of Millersburg and Their Descendants, with Kindred Families of Miller, McGee, Jameson, Read, Scott, Wyatt, Donnelley, White, Washington, Blackwell, Smith, Mayfield, Johnson, Kuykendall, Beene, Sadler, Clark, Myers.* Nashville, TN, Brandon Print. Co., 1923. xix, 485p. [L11882; NG71].

MILLER -- Sell, Jeanne Lyle. *The Miller Family of Knob Creek, Washington County, Tennessee.* Johnson City, TN, J.L. Sell, c1985. 257p. LC CALL NUMBER: CS71.M65 1985b

MILLION -- Hayes, Carl N. *Million-aires (Heirs) the Descendants of Edward Million of Tennessee.* Chuckey, TN, Author, 1971. 100p. [X653-FW].

MIMS -- Mins, Cora M. *The Families of Mims and McSween in Cocke County, Tennessee.* NPO., 1950. Unpaged. [X655-FW].

MITCHELL -- Allen, Estill Franklin. *Cousins: Handbook and Family History of Mitchell, Allen, Gilleland, and Related Families from Virginia into Georgia, North Carolina, Kentucky, Tennessee, Missouri, Mississippi, Illinois, Iowa, Arkansas, Louisiana, Oklahoma, New Jersey, Texas, California, Florida, and Idaho, mid-1700's to 1980.* Brownwood, TX, Howard Payne University, 1981. xxiv, 347p. [C477; VV132].

MITCHELL -- Goggans, Helen Mitchell and Mavis P. Kelsey, Sr. [G458-1]. See above: . BISHOP: [G58-1; NGN17-6-91].

MITCHELL -- Smith, Austin Wheeler. *Mitchell - McGlocklin and Allied Families.* Cookeville, TN, Smith, 1940. 87 leaves. [L11985; D8863].

MOAK -- Moak, Lennox Lee. *The Moak and Related Families of South Carolina and*

*Mississippi, 1740-1960; with Notes as to Members of the Family in Tennessee and Illinois. Also, Notes as to Other Noah Families in New York, Pennsylvania, Maryland, and Virginia.* Fort Washington, PA, 1960. 310 leaves. [L11996; VV132; VP157].

MONEY -- Eppard, Sarah E. *The Moneyhuns of Cooper Ridge, Hawkins County, Tennessee.* Parul Revere Chapter (Ind.) DAR, G.R.C., 1995. 286p. [DC2594].

MONTGOMERY -- Anderson, Beulah Henry. *John and Esther Montgomery, 1719-1973.* Maryville, TN, Anderson, et al., 1974. 512p. D gives underscored part of title. [S1787; D8997].

MONTGOMERY -- Hoover, Frances M. *Castle O'Montgomery.* Nashville, TN, Parthenon Press, 1974. 228p. [S1787a].

MONTGOMERY -- McMurry, Rhuy K. Williams. *The Tennessee Colony. Montgomery and McMurray.* Greensburg, KS, 1966. 195p. [NG72; X661-FW].

MOODY -- Massey, Pauline S. *Descendants of Spencer Moody and Susanna Hendricks and Allied Families, Tenn., Ill., Mo., Kans.* Wichita KS, 1937. 108 l. [X663-LA].

MOON -- Moon, Anna Mary. *Sketches of the Moon and Barclay Families Including the Harris, Moorman, Johnson, Appling Families.* Chattanooga, TN, Moon, 1938, c1939. 108p. [L12091; D8915].

MOONEY -- Mooney, Russell E. & Marianne Turpin Burk. *A Mooney Genealogy and Miscellany with Some Allied Lines.* Knoxville, TN, Knoxville Chapter D.A.R., 1964. 191 leaves. [DC2606; X636-FW,NY].

MOORE -- NAS. *John Trotwood Moore Papers.* Nashville, TN, Tennessee State Library and Archives, Manuscript Division, 1964. 33p. [X665-FW].

MOORE -- O'Neal, Rosetta Crenshaw. *The Moore Generations: Genealogy and Directory: Family Reunion, July 19, 21, 21, Paris Landing State Park, Buchanon, Tennessee.* Carbondale, IL, R. O'Neal, 1985. 39p. 1. Moore family. 2. Afro-American-Genealogy. [G464-1].

MOORE -- Sherwood, Waring. *The Story of Sarah (Sally) Moore.* Memphis, TN, James Jackson, 1970. 71p. [D8948].

MOORE -- Snyder, Maud M. *The A. A. Moore Family.* Knoxville, TN, 1962. 195p. [X664-NY].

MOORING -- Algee, Isabelle Rogers. *Moorings Past and Present: Family of Wyatt Mooring, Sr., and Allied Families.* Tiptonville, TN, Printed by Banner Printing Co., 1982, c1981. 1 v. (various pagings). [DS501].

MORGAN -- Britton, Eudine Morgan. *John Morgan (b.1784) and His Family in Georgia: His Sons, William, Richard, James J., Samuel J., and John B. Morgan: His Daughters, Lucinda M. Cannon, Nancy M. Vicerky[sp?] Emma M. Adams, Lodoizkly M. Boss. and Diedamy M. Jackson and Appendix, Samuel Morgan, Sr. Family, Miscellaneous Morgan Notes.* Chattanooga, TN, E.M. Britton, 1989. v, 264, 52, leaves. DC gives underscored part of title and 1 vol. various foliations. 1. Morgan family. 2. Morgan, John, b. 1784-Family. 3. Georgia-Genealogy. [G465-3; DC2625].

MORRIS -- Beeler. Flora M.D. *Morris and Jaretts of West Virginia, Descendants and Connecting Families.* Knoxville, TN, Campbell, Inc. 1974. 283p. D gives underscored part of title. [D8991; X668-FW,LA; VV134].

MORRIS -- Grimes, Jay Cook. [G467-3]. See above: COOK. [G155-1; D5326].

MORRIS -- Morris, Phillip Stephen. *Morris - Walden: Family Group Records of the Ancestors*

*and Descendants of Hiram Morris and Sarah
Walden Morris.* Memphis, TN, Morris, 1980.
ii, 22 leaves. [C487-1].

MORROW -- Hailey, Naomi Morrow. *Five Morrow
Men.* Nashville, TN, Hailey, c1975? v.
(various foliations). [D9025].

MORROW -- Hailey, Naomi Morrow. *Five Morrow
Men: With Some Descendants and Allied
Families -- 1982 rev. ed.* Nashville, TN, N.M.
Hailey, 1982. viii, 153p. [C487].

MORROW -- Morrow, Joe. *Ancestors and
Descendants of George & Ethel ( Scaggs )
Morrow.* Memphis, TN, J. Morrow, 1984. 159p.
[C488].

MORTON -- Buckley, Shirley G. *Index to
Genealogy of John Morton, Henrico Co.*
Martin, TN, S.G. Buckley, 1990. 13 leaves.
[DC2648].

MORTON -- Morgan, Donna Morton. *The Lookout
Mountain Mortons and Their Descendants: Plus
Ancestors and Relatives from York Co.,
Pennsylvania, Mecklenburg Co., North Carolina,
Blount Co., Tennessee, and Walker Co.,
Georgia.* Baltimore, Gateway Press, New
Orleans, LA, D. M. Morgan, 1989. viii, 265p.
1. Morton family. 2. Georgia-Genealogy. D
gives underscored part of title.
[G468-3; D2650].

MORTON -- Haas, Bishop Elijah Embree. *David
Morton, A Biography.* Nashville, TN,
Publishing House of the Methodist Episcopal
Church, Smit, Smith & Lamar, agents, 1916. x,
214p. [L12244].

MOSELEY -- Moseley, Alexander. *Descent of
Alexander Moseley.* Nashville, TN, 1967. 9p.
[X671-FW,MH].

MOSELEY -- Vicki, Velma G. (B.). *Descent of
Alexander Moseley.* Nashville, TN, 1967. 9
leaves. [X671-SU].

MOSER -- Bernard, Beaulah Moser. *Genealogy of Abraham Moser - Marie Hofstetter - Mary Leatherman - Abraham, Son of Ulrich Moser - Anna Bogli - Grandson of Hans Moser - Elizabeth Althaus.* Lascassas, Tenn. : B.M. Bernard, c1987. 42 leaves.
LC CALL NUMBER: CS71.M899 1987

MOSS -- Moss, T. C. *The David Moss Family; Warren and Granville Co., N.C. Green, Adair, Mercer, Boyle, Barren, Hart and Warren County, Ky. Williamson and Maury Co., Tenn. Mississippi.* Memphis, TN, Print by C. Johnson and Assocs., 1968. 79p. [L12274].

MOTLEY -- Motlow, Feliz Waggoner. *The Motley Family.* Tullahoma, TN, Mrs. Motlow, 1954-1958. 91p. [D9065].

MOTTERN -- Mottern, Hugh H. *William Mottern Family of Turkeytown, East Tennessee (Elizabethton, Carter County).* Glenview, IL, 1962. Various Pagings. [X672-FW,NY].

MOULDER -- Moulder, George B. *The Moulder Family Tree and Early Family History in the United States.* Nashville, TN, 195__, 19 leaves. [L12284].

MUHLEMAN -- Muhleman, Ruth P. *Muhleman Family.* Chattanooga, TN, 1928, 111 leaves. [X674-04].

MULLICAN -- Kochanski, Lois Whidden. *The Mullican Family of Warren County, Tennessee: A History & Genealogy.* Bethesda, MD, L.Kochanski, c1991. xi, 120p.
LC CALL NUMBER: CS71.M9585 1991

MULLIGAN -- Kochanski, Lois Whidden. *The Mullican Family of Warren County, Tennessee: a History and Genealogy.* Bethesda, MD, L. Kolchanski, c1991. xi, 120p. Includes bibliographical references (p. 102-106) and index. 1. Mulligan family. 2. Tennessee-Genealogy. NGN gives underscored part of title. [G472-1; NGN18-1-92].

MURPHY — Murphy, Marion Emerson. *Tennessee Murphys - Murpheys and Allied Families*. 1st ed. NP, 1968. v. Contents: Braceys, Gossetts, Heads, Justices, Mitchells, Morgans, Murpheys, Murphys, Parkers, Wineter, and Others. [L12364].

MURPHY -- Murphy, Marion Emerson. *Early Murphys - Murpheys in Pittsylvania County, Virginia, Robertson and Carroll Counties, Tennessee*. San Diego, CA, 1974, c1975. xvii, 249p. [D9129; VV136].

MYERS -- Dress, Alice Amelia. *Myers, Pritchard, Cooper and Allied Families*. Knoxville, TN, A.A. Dress, 1990. 103p. [DC2684].

MYNATT -- Hubbs, Mrs. Ferol Frost. *The Mynatt History*. Greenville, TN, Hubbs, 1941. 1 v. (various foliations). [D9150].

# N

NASH -- Nash, James Henry. *The Georgia Descentants of Edward Nash of Greenville County, South Carolina*. ?Somerville, TN, 1973. 111p. [S1802b; NG73].

NEAL -- Neal, Thomas Howe R. *The Neal, Harbison, Snodgrass, Miller, and Related Families*. Knoxville, TN, 1971. 267p. S gives 230p. [S1803; NG74; D9181].

NEALE -- Neal, Thomas Howe R. *The Neal, Harbison, Snodgrass, Miller, and Related Families*. Knoxville, TN, 1971. 230p. [S1803].

NEELY -- Renshaw, Grace Parke. *Neely Narrative*. Memphis, TN, Renshaw, 1976. 137p. [D9189].

NEFF -- Neff, Robert Owen, Jr. *Neff - Wiren: The Story of Our Family*. Murfreesboro, TN,

R.O. Neff, 1980. 325p., 38p. of plates.
[C502].

NELMS -- Hooker, Ruth N. *Presley Nelms, Jr.
His Ancestors and Descendants in America from
November 25, 1652 to the Present.* Memphis,
TN, 1946. 55 l. [X684-MH].

NELSON -- Alexander, Thomas B. *Thomas R. R.
Nelson of East Tennessee.* Nashville, TN,
Tennessee Historical Commission, c1956. 186p.
[D9209].

NELSON -- Braden, Harold J. [G478-2]. See
above: BRADEN. [G81-1].

NETHERLAND -- Spoden, Muriel M. C.
*Ancestry and Descendants of Richard
Netherland, Esquire (1764-1832).* Kingsport,
TN, Spoden, 1979. x, 332. [D9220].

NICHOLS -- Allen, Chris E. *Nichols Family
Genealogy; Hardin Co., Tenn. to Sebastian Co.,
Ark.* Fort Smith, AR, 1973. 30 l. [X689-FW].

NICHOLS -- Bevan, Thelma K, Owen N. Meredith
& Robert M. McBride. *The Nichols Family of
North Georgia and Related Cansler, Black,
Puett, Coffey, and Boone Families: Outline
for a Family History.* Nashville, TN, 1960.
139p. [L12558].

NICHOLS -- Nichol, Bromfield Bradford.
*Nichol of Nashville: An Ulster Scot Family,
circa 1689-1989.* Baltimore, MD, Gateway
Press. 1990. ix, 339p. 1. Nichols family.
2. Scots-Irish-Genealogy. [G481-2].

NICHOLSON -- Fort, Robert C. *Britton
Nicholson and Mary ( Harris ): Progenitors
and Progeny.* Cookeville, TN, R.C. Fort,
c1989. 245p. 1. Nicholson family. 2.
Nicholson, Britton-Family. [G481-3].

NOLEN -- Nolen, Jewell. *The Nolen Story.*
Cookeville, TN, Nolen, 1976. 436p.
[C509; X692-NY].

MUNGEZER -- Bainbridge, Edith Nichols.
*Related Families of the Atlantic an Gulf
Coasts including Mungezer, Nichols, Krebs,
Grant, Davis, Sarrazin, Demas, and Bainbridge.*
Kingsport, TN, T.K. Bainbridge, c1985. 263p.
[DC2755].

O

OAKES -- Oaks, William Bryant. *Descendants
of Isaac Oakes/Oaks, Born in North Carolina in
1777, Died in Tennessee in 1870.* Renton, WA,
W.B. Oaks, Jr., 1985. 1. Oakes family. 2.
Oakes, Isaac, 1777-1870-Family. [G488].

OAKLEY -- Simms, Vivian York. [G488-2]. See
above: McKIBBEN. [G443-1].

OCHS -- Ochs, Grace Lillian. *Up From the
Volga: The Story of the Ochs Family.*
Nashville, TN, Southern Publishing
Association. 1969. 128p. [A500].

ODELL -- Drinnen, Evelyn Spitzer. *All Our
Yesteryears.* Knoxville, TN, E.S. Drinnen,
1982-<1987 > v. <1-2 >. Contents: Pt. 1.
A history of the Odell's and related families.
2. a collection of genealogical records of
Spitzer and related families. 1. O'Dell
family. C gives Pt. 1 only with pub. date of
1982 and v. <1 >. [G490-1; C514].

ODIL -- Bracy, Gladys Elizabeth Odil. *Odil,
Kerr and Cowsert Families.* Nashville, TN,
Bracy, 1964. 110 leaves. [D9382].

ODOM -- Odom, Mary Thelma Cloud. *Descendants
of George & Jane ( Russell ) Odom, Who Settled
in the Second Civil District of Hancock
County, Tennessee.* Morristown, TN, M.T.C.
Odom, 1987. 1 v. (various pagings).
LC CALL NUMBER: CS71.025 1987

OSBORNE -- Harrell, Elizabeth J. [G495-3].
See above: FAULK. [G223-2].

OUSLEY -- Anderson, Ollie Mae Ousley. *From Tennessee to Texas.* N.P., O.M.O. Anderson, 1980. 400 l. [C520].

OVERALL -- Britton, Eudine M. *The Family of William Jefferson Overall, 1838-1908.* Chattanooga, TN, Britton, 1977. 100 leaves. [D9479].

OVERALL -- Kiger, Wenzola R. *Overall Family.* Chattanooga, TN, Kiger, 1978. X gives 1976. xxii, 438p. [D9480; X707-FW].

OWEN -- Lasater, Lee. *Ancient Owners of Marion Farms & Early History of Owen Methodist Church.* __, TN, M.S. Harris, c1985. iii, 56p. Compilations of writings originally published in the Sequatchie Valley news, located at Sequatchie, Tenn. in 1946-47. 1. Owen family. 2. Sequatchie County (Tenn.)- Biography. 3. Sequatchie County (Tenn.)- Genealogy. [G498-2].

OWEN -- See above: CAMPBELL. [L2939; D2108].

OWNBY -- Morgan, Boyce M. *The Ownby - Ownbey Families of Rutherford and Buncombe Counties, North Carolina, and Eastern Tennessee.* El Paso, TX, B.M. Morgan, 1988 [1989]. 63, 233p. Some copies may be imperfect: p176 blank. 1. Ownby family. 2. North Carolina-Genealogy. 3. Tennessee-Genealogy. [G498-3].

OWNBY -- Park, Percival David. *Ownby - Watson Family History, with Information on the Bradley, Cardwell, Wilson, and Other Allied Families of Sevier County, Tennessee.* Atlanta, GA, P. D. Park, 1985. ii, 149 leaves. [C522].

## P

PACK -- Soyars, Crystine Yates. *The Thomas M. Pack Clan, 1836-1977.* Madison, TN, Madison Print Shop, 1977, 103p. [C523].

PAFFORD -- Pafford, John Williams. A Pafford Line in Review. Nashville, TN, 1971. 101p. [NG76].

PAINTER -- Painter, Harold Nelson. Painter Families. Signal Mountain, TN, J.L. Douthat, 1982. 61p. Reprint. Originally published: Sedalia, MO, H.E. Painter, 1978 with additions by James L. Douthat. -- Second entry at same location indicates 64p. and Cover title of: "Painter Records". [C524].

PAMPLIN -- Pamplin, William E., Jr. The Pamplin Family Connections. - 1st and 2nd. ed. Baltimore, MD, Gateway Press; White Bluff, TN, 1984-<1986 > v. <1-2 >. 1. Pamplin family. [G501-2].

PARK -- Moss, Ernestine Parke. Thomas Parke and Rebecca Hooper of Chester County, Pennsylvania: Abiah Taylor, Aaron Bullock, John Hannum, John Chalfant, Ernestine Parke Moss. Memphis, TN, E.P. Moss, 1982. 271p., 4 leaves of plates. [C526].

PARKE -- Moss, Ernestine Parke. Thomas Parke and Rebecca Hooper of Chester County, Pennsylvania. Memphis, TN, Moss, 1982. 271p. [DS527].

PARKER -- Jones, Daniel W. The House of Parker: Dempsey C. Parker of W. Tenn., 1800-1991. Dyersburg, TN. D.W. Jones, 1991. 196 leaves.
    LC CALL NUMBER: CS71.P24 1991

PARKHURST -- Parkhurst, Charles B. The Old Log Church. A Biographical Sketch of the Author. Genealogies in the Appendix. Nashville, TN, Cumberland Presbyterian Pub. House. 1928. 51, 7p. [X718-GF].

PARROTT -- Kelsey, Mavis Parrott. Benjamin Parrott, c1795-1830 and Lewis Stover, 1781-1850/60 of Overton County, Tennessee and Their Descendants. Houston, TX, Dr. & Mrs. Mavis Parrott Kelsey, 1979. 133p. [NG77; D9619].

**PARSLY** -- Parsly, Lewis Fuller. *Ancestry of Lewis Fuller Parsly.* Oak Ridge, TN, Parsly, 1981. 208 leaves. [D9626].

**PATTEN** -- Sinnett, Charles N. *Patten Family.* Fertik, MN, 1925. 6 vols in 1. Typed. Contents: Actor Patten; George Washington Patten, Chattanooga, Tenn. John Patten, Herkimer Co., N.Y., Robert Pattern; William Patten of Argyle, N.Y. [X721-NY].

**PATTERSON** -- Patterson, Jefferson. *Family Portraits.* Nashville, TN, Priv. Print. Baird-Ward Print Co., 1967. xii, 63p. [S1906].

**PATTON** -- Patton, Joseph W. *John Patton and His Descendants.* Jackson, TN, Long-Johnson Prtg. Co., 1922. 98p. [X722-FW,NY].

**PAULETT** -- Garrett, William Robertson. *The Father of Representative Government in America.* Nashville, TN, 189_. 31p. Cover Title: History of the First Legislative Assembly Even Convened in America. Also published with Cover Title: The Paulett Family. Includes mention of a few members of the Paulett family. [L13167].

**PAYNE** -- Paine, Grace Hillman Benedict. *Ancestors of Thomas Fite Paine, Jr. and Grace Hillman Benedict Paine: with Sketch of David Campbell, Pioneer of "Royal Oak," Virginia: (documented biographical notes, illustrations, and index).* Nashville, TN, 1982. ix, 46 leaves. [C531; VV143].

**PAYNE** -- Payne, Lois Wittenbracker. *The Paynes of Wabash County, Illinois and Wilson County, Tennessee.* Effingham, IL, L.W. Payne, 1984. 160p., one folded leaf containing additions attached to p.[2] of cover. [C531].

**PAYNE** -- Thomas, Alice I. (P.). *Descendants of Margaret Couch Payne and Micajah Payne,*

*1824-1968.* Chattanooga, TN, Author, 1968, 95p. [X724-LT].

PEARSON -- Pearson, Eugene L. *Pearson Family History.* Nashville, TN, Author, 1962. 57p. [X725-FW].

PEARSON -- Pearson, Frank Elmer. *Just a Few Pearsons: A Biographical, Historical, Genealogical Sketch of Thomas Pearson, Born 22 April, 1805, Tennessee, His Ancestors and Descendants.* - 1st ed. ___, CA, F.E. Pearson, 1989, c1988. xviii, 479p. 1. Pearson family. 3. California-Genealogy. [G508-3; NGN17-6-91].

PEARSON -- Smith, Jonathan K. T. *A Genealogical Memoir: The Pearsons.* Memphis, TN, c1974. 63p. D gives underscored part of title. [S1913; D9712].

PERES -- Shankman, Sam. *The Peres Family.* Kingsport, TN, Southern Publishers, 1938. xiv, 241p. Speeches and essays of Hardwig Peres. [L13338; D9801].

PERKINSON -- Perkinson, Eula Thomas. *Good Morning -- Mrs. Featherstone?: 700 Years of Perkinson Family History.* Riceville, TN, D.D. Perkinson, 1983. 250p. 1 leaf of plates. [C538].

PERRY -- Miller, Mildred Perry. *Perry Portraits.* Chattanooga, TN, M.P. Miller, 1983. 337p. [DC2877].

PERRYMAN -- Bruhn, Reva Hopkins. *"Lest We Forget, the Perriman Story." 1707-1987: Maryland, North Carolina, Tennessee, and Missouri.* Visalia, CA, R.H. Bruhn, 1987. 79 leaves, 52 leaves of plates. 1. Perryman family. 2. Southern States-Genealogy. [G513-1].

PETTY -- Watt, Irene. *Pettys in America and Some Kith and Kin.* Monoville, TV, Author, 1969. 87, 10p. [X735-FW].

PETTYPOOL -- Pettypool, Edward H. *The Pettypools Family History.* Nashville, TN, D.B. Pettypool, 1960. 225p. [D9866].

PEYTON -- Ross, Helen Pate. *Pait, Payte, Pate: Virginia, North Carolina, Tennessee, Georgia.* Sturtevant, WI, H. P. Ross, 1986. 53p. 1. Peyton family. [G515-2].

PHILLIPS -- Lovell, Eloise Groover. *The Richard Phillips Family History, 1791-1983: An Incomplete History of the Reverend Richard Phillips, His Wife, Delilah Rainwater, and Their Descendants through Eight Generations.* Hermitage, TN, E.G. Lovell, 1983. xi, 340p. Cover title: The Richard Phillips Family, 1791-1983. [C543].

PHILLIPS -- Phillips, Harry. *Phillips Family History; A Brief History of the Phillips Family, Beginning with the Emigration from Wales and a Detailed Genealogy of the Descendants of John and Benjamin Phillips, Pioneers of Wilson County, Tenn.* Lebanon, TN, Lebanon Democrat, Inc., 1935. 3, 242, xix p. NG gives underscored part of title. [L13562; NG79].

PHILLIPS -- Phillips, Harry. *History of the Phillips Family, Beginning with the Emigration from Wales and a Detailed Genealogy of the Descendants of John and Benjamin Phillips, Pioneer Citizens of Wilson County, Tennessee.* 2nd ed. Washington, DC, Heritage Press, 1971. 242p. [X737-OS].

PHILLIPS -- Price, David. *A Short Genealogy of the Families Phillips and Price Beginning in the Eighteenth Century in South Wales.* Brentwood, TN, 1977. pni. [NG79].

PHIPPS -- Young, Asher Leon. *The Phipps Tree II: A Supplement to The Phipps Tree.* Nashville, TN, A.L. Young, 1989. iii, 332p. 1. Phipps family. 2. Kentucky-Genealogy. C gives: iii, 316p. and " An expansion and updating of the chapter on the Phipps that

was in my book Washington Young of Wayne
County, Kentucky and His Descendants...
written in 1976. [G518-1; C544].

PICKENS -- Anderson, Nellie Pickens (E.)
*The John Pickens Family; A History of John and
Letitia Hannah Pickens and Their
Descendants... and Related People*. Rockford,
TN, Anderson, 1951. 256, 16p. D gives
underscored part as title.
[D9923; X738-FW].

PICKENS -- Sharp, S. M. *Pickens Families of
the South*. Memphis, TN, Sharp, 1963. 152p.
[D9927; X738-DP].

PINKERTON -- Chandler, Melvin Leon.
[G520-1]. See above: CHANDLER. [G132-1].

PLANT -- Kniker, Rosemary Connelly. *Plants
Unlimited: Descendants of Williamson Plant
(1763-1830) and Frances Watts, b. 1760-1770,
d. after 1830. Humphrey County, Tennessee and
Bond County, Illinois*. Fairview Heights, IL,
Kniker, 1980. xv, 365p., 38 leaves of plates.
[C548].

POINTER -- Pointer, Zola. *Pointer and
Quarles Families*. Baltimore, MD, Gateway
Press, Cookeville, TN, Z. Pointer, 1986.
viii, 535p. 1. Pointer family. 2. Quarles
family. [G523-2].

POLK -- NAS. *A Genealogical Tree of the Polk
Family*. ___, TN, J.B. McDowell, 1849.
Broadside. [X745-MH].

POLK -- Angellotti, Mrs. Frank M. *The Polks
of North Carolina and Tennessee*. Easley, SC,
Published for the James K. Polk Memorial
Association, by the Southern Historical Press.
1984. viii, 105p. "Reprinted from the New
England historical and genealogical register,
volume 77...volume 78". 1. Polk family. 2.
North Carolina-Genealogy. 3. Tennessee-
Genealogy. NGS gives only title, author, and
105p. [G524; NG80].

POLK -- Rogers, Wilmot Polk. *Ezekiel Polk and His Descendants*. San Francisco, CA, 1939. 114, 32 numb. leaves. "Some of this material was included in a series of articles "The Polks of North Carolina and Tennessee", which appeared in the New England historical and genealogical register beginning with the issue of April, 1923 and concluding in the issue of July, 1924" - Foreword. "Vindication of the revolutionary character and services of the late Colonel Ezekiel Polk of Mecklenburg, N.C..." Also includes the Alexander, Campbell, McNeal, and Rogers families. [L13714].

POPE -- Pope, William R. *Histories of the Pope, Charter, and McFerrin Families of Middle Tennessee*. Nashville, TN, McQuiddy Print, 1950. 223p. [X747-FW,NY].

POTTS -- Potts, J. Ivan. *The Potts Family Descendants of Oswalt Potts in Bedord County, Tennessee*. Shelbyville, Tn, J.I. Potts, Jr. 1983. v, 131, 1 leaf of plates. [C554].

POWELL. -- Lucas, Silas Emmett. *The Powell Family*. Sewanee, TN, University Press, 1961. xiv, 305p. See also: Powell families of Virginia and the South / Lucas 1977. [D10097].

POWELL -- Lucas, Silas Emmett. *Powell Families of Virginia and the South*. Vidalia, GA, Lucas, c1969. 584p. [D10098].

POWELL -- See above: CAMPBELL. [L2939; D2108].

POYNOR -- Poynor, Marion Joyce. *History and Genealogical Data of the Poynor, Burns, Meadows, and Conyer Families*. Columbia, TN, M.J. Poynor, 1982. 158p. [C556].

PRATHER -- Prather, Douglas H. and Ralph E. *Thomas Prather, Sr., McNairy County, Tennessee: Ancestors and Descendants*. Ramer, TN, Douglas H. Prather, 1989. 1 v. (various pagings). Caption title: Ancestors and descendants of Thomas Prather, Sr. 1. Prather family. 2. Tennessee-Genealogy. 3. Prather, Thomas, 1673-1912-Family. [G523-1].

PRIEST -- Ayres, Nellie F. *Genealogy of the Priest, Harris, Stubblefield Families.* Memphis, TN, 1945. Various Pagings. [X757-FW].

PRIEST -- Ayres, Nellie F. *Genealogical Notes of the Priest, Stubblefield, Brown, Hockley, Matt, Shippey and Allied Families.* Memphis, TN, 1961. 84, 23, 42p. Originally drafted in 1945. [X757-NY].

PRINCE -- Prince, Pete. *Prince Family Prince: The Story of 1400 Princes Across America.* Morristown, TN, Lakeway Publications, 1882. 168p. [C559].

PRITCHARD -- Symmonds, Dorothy. [G532-3; C559]. See above: JACOBS. [G345-1; DC2965].

PROCTOR -- Fahrni, Margie Proctor. *Nathan Proctor / Proctor and His Descendants, 1786-1981.* Russellville, MO, M.P. Fahrni, 1981. 146p. [C560].

PRUITT -- Hagan, Imogene Hoover. *The Pruitts, Pattersons, and Their Rhodes Relatives.* Columbia, TN, 'P-Vine Press', 1978. 166p. [C561; D10205].

PRUITT -- Prewitt, Richard A. *Prewitt - Pruitt Records of [name of state].* R. A. Prewitt, <1981-1988 > <5 > v. Contents: [1] Georgia- [2] South Carolina- [3] Tennessee- [4] Texas- [5] Virginia. 1. Pruitt family. 2. Southern States-Genealogy. [G533].

## QR

QUARLES -- Pointer, Zola. [G537-3]. See above: POINTER. [G523-2].

QUISENBERRY -- Brigance, Albert H. *Christenberry / Christenbury Genealogy.* Maryville, TN, Brigance Enterprises, c1988. ii leaves, 231p. 1. Quisenberry family. [G539-1].

RAGLAND -- Davis, David Ragland. [G540-2]. See above: DAVIS. [G177-2].

RAINES -- Rhine, Nanneitta Raines & Mary Sue R. Moseley. [G541-1]. See above: MARKS. [G424-1].

RAINES -- Threatt, Fredna Raines. *Raines of Cocke County, Tennessee.* Dallas, TX, Threatt, 1965. 38 leaves. [D10272].

RALSTON -- Raulston, J. Leonard. *The Ralstons.* South Pittsburg, TN, 1970. 284p. 1. Ralston family. [G541-3].

RAMBO -- Clardy, L. L. *Ancestors of David Henry Rambo, Texas-Tennessee, 1842-1916, and Mary Jane Bills, Brown County, Texas-Tennessee, 1853-1942.* Alpharetta, Ga, L.L. Clardy, 1992. 230p.
 LC CALL NUMBER: CS71.R175 1992

RAMSEY -- Bivins, Willie Hardin. *The Family of Reynolds Ramsey, Revolutionary Soldier.* Oklahoma City, OK, Mrs. W.V. Bivins. 1987. xi, 144p. 1. Ramsey family, 2. Ramsey, Reynolds, 1736-1816 or 17-Family. 3. Tennessee-Genealogy. [G542-2].

RAMSEY -- Ramsey, Elizabeth R. *Links: Descendants of James Ramsey of Habersham County, Georgia and Thomas Ramsey of Maury County, Tenn., Plus Allied Lines of Alexander, Baldridge, Clanton, Dorsey, Durham, Fleming, Grier, Henderson, Herrin, Kerr, McKnight, Oliver, Pardeu, Shields, Scrantao, Simonton, West, and Others.* Richland, WA, Ramsey, 1974. 188, x p., 14 leaves. of plates. [S2038].

RANDLE -- Durham, Mary Kate Randle. *Randle in Virginia, North Carolina, Tennessee, Texas,*

RANDOLPH  --  Randolph, Wassell.  *William Randolph of Turkey Island, Henrico County, Virginia.*  Memphis, TN, Seebode Minac Service, 1949.  115p.  [NG81; D10295].

RANDOLPH  --  Randolph, Wassell.  *Henry Randolph I, 1623-1773 (sic) of Henrico County, Virginia, and His Descendants.*  Memphis, TN, 1952.  105p. [NG81].

RANDOLPH  --  Randolph, Wassell.  *Pedigree of the Descendants of Henry Randolph I  (1623-1673) of Henrico County, Virginia.*  Memphis, TN, 1957.  277p.  Sequel to Henry Randolph I.  1623-1673 of Henrico County, Virginia and his descendants.  D gives underscored part of title.  [L10499; NG81; D10294].

RANEY  --  Waldenmaier, Inez.  *One Branch of the Raney Family.*  Tulsa, OK,  I.R. Waldenmaier, 1985-  .  3 v.  Contents: part 2 Traveling westward from New Jersey to North Carolina, through Tennessee and Indpendence County, Arkansas.  [DC3009].

RANSOM  --  Ransom, Robert G.  *The Ransom Family of Western Kentucky:  A History and Genealogy.*  Murfreesboro, TN, Ransom, 1977.  vii, 386p.  [C570].

RATLIFF  --  Ratliff, Carl M., Jr., Ed.  *Ratliff - Keller, Book Two:  Louisville, Tennessee and Memorabilia.*  Gradyville, PA, C.M. Ratliff, Jr., 1880.  1 v, (various pagings).  Genealogical Table.  [C571].

RATLIFF  --  Ratliff, Carl M., Jr., Ed.  *Ratliff - Keller, Book Two:  Louisville, Tennessee and Memorabilia.*  Gradyville, PA, C.M. Ratliff, Jr., 1882.  211p.  Contains the Ancestors and Descendants of Carl Marcus Ratliff (1886-1972) and Ethel Keller Ratliff

(1888-1975), his Wife, with Some Collateral Lines, 1980. [C571].

RAULSTON -- Raulston, J. Leonard. *The Raulstons*. South Pittsburg, TN, Raulston, 1970. 284p. [A555; D10321].

RAY -- Franklin, Della P. *Ray Connections*. Cookeville, TN, D. P. Franklin, 1990. iv, 459, 60p. 1. Ray family. 2. Tennessee-Genealogy. 3. Kentucky-Genealogy. [G544-1].

RAYLE -- Jones, Jean E. *The Rayle Family of Chester County... Guilford... East Tennessee*. Thousand Oaks, CA, Jones, 1980. 203p. [DC3020].

REAGAN -- NAS. *Reagan Family Journal: The Quarterly Newsletter of the Reagan Family Association*. Knoxville, TN, The [Reagan Family] Association, 1984- --v. Check shelflist for DAR Library holdings. [DC3026].

REAGAN -- Reagan, Donald B. *Smoke Mountain Clans*. Knoxville, TN, Reagan, c1978-c1983. 3 vols. [C572].

RECTOR -- King, Larry. *Rector Records: Ancestors and Descendants of John Jacob Rector and Elizabeth Fischbach: 1714 Immigrants from Trupbach, Germany to Germanna, Virginia*. Hendersonville, TN, L. King, c1986. vi, 474p. 1. Rector family. 2. Rector, John Jacob, 1674-1729-Family. [G545-2].

REED -- Reed, Forrest F. *A Reed Family in America*. Nashville, TN, Tennessee Book Co., 1962. 83p. [D10380].

REED -- Reid, Mildred H. *Reid, Reed Family History: Descendants of Isaac Reed, Born, 1800. Died, 1873*. Sewanee, TN, University Press, 1984. 39p. [C574].

REEDER -- Marvin, William. *A Brief History of the Reeder Family*. Knoxville, TN, Marvin: Reeder, 1956. 247 leaves. [D10392].

REEVE  --  Runions, Judy Ferguson.  *The Descendants of Peter Reeves, 1775-1980*. Columbia, TN, P-Vine Press, 1981.  56p., 25 leaves of plates.  [C575].

REEVE  --  Reaves, Timothy O.  *The Reeves Family Tree*.  Greenville, TN, T. O. Reaves, 1983.  v, 301p.  [C576].

REEVES  --  NAS.  *Ancestral Sketches.  (A Chronicle of the Pioneer East Tennessee Families: Reeves, Miller, De Vault, and Range of Washington County; Robeson of Sullivan and McMinn Counties; Easley, Hamilton, Acuff, and Vincent, of Sullivan County; and Certain of Their Antecedents in New Jersey, Pennsylvania, Maryland, Virginia, and North Carolina)*.  Lynchburg, VA, J.P. Bell Co., 1951.  ix, 113p.  [L14226; VV155].

REEVES  --  Bivins, Willie Hardin.  *Descendants of Edward Reeves and Jane Melvin*.  Oklahoma City, OK, W.V. Bivins, c1984.  39 leaves.  1. Reeve family.  2. Reeves, Edward, 1791-1826-Family.  [G547-2].

REEVES  --  Bivins, Willie Hardin.  [G547-3].  See above:  HARDING.  [G297-3].

RENSHAW  --  Renshaw, Grace Parke.  *Renshaw Reflections*.  Baltimore, MD, Gateway Press, Memphis, TN, G.P. Renshaw, 1983.  176, viii p., 3p. of plates.  [C577].

REVELEY  --  Hudgins, Sally Reveley.  *The Inhabitants of Woodend*.  Martin, TN, Hudgins, 1981.  viii, 254p.  [DS594].

RHEIN  -  Rhine, Nanneitta Raines & Mary Sue R. Moseley.  [G552-1].  See  above:  MARKS.  [G424-1].

RHODES  --  Rhodes, Troas Etta.  *Some of the Early Settler of Pennsylvania, Virginia, Missouri, North Carolina, Indiana, Ohio, Illinois*.  Palm Desert, CA, Artisan Printing Co., 1977.  iii, 236, iv p.  [D10465; VV156].

RICE -- Calhoun, William Gunn. *The Rice Family, 1680-1973.* Washington College, TN, Washington College Academy, 1973. x, 169p. [D10469].

RICE -- Little, Melvin Weaver. *Henry Rice (1717-1818), the Pioneer Tennessee Grismiller and His Twelve Children.* Arlington, ?, M.W. Little, c1984. xi, 312p. [DC3064].

RICH -- Hogan, Julia R. *William Rich (Richee) Sr., The Record of Some Rich Families in Maryland, Pennsylvania, North Carolina, Tennessee, Indiana and Utah.* 2d. ed. Houston, TX, Rich Family Assoc. 1968. -- _ vol. LA has vol. 3. [X783-LA/SU].

RICHARDSON -- Bragg, Emma W. [G553-2; C581]. See above: CARTER. [G124-2; C581].

RICHARDSON -- Richardson, Thomas F. *Richardson - Hartley - Arender and Related Families; A List of the Known Descendants of Elijah Richardson of Tennessee and Frank Hartley of South Carolina, Both of Whom Moved to Mississippi about 1815.* NP, 1969. 399p. [L14361].

RICKS -- Stine, Annibel. *Descendants of the Ricks Family in the Tennessee Valley.* NP, 1936. 71 leaves. [D10521].

RIGBY -- McConnell, Grace Conn. [G556-1]. See above: BREWER. [G87-3].

RIGBY -- Rigsby, Homer J. *The Rigsbys of Bledsoe County, Pikeville, Tennessee.* Safety Harbor, FL, Grey Goose Press, c1984. viii, 56 leaves. 1. Rigsby family. 2. Tennessee-Genealogy. [G556-1].

RIGGS -- Duggan, Clara Nichols. <u>More About the Riggs Family, 1590-1973</u>; *With Cognate Ogilve, Haley, and Brittain Families, Descended from Edward Riggs, Born About 1590.* Holtland, TN, Duggan: Duggan, 1974. viii, 254p. Based partly on a continuation of J.H.

Wallace's Genealogy of the Riggs Family, published in 1901. D gives underscored part of title. [S2092; D10535].

RIPPER -- Symmonds, Dorothy. [G557-1]. See above: JACOBS. [G345-1; DC2965].

RINDLAUB -- Anderson, Beverly D. [G557-1]. See above: GUSS. [G282-2; DC1539].

RINEHART -- Henning, Emma. *The Ulrich Reinhart Family and Descendants, 1704-1985.* Dayton, TN, E.A. Henning, 1986. x, 422p. 1. Rinehart family. 2. Rinehart, Ulrich, 1704-1787-Family. 3. Ohio-Genealogy. [G557-1].

RITCHIE -- Richey, James. [G558-3]. See above: LEAR. [G392-2].

RIVES -- Rives, John Robert Thomas. Green Rives of Dinwiddie County, Virginia and Lincoln County, Tennessee, *and His Descendants.* Birmingham, AL, A. H. Cather Pub. Co., 1958. v, 103p. D gives underscored part of title. [L14436; D10565; VV157].

RIX -- NAS. *Descendants of the Ricks Family in the Tennessee Valley, with Excursions on Many Allied Families, 1820-1936.* Tuscumbia, AL, 1936. 5p., 71 numb. leaves. Typed. "The data has been supplied mostly by Miss Ethel Ricks Clark". [L14441].

ROBERTS -- Hays, Maude Calloway. See HAYES. [L8051].

ROBERTS -- Roberts, Laney James. *The Generations of Reuben.* Chattanooga, TN, Roberts, 1977. xi, 268p. [C587].

ROBERTS -- Roberts, Snyder E. *Roberts Families of Roane County, Tennessee.* Olive Springs, TN, Roberts, 1968. iv, 323p. [A564; D10591].

ROBERTS -- Turbett, James A. *The Roberts-Smith Book: The Roberts and Smith*

*Families of Upcountry South Carolina, Bedford County, Tennessee, Coffee County, Tennessee, Hamilton County, Tennessee, and Boone County, Arkansas.* Alexandria, VA, J.A. Turbett, 1994. 1 v. (unpaged). [NGN SEP/OCT 94].
LC CALL NUMBER: CS71.R64 1994

ROBERTSON -- Harrell, Elizabeth J. [G561-3]. See above: FAULK. [G223-2].

ROBERTSON --- Kelley, Sarah Foster. *The Family Tree of General James Robertson (1742-1972).* Nashville, TN, Blue & Gray Pres, 1972. 218p. [S2104].

ROBERTSON --- Kelley, Sarah Foster. *Children of Nashville: Lineages from James Robertson.* Nashville, TN, Blue & Gray Press, 1973. x, 447p. [S2105; NG84: D10604].

ROBERTSON -- Kelley, Sarah Foster. *General James Robertson.* Nashville, TN, c1980. ii, 80p. [D10605].

ROBERTSON -- Matthews, Thomas E. *General James Robertson, Father of Tennessee.* Nashville, TN, Parthenon Pr., 1934. 588p. [X794-FW,IG].

ROBERTSON --- Randolph, Wassell. *The Reverend George Robertson (1662-1739) Rector of Bristol Parish, Virginia (1693-1739) and His Descendants.* Memphis, TN, Distributed by Cossitt Library. 1955. 93p. "Compliment to the author's prior publication "The Reverend George Robertson and Bristol Parish Virginia". [L14494; NG84; D10609].

ROGERS -- Brabson, Estalena Rogers. *Rogers Relatives with Origination in Blount County, Tennessee.* Sevierville, TN, Tri-County News, 1970. 176p. [D10677].

ROMINE -- Romine, William Bethel. *The Romine Family.* Pulaski, TN, Pulaski Citizen, 1930. 13p. [L14637; NG85].

ROPER -- Super, Mary Waller. *The Roper Family Bible Record*. Winchester, TN, Franklin County Pub. Co., 1982. 424p. [C594].

ROSE -- Rose, Christine. *Ancestors and Descendants of Frederick Rose of Sussex County, Virginia, Orange County, North Carolina, and Hardin County, Tennessee*. San Jose, CA, Rose Family Bulletin, 1980. 77p. [D5818; VV160].

ROSE -- Rose, Virginia. *Colonel William Rose of Tennessee*. Jonesboro, AK, Sammons Printing Co., 1939. 281, 3p. Index bound separately. [D10747].

ROTHWELL -- Fischer, Myra Smith. *A Rothwell Book. Comprising the Descendants of Claiborne Rothwell of Albermarle County, Virginia, Through Nine Generations, and Interesting Sketches About Some of His Descendants*. Memphis, TN, Fischer, 1964. xviii, 434p. [ gives underscored part of title. [L14732; D10773].

ROWE -- Davis, David Ragland. [G572-1]. See above: DAVIS. [G177-2].

ROWLAND -- Johnson, Lillian Vesta Brown. [G572-2]. See above: BROWN. [G99-3].

ROWLAND -- Sheridan, Richard C. *Richardson Rowland (1791-1872) and His Family... Tennessee and ... Kentucky*. Sheffield, AL, Sheridan, 1975. 47p. [X809-DP].

ROYAL -- Wilkinson, A. Mims. [G573-1]. See above: DERRYBERRY. [G187-1].

RUBLE -- Ruble, Roy Clark. *The Ruble Family*. Memphis, TN, Riverside Press, 1970. 56p. [D10811].

RUCH -- NAS. *Sarah Verena Ruch and Charles Orin Ruch, Jr.; Ancestral and Family Records, Showing Lineage Through the Following Families: Ruch, Fuller, Ross, Stalder,*

*Bonham, and Johnson. Also Partial Records Giving Kampf, Bryan, Phillips Connection.* Chattanooga, TN, 1952. 1 v. [L14779].

RUCKER -- Whitley, Mrs. Edythe Hones Rucker. *History of the Rucker Family and Their Descendants. Sketches of Carter, Barton, Early, Johns, Lee, Martin, Pendelton, Reade, Seldon, Taliaferro, Witt, and Wyatt Families.* Nashville, TN, Hermitage Print Co., 1927. 2, iii-ix, 308p. Half-Title: Ruckers and connections. [L14780].

RULE -- Rule, William III. *The Rule Family of East Tennessee and Extended Points.* Knoxville, TN, W. Rule, 1984. v, 218p., 2p. of plates. [C602].

RUNYAN -- Wright, Marie Runyon. *Tracking Barefoot Runyon: Descendants of Isaac Barefoot Runyon: Tracing the Path of These Runyons from the Shenandoah Valley Through Tennessee and Alabama and Their Journey Westward.* Baltimore, MD, Gateway Press, 1980. xiii, 292p., 1 leaf of plates. [C603].

RUSH -- Ayres, Nellie F. *Genealogy of the Rush Family of Virginia and the Terrell Genealogy.* Memphis, TN, 1946. pni. [VV162].

RUSH -- Ayres, Nellie F. *Genealogy of the Rush Family of Virginia.* Memphis, TN, 1963. pni. [VV162].

RUSSELL -- Boals, Prudencia, Ed. and Publ. *Candelwicks.* Ripley, TN, Boals, 1979. xxv, 313p. [C604].

RUSSELL -- Pilcher, Margaret Campbell. See above: CAMPBELL. [L2939; D2108].

RUTLEDGE -- Grigsby, Frances Cate. *The Rutledges of Rose Holl: Rutledge Hill Remembered.* Nashville, TN, F.C. Grigsby, 1980. 37p. [C605].

RUTLEDGE -- Wheeler, Mary Bray & Genon
Hickerson Neblett. *Hidden Glory: The Life
and Times of Hampton Plantation, Legend of the
South Santee* -- 1st ed. -- Nashville, TN,
Rutledge Hill Press, 1983. xvi, 186p., 4p. of
plates. [C695].

RYAN -- Stout, Mildred Bochner. *More Ryan
Roots: Descendants of William and D. Ryan of
Virginia Through Their Sons: William, John,
Philip, Joseph, Thomas Who Lived in Kentucky,
Tennessee, and Alabama.* Pullman, WA, M.B.
Stout, c1994. x, 528p.
  LC CALL NUMBER: CS71.R98 1994


# S

SANDERS -- Sanders, Charles Richard. *A
History of the Family of Dr. William Josiah
and Fannie Adams Sanders of Rutherford County,
Tennessee.* Durham, NC, C.R. Sanders, 1982.
77 leaves. [DC3201].

SANFORD -- NAS. *Register, Henry Shelton
Sanford Papers. Henry Shelton Sanford
Memorial Library, Sanford, Florida.*
Nashville, TN, Tennessee State Library and
Archives, Manuscript Division, Registers, n.d.
72p. [X822-FW].

SAPP -- Goff, Bob Baker. *Some Leaves From
the Sapp Family Tree and Related Families of
Skillern, Anderson, Fraser.* Knoxville, TN,
B.B. Goff, 1983 or 1984. iii, 123p. [C611].

SARGENT -- Harpole, Agnes S. *Major Sargents
and Their Minors: from James Sargent, ca.
1765-ca. 1845, North Carolina through
Tennessee, Mississippi, and West.* West Point,
MS, 1961. 47 leaves. [X823-FW/MH/NY/PH].

SAUNDERS -- NAS. [G583-2]. See above:
CLARK. [G141-2].

SAUNDERS -- Hooker, Ruth N. *Edward
Saunders, Sr. Chirurgeon, Captain, Justice.*

*1621-1672.* Memphis, TN, 13 leaves. "Supplement to Presely Nelms, Jr. by Ruth N. Hooker, 1946. See NELMS: X684-MH above. [X824-MK].

SAUNDERS -- Terrell, Rufus. *Newell Sanders; A Biography.* Kingsport, TN, Priv. Print., Kingsport Presss, Inc., 1935. xvii, 310p. [L15025].

SAUNDERS -- Whitley, Edythe. *Lineage of Mrs. Josephine Saunders Gourley of Nashville, Tennessee.* NP, 1969. 1 v. [DS639].

SAWYER -- Jones, Daniel W. *John Sawyer, the Emmigrant of Dyer County, Tenn.: Genealogical History of John Sawyer and Families.* Dyersburg, TN, D.W. Jones, 1988. 82 leaves. 1. Sawyer family. 2. Sawyer, John, 1830-1906-Family. 3. Tennessee-Genealogy. 4. Southern States-Genealogy. [G585-2].

SAWYERS -- Harris, Madison Monroe. *Family History of Col. John Sawyers and Simon Harris and Their Descendants.* Knoxville, TN, Knoxville Lithographic Co., 1913. 195p. [D10992].

SAWYERS -- NAS. *Colonel John Sawyers.* NP, Tennessee DAR, G.R.C., 1945. 4 l. [D10993].

SCALES -- Scales, Cordelia Lewis. *"Dear Darling Loulie": Letters of Cordelia Lewis Scales to Loulie W. Irby During and After the War Between the States.* Including Dabney Minor Scales' letter written from the deck of the Arkansas. Martha Neville Lumpkin, ed. Clarksville, TN, 1972. 157p. [NGS10].

SCHILD -- Taylor, Dola Schild. *Genealogy of the Schild Marugg Families, Settlers in 1869 of the Swiss Coloney [sic] of Gruetli, Grundy County, Tennessee.* Winchester, TN?, Taylor, 1986. 64 leaves. [DC3221].

SCHULTZ -- Reagan, Donald B. *Early History of Doctor Martin Shultz and Julianna Stentz.*

Knoxville, TN, D.B. Reagan, c1989. 47 leaves.
1. Schultz family. 2. Shultz, Martin, ca.
1740-1787-Family. 3. Tennessee-Genealogy.
[G591-3].

SEMMES -- Humphreys, Anderson & Curt
Guenther. *Semmes America*. Memphis, TN, A.
Humphreys, c1989. xxvi, 669p. [DC3262].

SEVIER -- Sevier, Cora Bales and Nancy S.
Madden. *Sevier Family History, with Collected
Letters of General John Sevier, First Governor
of Tennessee and 28 Collateral Family
Lineages*. Washington, DC, 1961. xvi, 558p.
[L15315].

SEVIER -- Armstrong, Zella. *The Sevier
Family*. Chattanooga, TN, The Lookout Pub. Co.,
1926. (16), 325p. (Her Notable southern
families, V. 4. See also V. 1. [L15316].

SHANNON -- Stimpson, Roberta Shannon.
*Shannon Family Research: Kentucky, Tennessee,
Virginia and Other States*. Berkley, VA, R.S.
Stimpson, 1987. 253p., 3 leaves of plates.
1. Shannon family. [G601-2; DC3275].

SHAPARD -- Shapard, Sarah Marsh. *A Shapard
Family, 1623-1980*. Columbia, TN, P-Vine
Press, Mrs. Polly C. Warren, 1980. 68p.
[D11224].

SHAPPLEY -- Shappley, Ora Estelle McMillin.
*Shappley Family Tree*. Memphis, TN, O.E.
Shappley, 1986. 73p.
    LC CALL NUMBER: CS71.S5567 1986

SHARP -- Hill, Euel Ray. [G601-3]. See
above: COKER. [G148-3].

SHECKLER -- Heiss, Joyce Sheckler. *Sheckler
( Schäckler )*. Jefferson City, TN, J.S.
Heiss, 1988. vi, 618p. 1. Sheckler family.
[G603-2].

SHELBY -- Galloway, Howard S. *The Shelby
Family: Ancestors and Descendants of John*

*Shelby and His Son David Shelby, Pioneers of Tennessee.* Mobile, AL, Printed for Author by Grill Print Co., 1964. xxxi, 352p. [L15439].

SHELLENBARGER -- Whitley, Edythe J. (R.). *Shellenbarger Family.* Nashville, TN, 1946. 134 leaves. [X849-FW,LA,SU].

SHELLY -- Whitley, Edythe. *Shelly Family of Scott County, Virginia, and Franklin County, Tennessee, Data.* NP, 1964. 21 leaves. [D11270].

SHELTON -- Brown, Kathryn Morris. *The Sheltons Lineal Descendants from Ancient, Medieval, and Modern Kings and from Fifteen Sureties of the Magna Charta.* Knoxville, TN, Keith Press, 1981. ix, 133p. [C630].

SHELTON -- Shelton, Arthur Paul. *The Family of James Shelton of McMinn County, Tennessee.* Doraville, GA, Shelton, 1980. 230 pages, 1 leaf of plates. [C631].

SHEPARD -- Shepard, Sarah Marsh. *A Shapard Family, 1623-1980.* Columbia, TN, P-Vine Press, P.C. Warren, 1980. 68p. [C631].

SHERARD -- Sherard, Gerald E. *The Descendants of James Sherard and Nancy Cornelison.* Baltimore, MD, Gateway Press, Knoxville, TN, G.E. Sherard, 1984. iii, 200p. [C631].

SHERERTZ -- Sherrod, James Andrew. *The Sheretz - Sherrod Family, 1714-1984.* Nashville, TN, William Printing, 1984. 864p. [C632; DC3297].

SHERRILL -- Sherrill, Charles A. *Henry Hunt Sherrill of Tennessee and His Descendants.* Cleveland, TN, C.A. Sherrill, 1989. 116, i.e. 235p., 17 columns. 1. Sherrill family. 2. Sherrill, Henry Hunt, 1830-1850-Family, 3. Tennessee-Genealogy. [G605-3].

SHERROD -- Sherrod, Charles C. The Genealogy of the Henry Sherrod Family, 1788-1956. Knoxville, TN, C.C. Sherrod. 1956. 164p. Includes: Beal, Leti, Luttrell, Tindell families. [X851-MH].

SHIELDS -- NAS. The Shields Family. Chattanooga, TN,1916. 3p. (Notable southern families). Detached from the Lookout of Dec. 16, 1916. [L15528].

SHIELDS -- Harmon, Katherine Susong. Research on the East Tennessee Shields Families. Greenville, TN, K.S. Harmon, c1963. 164p. [A609; DC3304].

SHIELDS -- Shields, Arthur Randolph. The Descendants of Robert and Margaret Emmett Shields of Cades Cove, Tennessee. NP, A.R. Shields, 1986. vi, 321p. Title from Spine: Shields Descendants. 1. Shields family. 2. Shields, Robert, 1784-1850-Family. 3. Tennessee-Genealogy. [G606-1; DC3305].

SHOFFNER -- Shoffner, C. L. A History of One Branch of the Shoffner Family, or, John Shoffner and His Descendants, Including Also Records of the Shoffner Reunions. Nashville, TN, McQuiddy Printing Co., 1905. 131p. [D11353].

SHOUN -- Neal, Carl B. Leonard Shoun and His Wife, Barbara Slemp Shoun, of Johnson County, Tennessee (JCT), and Their Descendants. Olympia, WA, 1957. a-q, 359p. [X855-GF,NY.OF,PP,SP].

SHOUN -- Neal, Carl B. Leonard Shoun and His Wife, Barbara Slemp, of Johnson County, Tennessee, and Their Descendants. Johnson City, TN, Overmountain Press, 1985. viii, 275p.
    LC CALL NUMBER: CS71.S5592 1985

SHRODE -- Taylor, I. T. America's Greatest Pioneer Family. History of the Shrode Family *in America.* Nashville, TN, McQuiddy Print. Co., 1945. 9, 345p. Includes Taylor, Duffey, and Jamison families. [L15591].

SHULTZ -- Reagan, Donald B. *Early History of Doctor Martin Shultz and Julianna Stentz.* Knoxville, TN, D.B. Reagan, 1989. 47 leaves.
    LC CALL NUMBER: CS71.S3887 1989

SIBERT -- Sibert, Vasco B. *The Sibert Family of South Carolina, Alabama, Tennessee.* NP, 1967. 116 leaves. [D11391].

SIEVERS -- Seivers, Edna Wallace. *The Robert & Harriet Wallace Family: Anderson County, Tn. and Knox County, Tn. 1800's & 1900's.* Knoxville, TN, E.W. Seivers, 1986. 37 leaves.
    LC CALL NUMBER: CS71.W22 1986

SIMCOX -- Seivers, Edna Wallace. *Simcox.* Knoxville, TN, E.W. Seivers, 1989. iv, 257p. 1. Simcox family. 2. England-Genealogy. [G610-2].

SIMMS -- Humphreys, Anderson & Curt Guenther. *Semmes America - 1st ed. -* Memphis, TN, Humphreys, Ink., c1989. xxi, 699p. 1. Simms family. 2. Semme, Marmaduke, ca. 1635-1693-Family. [G611-2].

SIMMS -- Simms, Vivian York. [G611-2]. See above: McKIBBEN. [G443-1].

SIMMONS -- Jenkins, Jack Simmons. *William Simmons of Wayne County, Tennessee and Descendants.* San Antonio, TX, 1987. 96p. [DC3338].

SIMPSON -- Simpson, Edna G. *The Family of John Simpson (1795-1887) of Virginia and Tennessee.* Knoxville, TN, E.G. Simpson, 1982. 12 leaves. [C639].

SIMS -- Sharp, E. M. *A History of the Sims Family: Descendants and Antecedents of Nathan Sims of Coronaca Community in Greenwood*

County, South Carolina. Memphis, TN, Greenwood County Historical Society, 1971. 97 leaves. [DC3348].

SIMS -- Sims, Almon J. *The Paris (Pariss - Parish) Henry Sims Branch of the Sims of Scotland, England, Ireland and America.* Knoxville, TN, 1948. 38 leaves. [L15683].

SIMS -- Sims, Almon J. *The Pariss Sims Family and Related Families, 1766-1965.* Knoxville, TN, Sims, 1965. 114p. D gives 14p. and underscored part of title. [L15683; D11445].

SISK -- Sisk, Luther L. *The Sisk Family: Virginia--North Carolina--South Carolina-- Kentucky--Alabama--Tennessee--Georgia-- Missouri--Texas.* Escondido, CA, 1980. 1 v. various foliations. [C640; VV170].

SIZEMORE -- Hankins, Edith Jackson. *Kin to "Old Ned" Sizemore.* Memphis, TN, E.J. Hankins, 1990. 42p. 1. Sizemore family. 2. Sizemore, Ned-Family. [G613-1].

SKINNER -- Adams, William Paul, Mrs. *The Tishomingo County Connection: History of Skinner - Welch & Allied Families of Tishomingo County, Mississippi.* Crump, TN, Mrs. W.P. Adams, 1980. 157, 152, 158-502, A-T p., 32p. of plates. [C641].

SLIGER -- Franklin, Della P. *Sliger and Related Families in America.* Cookeville, TN, D.P. Franklin, 1981. 410, 108p. [C643].

SMITH -- Carter, Sharon S. *The Descendants of Theodore Senter Smith, Hamblen County, Tennessee.* ___, TN, S.S. Carter, 1991. 51p. LC CALL NUMBER: CS71.S643 1991d

SMITH -- Collins, Sonja Jo Smith. *Elisha Smith and Family, 1814-1979.* Corryton, TN, S. J. S. Collins, 1979. 129p. [C644].

SMITH -- Masters, Jack. *Smith, Bowers, Hull & Beaty Family History*. Gallatin, TN, J. Masters, c1991. vii, 441p.
   LC CALL NUMBER: CS71.S643 1991

SMITH -- Reeves, Emma Barrett. *Tennessee Smithology*. NP, Reeves, 1975. viii, 153p. [S2338].

SMITH -- Smith, Austin Wheeler. *The Smith - Jarratt Genealogy*. Cookeville, TN, Smith, 1941. vii, 204 numb. leaves. [L15878; D11578].

SMITH -- Smith, Oma. *Smith, Garrett, and Allied Families of Overton, Fentress, and Pickett Counties, Tennessee*. Jacksonville, FL, Smith, c1979. xi, 549p. [D11607].

SMITH -- Smith, Wesley. *A Family History*. Nashville, TN, University Press Company, 1898. 167p. [D11614].

SMITH -- Smith, Wolbur Bell. *Smith Family, 1750-1990, Rowan County, N.C., Tipton County, Tn*. Dallas, TX, Baylor University, 1990. 186p. [DC3392].

SMITH -- Sorensen, Willa Thomas. *Tennessee Smiths*. Goodyear, AZ, Sorenseen, 1986. 207, 69p. 1. Smith family. 2. Tennessee-Genealogy. [G618-3].

SMITH -- Wilson, Ealon V. *Colorful and Eventful Life of St. Clare W. Smith, 19th Century Trail-Blazer, etc. with Account of Ancestors, Descendants*. Memphis, TN, 1967. 46p. [X871-FW].

SMITHSON -- Andrews, Ella Smith Johns ( Mrs. Forest Andrews). *The Descendants of Horatio Sharp Smithson & A18 Lydia Andrews*. Knoxville, TN, 1968. 14p. 1. Smithson family. [G619-2; A620].

SOPER -- Soper, Mary Waller Shepherd. *The Chronicles of a Clan, 1045-1977*. Sarasota,

FL., Soper, 1977.   336 leaves.   Chiefly
photocopy of holograph.  [C653].

SOPER  --  Soper, Mary Waller Shepherd.  Thrice
Three Times Told Tales.   Winchester, TN,
Franklin County Pub. Co., 1978.   355p., 228p.
of plates.  [C654].

SPENCER  --  Spencer, Donald.  Spencer Family
of Lincoln County, Tennessee.  Cullman, AL,
Gregath Pub. Co., c1991.  vii, 297p.
   LC CALL NUMBER: CS71.S745 1991

STACY   --   Scott, Mary & Edith.   Stacy, A
Record of Some of the Descendants of William
Stacy of Hawkins County, Tennessee and His
Wife Dolley Sizemore.   Salina, KS, M. Scott &
E. Scott, c1985.  163p.  1. Stacey family.  2.
Stacy, William, b. ca 1750-60-Family.  3.
Tennessee-Genealogy.  [G627-3].

STALCUP  --  Jones, Earl E.   The Stalcup
Family History, 1641-1986.  Madison, TN, E.E.
Jones, c1986.  3 v. (iii, 1505, 306p.)  1.
Stalcup family.  [G628-1].

STANFIELD  --  Hieronymous, Goldie Smith.
Descendants of Sampson Stanfield, Who Went
From Anson County, North Carolina into Knox
County, Kentucky, in the Early 1800's Was Son
of John Stanfield and Wife Mary.   Falls
Church, VA, Hieronymous, 1978.  158p.  Rev.
ed. Published as:   Descendants of Sampson
Stanfield, North Carolina via East Tennessee
into Knox County, Kentucky in the Early
1800's. Rev. ed. 1981.  [C661].

STARK  --  Abbott, Jane H.   Thomas Stark of
Virginia, to South Carolina, South Carolina to
Tennessee and Returned to South Carolina.
Genealogical Notes and Records.   NP, 1929.
pni.  [VV174].

STEELE  --  McConnell, Grace Conn.   [G631-1].
   See above: BREWER.
   [G87-3].

STEELE -- Steele, Newton Chambers, M.D. *Archibald Steele and His Descendants; A Short Historical Narrative of Archibald Steele the First ad His Descendants with Genealogical Tables Showing Their Proper Places in the Family of Every Member of It Whose Name Could Be Learned.* Chattanooga, TN, The MacGowan & Cooke Co., 1900. 143p. [L16226; D11878].

STEELE -- Steele, Newton Chambers, M. D.. *Captain Ninian Steele and His Descendants; A Short Historical Narrative of Archibald Steele the First ad His Descendants with Genealogical Tables Showing Their Proper Places in the Family of Every Member of It Whose Name Could Be Learned.* Chattanooga, TN, The MacGowan & Cooke Co., 1901. 100p. D gives 100, 31p. [L16227; D11879].

STEINSEIFFER -- Stonecipher, H. S. *The Descendants of Johannes Steinseiffer.* Helenwood, TN, H.S. Stonecipher, 1986. 1. Stonecipher family. 2. Steinseiffer, Johannes, 1692-1757-Family. 3. Steinseiffer family. [G632-3].

STEPHENSON -- Roberson, Susan McDonald. *The Stephenson Family, Past and Present.* Nashville, TN, Mrs. R.E. Roberson, 1984. 87p. [C665].

STEWART -- Blakemore, Mary S. *A Narrative Genealogy of the Stewarts of Sequatchie Valley, Tennessee, and Allied Families.* Richmond, VA, Dietz Press, 1960. xvi, 227p. X gives 226p.
[L16313; D11948; X901-FW; VV176].

STEWART -- Boyd, William J. *An Introduction to the Stewarts -- 2nd ed. --* Nashville, TN, W.J. Boyd, Sold by Clan Stewart Society, c1988. 12p.
LC CALL NUMBER: CS71.S93 1988a

STIMSON -- Stinson, Ulery & Edna. *Our Stinson's [sic].* Columbia, TN, U.,E., & R. Stinson, 1981. 521p. [C668].

STOLTZFUS -- Yoder, Paton, comp. *Tennessee John Stoltzfus: Amish Church-Related Documents and Family Letters.* Lancaster, PA, Lancaster Mennonite Historical Society, 1987. 296p. (Mennonite sources and documents; no. 1). 1. Stoltzfus, Tennessee John, 1803-1877--Correspondence. 2. Amish-Pennsylvania--Correspondence. 3. Amish-Tennessee--Correspondence. 4. Amish-United States--History-Sources. 5. Stoltzfus family. [G636-3].

STONE -- Stone, Dolly Mary. *Samuel Stone and His Wife, Mary Ann Chunn: A Story of Their Lives, Including Early Residence in Virginia, Tennessee, and Alabama, Their Migration to Missouri and later to the Republic of Texas, with Data Concerning Their Family and Descendants, and Also Including Some Genealogical History Proving the Ancestry of Mary Ann Chunn.* San Antonio, TX, 1955. pni. [VV176].

STONE -- Stone, Martha Jane. *A History of the Stone Family Who Settled in the South and the Cherry Family of Tennessee.* Lexington, KY, M.J. Stone, 1993. 481p.
  LC CALL NUMBER: CS71.S88 1993

STONECIPHER -- Stonecipher, H. S. [G637-1]. See above: STEINSEIFFER. [G632-3].

STRANGE -- Strange, M. Robert. *A Strange History.* Clarksville, TN, Josten's, c1977. 144p. [C672; DC3516].

STUART -- Boyd, William J. *An Introduction to the Stewarts - 2nd ed.* - Nashville, TN, W.J. Boyd, Sold by Clan Stewart Society, c1988. 12p. 1. Stuart family. [G642-3].

STURMAN -- NAS. *Thomas Sturman and Ann; Col. William Hardwick and Elizabeth Sturman; Jeffrey Johnson and Margaret of Virginia, and Their Descendants in North Carolina and Knox County, Tennessee.* NP, 1974. 98 l., 99-110p. [S2424].

SULLIVAN -- Simpson, Edna Grant. *The Family of Daniel Asbury Sulliven (1839-1913) of Georgia and Tennessee*. Knoxville, TN, E. G. Simpson, 1982. 62 leaves. [C676].

SULLIVAN -- Simpson, Edna Grant. *The Sullivan Family of Virginia, North Carolina, and Georgia*. Knoxville, TN, Simpson, 1975. ca. 450 leaves. [DC3546].

SUMNER -- Sumner, Williams S. *History of Sumner Family*. Nashville, TN, Parthenon Press, c1932. 79p. [D12157].


T


TALIAFERRO -- See above: CAMPBELL. [L2939; D2108].

TALIAFERRO -- NAS. *The Taliaffero Family*. Chattanooga, TN, 1916. 2p. (Notable southern families). Detached from the Lookout. [L16745].

TANNER -- Hussey, Marguerite Carleton. *The Family of Rev. John Tanner - Baptist Preacher; Virginia - North Carolina - Kentucky - Missouri*. Berkeley, CA, 1972. 52 leaves. [S2446; VV181].

TARWATER -- Tarwater, Charles B. *A Brief History of the Tarwater Family*. Knoxville, TN, Tarwater, 1957. 72p. [D12267].

TATE -- Carpenter, Evelyn Yates. *Tate and Allied Families of Robertson County, Tennessee*. Clarksville, TN, Jostens Printing and Publishing Division, 1987. 129p., 55p. of plates, [DC gives 128p]. "Includes the nearby Tennessee Counties of Davidson, Sumner, and Wilson. Includes Virginia and North Carolina, the states of Tate family origin. Includes Counties in Arkansas, Illinois, Missouri, and throughout the United States were many Tate families migrated." 1. Tate family. 2. Tennessee-Genealogy. [G651-3; DC3587].

TATUM -- Castleberry, Amelia A. *The Tatum Family of Tennessee.* NP, 1948. 36 leaves. [D12675].

TAYLOR -- NAS. *The Taylors of Tabernacle: The History of a Family Including the Genealogy of Its Descendants with Biographical Sketches and Family Journals and Daily Accounts of Life in Haywood County, Tennessee, For Over a Century.* Brownsville, TN, The Taylor Kinfolk Assoc. at Tabernacle Church, 1957. 682p. D gives underscored part of title. [L16834; D12314].

TAYLOR -- Armstrong, Zella. *Taylor of Tennessee. Pamphlet Edition.* Chattanooga, TN, Lookout Pub. Co., 1933. 36p. (Notable southern families). [L16824].

TAYLOR -- Ford, Ethel M. T. *Thomas Taylor and Benjamin Branch of Nashville, Tenn. and Related Families.* Amarillo, TX, 1972, x, 214p. X gives date as: 196_. [S2458; X926-FW].

TEMPLIN -- Templin, Ronald R. *The Templins of Tennessee.* Fort Myers, FL, R.R. Templin, 1989. a-g, 159, xxiv p. 1. Templin family. 2. Tennessee-Genealogy. [G654-2].

TERRY -- Terry, George Alvin. *The Terrys of Scott County, Tennessee.* Huntsville, TN, Scott County Historical Society, [DC gives: Goodlettsville, TN, G.A. Terry], 1984. 29, xv leaves. 1. Terry family. 2. Tennessee-Genealogy. [G656-1; DC3613].

TERRY -- Terry, Woodford. *James Terry of Tennessee: A Door to His Ancestry and Progeny.* Oak Ridge, TN, W. Terry, 1986, xiii, 737, 13p. of plates. 1. Terry family. 2. Terry, James, 1768-1828-Family. 3. Tennessee-Genealogy. [G656-2].

THARPE -- Hope, Mildred Tharpe. *Col. William A. Tharpe of Tennessee.* Shelbyville, TN, Hope, 1973. 98p. [D12355].

THOMAS -- James, Larry A. [G658-1]. See above: JEWELL. [G350-1].

THOMAS -- Wynn, C. B. *Isaac Thomas of Sevierville, Tennessee.* Gatlinburg, TN, Buckhorn Press, 1980. 94p. [D12392].

THOMPSON -- Billington, Harry Lee. *An Amazing Lady; The Life Story of Irene Ward Thompson.* Franklin, TN, H.L. Billington, 1988. 60p. [DC3628].

THOMPSON -- Brown, Emma Catherine Champion & Jonathan Kennon Thompson Smith. *These Many Hearths.* Eva, TN, 1972. ii, 71 leaves. [S2483].

THOMPSON -- Brown, Emma Catherine Champion. *Thompson Kin of Yellow Creek Valley.* Memphis, TN, Smith, 1974. 115, 9p. [S2486; D12402].

THOMPSON -- Buchanan, Jane Gray. [G659-1]. See above: FINNEY: [G229-3; NGS11; DC3630]. LC CALL NUMBER: CS71.T47 1987a

THOMPSON -- Eberle, Marie Thompson. *Thompson Twigs: Some Descendants of Sheldon and Ann Thompson of Washington County, Virginia: with Allied Families of Allen / Daily; Bowman / Whitaker; Crawford, Johnson / Dickinson, Linder, McCulloch, White.* Edwardsvile, IL, 1981. pni. [VV183].

THOMPSON -- Hankins, Edith Jackson. *Thomas Begat: An Accounting of the Family of Thomas Thompson.* Memphis, TN, E.J. Hankins, 1989. 131, 29p. 1. Thompson family. 2. Thompson, Thomas, 1780-1863-Family. [G659-2].

THOMPSON -- Johnson, Katherine Baker. *The Thompson, Epperson, Langrord, and Haynes Families of Albermarle County, Virginia and Knox County, Tennessee.* NP, 1940. 31 leaves. [D12411].

THOMPSON -- Thompson, Mary Ann Morris. *Samuel Thompson of McMinn County, Tennessee*

and Some of His Descendants. Including the
Related Families of Cobb, Cooke, Derrick,
Lattimore, and Rogers. 1st ed. Plano, TX,
M.A.M. Thompson, 1993. viii, 513p.
  LC CALL NUMBER: CS71.T47 1993

THORNTON -- Whitley, Edythe R. *Thornton
Family of Virginia.* Nashville, TN, 1944.
39p. Typed. "As copied with additions, etc.
by Elmer T. Randle...1955.". [X938-SP].

THRASHER -- Thrasher, Marion. *Thrasher
Family.* Nashville, TN, J.C. Barnett, 1956.
54 leaves. [D12453].

THRUSTON -- Thruston, Gates Phillips. *A
Sketch of the Ancestry of the Thruston -
Phillips Families; With Some Records of the
Dickinson, Houston, January Ancestry, and
Allied Families.* Nashville, TN, Brandon
Printing Co., 1909. viii, 64p. D gives 60p.
and underscored part of title.
[L17057; D12465].

TILLMAN -- Tillman, George Newton. *Tillman
Genealogy; Marshall, Clay, Martin, Davidson.*
Nashville, TN, McQuiddy Printing Co., 1905.
42p. [D12499; X941-LT].

TILLSON -- Alderman, Pat. *The Tilson Grist
Mill: A Mountain Folklore Genealogy.* Johnson
City, TN, P. Alderman, 1981. 48p. [C694].

TIPTON -- Heinemann, Charles Brunk. *Tipton
Family of Maryland, Virginia, Tennessee,
Kentucky, Ohio, Indiana, Illinois, Missouri.*
Washington, DC, 1934. 1, 29, 1, 2, 10 numb.
leaves. [L17127; VV185].

TIPTON -- Heinemann, Charles Brunk. *Tipton
Family of Maryland, Virginia, Tennessee,
Kentucky, Ohio, Indiana, Illinois, Missouri.*
Chicago, IL, 1937. 1, 40, 11 numb. leaves.
Typed. [L17128].

TIPTON -- Heinemann, Charles Brunk. *Tipton
Family of Maryland, Virginia, Tennessee.*

*Kentucky, Ohio, Indiana, Illinois, Missouri.*
Washington, DC, 1941. 1, 48 numb. l. Typed.
[L17129].

TIPTON -- Heinemann, Charles Brunk. *Tipton
Family Records in the Present Boundaries of
the United States from Colonial Times to 1950.*
Washington, DC, 1950. 332, 49 leaves. Typed
(carbon copy). [L17131].

TOWNSEND -- Townsend, Edward E. *Sam
Townsends of North Georgia.* Cleveland, TN,
1974. 138p. [X948-FW].

TOWNSEND -- Townsend, Kathy. *The Townsend
Heritage.* Sevierville, TN, K. Townsend, 1984.
vi, 135p. [C700].

TRABUE -- Yates, Julie Trabue & Charles C.,
IV. *The Trabue Family in America, 1700-1983.*
Baltimore, MD, Gateway Press, Nashville, TN,
Mrs. D.J. Yates, 1983. xi, 515p. [C700].

TROTTER -- Trotter, Susie Eager (Mrs. Isham
Patten Trotter, Jr. *Trotter Genealogy. The
Virginia - Tennessee - Mississippi Trotter
Lines, 1725-1948.* Louisville, KY, Mayes
Printing Co., 1948. 225p. [L17332; D12664].

TRENTHAM -- Russell, Gladys T. *Call Me
Hillybilly; A Personal Account of Growing Up
in the Smokies near Gatlinburg.* Alcoa, TN,
Russell Pub. 1974. 92p. [X951-FW].

TUCKER -- Tucker, Reuel Walter. *Memoirs and
History of the Peyton Tucker Family; Ancestors
and Descendants of England, Wales, Vermont,
Massachusetts, Maryland, Virginia, the
Carolinas, Georgia, Tennessee, Kentucky,
Illinois, Missouri, Arkansas, Louisiana,
Texas, Oklahoma, and California; and
Genealogy.* Baltimore, MD, Gateway Press,
1975. xxvii, 256 p. 2 fold. leaves of plates.
[S2558; VV187].

TUGWELL -- Rollins, Sarah Finch Maiden. *The
Tugwell and Finch Families of Tennessee and*

Allied Families of Virginia and North Carolina 1635-1993 : Bobbitt, Hockaday, Lang, Montgomery, and Powell. Houston, TX, S.F.M. Rollins, c1993. xii, 350p.
  LC CALL NUMBER: CS71.T92 1993

TURNER -- Turner, William B. *Early History of the Tucker Family and the Charles New Tucker Branch.* Nashville, TN, Parthenon Press, 1960. 47p. [X956-FW].

TURNEY -- Taylor, James C. *Pioneer Turneys and Allied Families of Henry and Francis in Tennessee.* Gulfport, MS, J.C. Taylor, 1989. xi, 43 leaves.
  LC CALL NUMBER: CS71.T946 1989

TURRENTINE -- HAS. *The Turrentine Family.* No. 112-113; July-Sept., 1969. Nashville, TN.

J.M. Turrentine. Ceased publication with Sept., 1969. [X956-NY].

TYREE -- Tyree, Forrest Hill. *A Tyree Genealogy.* Nashville, TN, F.H. Tyree, 1983. viii, 136p. [C708].

# U

UFFORD -- Davis, Sarah Marie Ufford, Frank W. and Marley H. Davis. *William Beers Ufford: The First Hundred Years.* Knoxville, TN, S.M.U. Davis, 1984. 169, 62p. [C709; DC3720].

UNDERWOOD -- Underwood, Burl. *The Underwoods from Roaring Gap (NC) to Duplin Valley (TN) and Onward and Related Families* - Rev. ed. - Knoxville, TN, B.H. Underwood, 1987. xiv, 356p. 1. Underwood. 2. Tennessee-Genealogy. [G679-2; NGN17-5-91].

UPSHAW -- Upshaw, Eugene. *The Upshaws of Essex County, Virginia and Giles County, Tennessee: The Jeremiah Line, the First 350 Years.* Farragut, TN, E. Upshaw, 1988. ii, 28p. 1. Upshaw family. 2. Upshaw, Jeremiah,

b. ca. 1704-Family. 3. Virginia-Genealogy. 4. Tennessee-Genealogy. [G680-1].

V

VALENTINE -- NAS. *Family Records of John Jackson Valentine.* Memphis, TN, 1957. Unpaged. [L17539].

VALENTINE -- Valentine, John Jackson. *John Valentine of Newberry District, South Carolina.* Memphis, TN, Valentine, 1957. 134 l. X gives 6, 134p. [NG98; D12807;X963-FW].

VANCE -- Dixon, Elizabeth Williamson. *The Vance Family of Virginia, Pennsylvania, North Carolina, Tennessee; the Brank Family of North Carolina and Kentucky.* NP, 1958. 315 leaves. [D12825; VP233; VV189].

VANDEREN -- Van Deren, H.S. *Van Deren.* Nashville, TN, Van Deren, 1930. 8, ca.125 leaves. [D12842].

VANDERBILT -- Archer, Verley. *Commodore Cornelius Vanderbilt, Sophia Johnson Vanderbilt and Their Descendants.* Nashville, TN, 1972. pni. [NG98].

VAN DYKE -- Van Dyke, Judge Thomas Nixon. *Tennessee Van Dyke Genealogy.* Washington, DC, 1940. 1p., 8 numb. leaves. Typed. [L17599].

VAN DYKE -- Battey, George Magruder. *The Van Dyke Graveyard and Its Occupants at Athens in McMinn County, Tennessee.* Washington, DC. 1940. 3 numb. leaves. [L17600].

VARNER -- Varner, Mary. *Harry Howard Varner: His Roots Are In Virginia.* Maryville, TN, M. Varner, 1987. 40p. 1. Varner family. 2. Varner, Harry Howard, 1855-1970-Family. [G686-2; DC3761].

VIVRETT -- Puckett, Mary Porter Vivrett. *Vivretts of Wilson County, Tennessee.* NP,

Puckett, c1976. 9op. 1. Vivrett family. 2.
Wilson County (Tenn.)-Genealogy. 3. United
States-Genealogy. [G691-2; C723].

WADDELL -- Broyles, Cathy B. The
Descendants of William "Bill" Waddle and Dora
Caroline Keller Waddle. Chuckey, TN, Broyles,
1988. 47p. [C723].

WADDINGTON -- Simons-Waddington, Andy.
Genealogy of the Waddington Family. Pulaski,
TN, 1980. 115 leaves. [A687].

WADE -- NAS. The Wades; The History of a
Family, Dealing with the Kith and Kin of
Zachary and Mary Hatton, Their Descendants and
Related Lines, Male and Female, in Maryland,
Virginia, Tennessee, South Carolina, North
Carolina, and Other States. Cairo, IL, 1963.
247p. [L17793; VV191].

WADE -- Wade, Ophelia R. Wade - Waid -
Waide; A Research Book primarily of
Census, Cemetery, and Courthouse Records for
the States of Ala., Ark., Ga., Ind., Ky.,
Mass., Mo., N.C., Okla., S.C., Tenn., Texas
and Va. Bragg City, MO, Author, 1975. 260p.
[X981-FW/MH].

WAHRER -- Ingersoll, A. M. Michael Wahrer
Family in America. Nashville, TN, 1970.
162p. [X983-FW].

WALDEN -- Walden, Kenneth E. [G695-2;
S2646]. See above; JOHNSON.
[G352-3; S2646].

WALKER -- Walker, Edward R. Walking with
the Walkers. Johnson City, TN, Overmountain
Press, c1981. xi, 113p. 1. Walker family.
[G696-2].

WALKER -- Walker, Mary Ellen Martin. The
Ten Children of William Walker. Pleasant

View, TN, M.E.M. Walker, 1989   80p.
   LC CALL NUMBER: CS71.W18   1989a

WALLACE   ---   Katz, Gertrude Price.   *The
   Tennesseans:   Family History of Dr. James
   Devol Wallis (1830-1904) and Wife, Frances
   Elizabeth Park (1842-1894) and Their Eight
   Children.*   2nd draft.  NP. n.d. 1 v. (various
   pagings).   [S2652].

WALLACE   ---   Seivers, Edna Wallace.   *The
   Ancestors and Descendants of Robert Wallace.*
   Knoxville, TN, E.W. Seivers, 1989.   iv, 328,
   28p.   1. Wallace family.   2. Wallace, Robert,
   1819-1897-Family.   [G697-1].

WALLACE   --   Seivers, Edna Wallace & Cheryl
   Edmonds Wallace.   *The Robert and Harriet
   Wallace Family: Anderson County, TN. and Knox
   County, TN, 1800's and 1900's.*   Knoxville, TN,
   E.W. Seivers, 1986.   37 leaves.   1.   Wallace
   family.   2. Wallace, Robert, 1819-1897-Family.
   3. Anderson County (Tenn.)-Genealogy.   4. Knox
   County (Tenn.)-Genealogy.   [G697-1].

WALLEN   --   Wallin, Carolyn D.  *Elisha Wallen:
   The Longhunter.*   Johnson City, Tennessee,
   Overmountain Press, c1990.   x, 890p.   1.
   Wallen family.   2. Wallen, Elisha, ca. 1732-
   1814-Family.   [G697-3].

WALLIS   --   Katz, Gertrude M. P.   *Dr. James
   Deval Wallis (b. 1830, d. 1904) of Ohio, Ky.,
   and Tenn. and Wife, Frances Elizabeth Park...
   of Franklin and Nashville, Tenn...*   NP, 1972.
   1 v. (various pagings).

WARD   --   Bell, Annie W.B.  *Ward Family History
   of the Records of the Eastern Cherokee Indian
   Tribe, Copied at the National Archives in
   Washington, D.C. to Honor the Famous Cherokee
   Woman, Nancy Ward of Tennessee.*   Washington,
   DC, 1988.   86 leaves.   FW gives date as 1961.
   [X992-FW/NY].

WARD   --   Burns, Annie Walker.  *Military and
   Genealogical Records of the Famous Indian*

Woman: Nancy Ward – 2nd ed. – Washington, DC,
A.W. Burns, 1966.   258   43 leaves.   1. Ward,
Nancy.   d.   1822.     2.   Cherokee   Indians-
Genealogy.   3. Ward family.   4. Indians of
North  America.     5.   Tennessee-Genealogy.
[G699-1].

WARD  --  McGhee, Lucy K.  Ward Family History
  of Virginia. Showing Their Links with the
  States  of  North  Carolina,  Tennessee  and
  Kentucky Branches of Wards.  Washington, DC,
  1957.   39+, 81, A-I leaves.
  [X992-FW/NY; VV193].

WARD  --  Whitley, Edythe.  Lineage of Mrs.
  Alice Arnold Greenlaw.  NP, 1960.   250 leaves.
  [D13135].

WARDIN -- Wardin, Albert W.  The Heritage of
  The Wardin Family of Oregon.  Nashville, TN,
  A.W. Wardin, Jr., c1986.   64p.   1. Wardin
  family.  2. Oregon-Genealogy.
  [G700-1].

WARE  --  Edwards, Olga Jones & Ina Wear
  Roberts.   Descendants  of  East  Tennessee
  Pioneers – 2nd ed.  –  Puyallup, WA, O.J.
  Edwards; Sevierville, TN, I.W. Roberts, c1986.
  382p.   1. Ware family.   2. Tennessee, East-
  Genealogy.  [G700-2].

WARREN  --  Waller, J. W.  Descendants of
  Daniel  Warren  (1788-1876)  Lincoln  County,
  Tennessee.   Batavia, IL, 1972.   13, 4p.
  [X995-FW].

WASSELL. -- Randolph, Wassell.  The Wassell
  Family And Its Several Branches in the United
  States.  Also a Pedigree of One Branch of the
  Spotts Family.  Memphis, TN, Distributed by
  Memphis Public Library, 1962.  63p.  U gives
  underscored part of title.
  [L18125; NG100; D13197].

WATERHOUSE  --  NAS.  Waterhouse Family of
  New Jersey and Tennessee and Allied Families.
  NP, n.d.  9 leaves.  [X999-LA].

WATERHOUSE -- Waterhouse, Carmack. *Certain Topics on the Ingraham, Waterhouse, and Allied Families...* Oak Ridge, TN, 1974. 272p. [S2669].

WATKINS -- Johnson, Donna Simpson. *Bible Records of Watkins, Casteel, Coats, Peterson; Southern Illinois and Tennessee, 1880-1938[?].* Omaha, NE, D.S. Johnson, 1983. 40 leaves. [DC3841].

WATKINS -- Watkins, William B. *The Watkins Family of North Carolina, Particularly Enumerating Those Descendants of Levin Watkins of Duplin County N.C. Who Emigrated to Alabama and Mississippi Early in the Nineteenth Century.* Jackson, TN, McCowat-Mercer, 1915. 85p. [L18147].

WATLINGTON -- Wolford, Mary Watlington. *Watlingtons of Madison County Tennessee and Dinwiddie County Virginia.* Oklahoma City, OK, M.W. Wolford, 1989. 1 v, various foliations. [DC3846].

WATSON -- Stephen, David. *A Genealogy of the Watson Family: Descendants of Jonathan Watson of Washington County, Tennessee.* Mansfield, OH, S.D. Watson, 1986. iv, 73p. 1. Watson family. 2. Watson, Jonathan-Family. 3. Tennessee-Genealogy. [G703].

WATSON -- Twain, Mark. [G703-2]. See above: DARNELL. [G175-1].

WATSON -- Watson, Annah Robinson. *"Oh Sceptered Race".* Memphis, TN, Early Print. and Pub. Co., 1910. 6, 379, 6p. [L18156].

WATT -- Brooks, Dorothy Claybroke Watts. *Thomas Watts and Alexander McElwain: Their Ancestors and Descendants, and Related Families.* Camden, TN, Brooks, 1980. vii, 220p. Cover title: Watts-McElwain and Related Families. [C736].

WATTS — Brooks, Dorothy Claybroke Watts. *Thomas Watts and Alexander McElwain.* Camden, TN, Brooks, 1980. vii, 220p. [D13253].

WEAKLEY — Saunders, Sara Bradford. [G704-2]. See above: BRADEN. [G21-1].

WEAR — Edwards, Olga Jones & Ina West Roberts. *Descendants of East Tennessee Pioneers.* Gatlinburg, TN, Brazos Printing, c1963. 315p. X omits place of publication. [D13248; DC3855; X1002-MH].

WEATHERBY — Allen, R. A. H. *Weatherby Family, 1700-1955.* Chattanooga, TN, 1956. 70p. [X1002-FW].

WEAVER — Nimmo, Sylvia. *Weaver, McKnight, Hagerty, and Clute Families of Texas, Alabama, Georgia, Tennessee, and North Carolina.* Papillion, NB, S.L. Nimmo, c1993. x, 256 p., 1 leaf of plates.
LC CALL NUMBER: CS71.W365 1993

WEBB — Freeman, Beth Ogle. *Entwining of Roots: Joseph & Barsheba Thomas Webb Genealogy.* Cosby, TN, B.O. Freeman, c1985. 246p. 1. Webb family. 2. Webb, Joseph, 1790-ca.1875-Family. 3. Tennessee-Genealogy. [G705-1; C737].

WEBB — Webb, Nonie. *The Family and Descendants of Levi and Vina Webb.* -- 1st ed. rev. -- Jasper, TN, N. Webb, 1984. 1 v. (various pagings).

WELCH — NAS. *Welch - Welsh - Walsh.* Knoxville, TN, The Association, 1959-61. 184. [D13312].

WELCH — NAS. *Welch - Welsh - Walsh. Vol. 1 - April, 1959 - .* Knoxville, TN, 3 vols. in 1. Semiannual. Official Publication of the W-W-W Assn. [X1008-NY,PH].

WESLEY — Wesley, Thomas Wyatt, Jr. *From the West Lea: A Wesley Family History.* --

1st ed. -- Brentwood, TN, Wesley, 1979. ca.
100 leaves in various foliations. [C744].

**WEST** -- Boyle, Blodwen W. *Isaac West's
Family of North Carolina, South Carolina, and
Dickson County, Tennessee, 1745-1850.* NP,
1974. 34 leaves. NG gives underscored part
of title and 34p. [NG101; X1014-FW,LA].

**WEST** -- Fox, Ann Woodard. *The Noble Lineage
of the Delaware West Family of Virginia.*
Memphis, TN, Seebode Printing Service, 1958.
241p. [D13367].

**WEST** --- Giulezan, Isabel S. *Notes on Amos
West (1776-1819) of Sumner County, Tenn., and
Logan County, Ky.* St. Louis, MO, 1960. 28
leaves. [X-FW].

**WEST** -- West, Hoke Holland. *What Is In A
Name? West: The Life of a Family, a People,
Their History, Their Homes, Their Lands, and
Their Hopes, Their Labors and Their Courage,
Their Faith, Their Devotion, and Their
Loyalty, Their Love and Their Dreams.*
Gallatin, TN, Quality Print Co., 1970. 365p.
[A697].

**WEST** -- Ikelman, Joy A. *Leonard West (1760-
1842) and Descendents (sic): A History of the
West Family in Sumner County, Tennessee,
Simpson County, Kentucky, and Pueble County,
Colorado.* ... Includes Information on
Couwenhoven, Dorris, Frost, Hendricks,
Holloway, McMurry, Morgan, Schenck, Wyckoff.
Longmont, CO, J. H. Ikelman, 1983. 64p. 1.
West family. 2. West, Lenoard, ca. 1760-1842-
Family. 3. Tennessee-Genealogy. 4. Kentucky-
Genealogy. 5. Colorado-Genealogy. [G710-2].

**WEST** -- Robbins, Kathleen West. *West Family
History Records.* Huntsville, TN, Scott County
Historical Society, 1985. 1. West family. 2.
Tennessee-Genealogy. [G710-3].

**WEYERMAN** -- Moss, Ernestine Parke. *William
Weyerman ( Wierman ) of Adams County,*

Pennsylvania Descendants and Allied Families.
Memphis, TN, E.P. Moss, 1983. 114p.
[DC3898]

WHITLOCK -- Roach, Thomas Edward. *Whitlock
Gleanings: A Genealogical Work Book*.
Rutledge, TN, T.E. Roach, 1982. 329p.
[C751].

WHIDDON -- Alexander, Virginia Wood.
*Whitten and Allied Families* - 2nd ed.
Columbia, TN, V.W. Alexander, Clemson, SC,
W.C.Whitten, Jr. 1984. 668p. 1. Whitten
family. 2. Witten family. 3. Whiddon family.
4. South Carolina-Genealogy. 5. Southern
States-Genealogy. C & DC list as WHITTEN.
[G712-3; C752; DC3931].

WHITE -- Bragg, Emma W. [G713-3]. See
above: CARTER. [G124-2].

WHITFIELD -- Whitfield, Vallie Jo.
*Whitfield History and Genealogy of Tennessee*.
Walnut Creek, CA, Whitfield, c1964. 237
leaves. [D13509].

WHITEHEAD -- Rhyne, Margaret Whitehead.
*Whitehead and Related Families*. Maryville,
TN, Printed by Marion R. Mangrum on the Brazos
Press, 1971. 256p. [S2699].

WHITESIDE -- Whiteside, Don. *Whiteside(s)
Listed in North Carolina Census for Selected
Counties, 1787-1880 and Other Papers on the
Whiteside Family*. Edmonton, Canada, 1965(-
1970). 1 v. (various pagings). On spine:
Whitesides listed in N.C., S.C., & Tenn.
census for selected counties.
[S2700].

WHITLEY -- Strader, Helen Whitley and
Benbow, Routh Whitley. *Our Wandering
Whitleys; Descendants of Sharp R. Whitley &
John Saunders Whitley of Virginia, Kentucky,
Tennessee, Illinois, Missouri and Texas and
Allied Families*. Clovis, NM. viii, 264 l.
[S2712; VV200].

WHITLOCK -- Roach, Thomas Edward. *Whitlock Gleanings: A Genealogical Work Book.* Rutledge, TN, 1982. 329p. [NG102].

WHITSETT -- Hays, Maud. *Harris Records and Allied Families of Claiborne, Gillison, Thompson, Whitsett.* Chattanooga, TN, 1953. Various pagings. [X1022-LA].

WHITTEN -- Alexander, Virginia Wood. [G716-1]. See above: WHIDDON. [G712-3; C752; DC3931].

WIEMER -- Potts, L. C. *Biographical Sketches and Family Records of the Gabriel Wiemer and David Wiemer Families.* Rockville, TN, Author, 1936. 270p. [X1024-FW].

WIERMAN -- Wierman, Ernestine Parke. *William Weyerman (Wierman) of Adams County, Pennsylvania: Descendants and Allied Families.* Memphis, TN, E.P. Moss, 1983. 114p., 3 leaves of plates. [C753].

WILCOX -- Albertson, Martha S. *A Willcox Family History, 1689-1977: Including Willcox, Wilcox and Allied Families of Pennsylvania, North Carolina, South Carolina, Georgia, Alabama, and Missouri.* Tucker, GA, M. S. Albertson, 1981. ca 550p. "Compiled to again update, enlarge upon and correct the author's previous volumes published in 1972 and 1977." - Preface. [C753].

WILEY -- Brown, Elois Renfro. *Wiley and Allied Families.* Columbia, TN, 1967. 168p. X gives 177p. [NG103; X1027-FW].

WILFORD -- Neel, Eurie Pearl Wilford. *The Wilford-Willford Family Treks in America and a Reprint of Counties of Christian and Tregg, Kentucky, Historical and Biographical, Edited by William Henry Perrin, 1884.* Nashville, TN, 1959. 2 pts. in 1 v. (Western Kentucky Pioneer Series in V. 2). D gives underscored part of title, Rich Printing Co., and 437p. [L18685: D13587].

WILHITE -- Greenwood, O. K. *The Wilhites and Associated Families: A Genealogical Publication.* Edited by Judy Stogner. Crossville, TN, O.K. Greenwood, 1981. iii, 107 leaves, 14 leaves of plates. [C754].

WILLIAMS -- NAS. *The Williams Family of Virginia.* Chattanooga, TN, 1917. 3p. (Notable southern families). Detached from the Lookout. [L18748; VV201].

WILLIAMS -- Brown, Christine R. [G730-1; C755]. See above: COLLAR. [G160-1; DC3958].

WILLIAMS -- Harris, Rebecca Williams. *Thomas Williams and His Descendants.* Memphis, TN, Harris, 1882. vi, 177p. [C755; DS762].

WILLIAMS -- Harris, Rebecca Williams. *Daniel Williams and His Kin.* Memphis, TN, R. H.[?] Harris, 1987. 2 v. [DC3959].

WILLIAMS -- Hughes, Nathaniel Cheairs. *Kentucky Memories of Uncle Sam Williams.* Chattanooga, TN, Hughes, 1978. xii, 135p. [D13649].

WILLIAMS -- King, James F. *The Benjamin Williams Family of Greene County, Tennessee: A History, Compiled from Public Records, Private Papers, and Family Tradition.* Gray, TN, J.F. King, 1982. 100 leaves. 1. Williams family. 2. Williams, Benjamin, ca. 1781-1848-Family. [G720-2].

WILLIAMS -- Long, Paul J. *Our Hill Country Heritage.* Oak Ridge, TN, Long, 1970, 1972. 2 v. Contents: V. 1. Williams and related families - V. 2. Longs and Related Families. [S2730; A715; D13655].

WILLIAMS -- Williams, E. Ray. *The Williams Families of Henry County, Tennessee.* Paris, TN, 1971. a-d, 159p. [S2731].

WILLIAMS -- Williams, Elisha M. *A Partial Historical and Biographical Genealogy of the Descendants of John Williams, the English Emigrant to America. Also, Chronology of the John H. Williams Family*, compiled by Laura Batdorf. "Henry Clay Williams, Son of Elisha and Hanna Williams": folded inserted leaf between p. 6 and 7. "Genealogies of the Descendants of Elisha Williams: The Laura Ann Williams Branch of the Family, compiled by E. M. Williams... Jacksonville, Tenn, 1932": 4 p inserted between p. 8 and 9. "Genealogies of the Descendants of Elisha Williams: the Jeremiah McLene Williams Branch of the Family: compiled by E. M. Williams, Jacksonville, Tenn. 1932": 4 p inserted between p. 12 and 13. "Genealogy of the Descendants of John Williams; the Jeremiah Williams, Jr. Branch of the Family: compiled by D.O. Williams, Gallion, O., 1932": 7p inserted at end. Jackson, TN, McCowat-Mercer, 1931. 24p. D gives underscored part of title: Insertions may be only in the Library of Congress edition. [L18754; D13672].

WILLIAMS -- Williams, Elisha M. *Genealogy of the Descendants of John Williams; the Jeremiah Williams, Jr. Branch of the Family*. Jackson, TN, 1932. 2 leaves. "Bulletin no. 11". [X1030-NY]. See immediately above.

WILLIAMS -- Williams, Joseph Vincent. *James Tate Williams, His Family and Recollections*. Kingsport, TN, 1938. xiv, 250p. [L18764; NG103; D13684].

WILLIAMSON -- Strickland, Frances Ann. *The Story of My Life*. Memphis, TN, Press of S.C. Toof & Co., 1910. 1, 21p. Notes on Williamson family, in manuscript at end of book. [L18790].

WILLIS -- Sherrill, Charles A. *Peter Willis of Tennessee and His Descendants* - Rev. ed. - Cleveland, TN, C.A. Sherrill, 1987. 237p., 72p. of plates. 1. Willis family, 2. Willis,

Peter. d. 1840-Family. 1. Tennessee-
Genealogy. [G723-2].

WILLOUGHBY -- Willoughby, Cleo Twilley.
*The Willoughbys.* Cleveland, TN, White Wing
Pub. House, 1977. 519p. [C757].

WILLIS -- Heal, Carl B. *The Wills Family of
Johnson County, Tenn.* Olympia, WA, author,
1960. 447p. [X1035-LA.OS.SP].

WILSON -- Wilson, Eugene D. *An Amite County
History: The Family & Descendants of John C.
Wilson.* E.D. Wilson, c1987. 95 p.
LC CALL NUMBER: CS71.W75 1987

WILSON -- Gillespie, Rollin Wilson. *William
Penn Wilson and Cynthia Wasson Who Brought
Their Children and Slaves in 1855-1856 from
Murfreesboro, Tennessee to Springfield,
Missouri - Their Ancestors and Descendants.*
Bellingham, WA, R.W. Gillespie, 1980. 198
leaves. [C758].

WILSON -- Kelsey, Mary Wilson. [G723-2].
See above: COOK. [G155-1; NGS12].

WILSON -- McQuiston, Leona B. *The "Wilson
Family of South Carolina to Tennessee".*
Washington, DC, 1943. 3p., 39 numb. leaves.
Typed, corrected in manuscript. Two slips
with additions inserted. [L18847].

WILSON -- Smith, Othella Boyd. *Descendants
of Hiram and Mariah Wilson of Marshall County,
Tennessee.* Nashville, TN, Smith, 1961. 91
leaves. [D13750].

WILSON -- Wilson, Earl J. *The Wilson Family
Tree, Our Branch, Tenn. & Va.* Potomac, MD,
Wilson, 1985. 51p. Typescript. [DC3980].

WILSON -- Wilson, Eugene D., Jr. *An Amite
County History: The Family and Descendants of
John C. Wilson.* Franklin, TN, E.D. Wilson,
c1987. 95p. 1. Wilson family. 2. Wilson,

John C. (John Croford), ca. 1775-1842-Family.
3. Amite County (Miss.)-Genealogy.
[G724-2].

WILSON -- Wilson, Gaines L. *Descendants of Dr. Isaac Alvis Wilson, Country Doctor, Union County, Tennessee.* Topeka, KN, Jostens, c1993. viii, 423p.
LC CALL NUMBER: CS71.W75 1993

WILSON -- Wilson, Marshall A. *You Take It From Here: Wilson and Related Families, Alexander, Blair, Hines, Humphries, Lawrence, McClurg, McVay, Moore, Rankin, Rice, Richardson, Shook, Tadlock, Taylor, Willett, Woods.* Knoxville, TN, 1958. 1 vol. (various pagings). [X1036_NY].

WINSTON -- NAS. *The Winston Family.* Chattanooga, 1917. 2p. (Notable southern families). Detached from the Lookout. [L18194].

WINTERS -- Winters, Ralph L. *Historical Sketches of the Winters Family.* Clarkesville, TN, R.L. Winters, 1965- . -- v. Check shelflist for DAR library holdings. [L18918; DC3996].

WITTEN -- Alexander, Virginia Wood. [G731-3]. See above: WHIDDON. [G712-3; DC3931].

WITTEN -- Jourdan, Elise Greenup. [G732-1]. See above: CECIL. [G129-1].

WOLLARD -- Dean, Frances F. *The Woollard Family of Virginia, Kentucky, and Tennessee Since 1650, and Allied American Families, Alston ...* Washington, DC, F.F. Dean & B.M. Malloy, 1992. 1 v. (various pagings).
LC CALL NUMBER: CS71.W9147 1992

WOMACK -- NAS. *Womack Genealogy.* McMinnville, TN, 1957-60. 5 parts in 1. DAR library lacks 1959 issue. [D13851].

WOMACK -- NAL. Womack Genealogy. Vol 1-4 (Whole No. 1-8. McMinnville, TN, 1957-60. 4 vols. in 1. Official publication of the Womack Family association. [X1045-NY,PH].

WOMACK -- Womack, Oscar B. Descendants of Thomas and Louvisa Rice Womack. McMinnville, TN, 1970. 50p. [X1045-FW].

WOOD -- Duckworth, Veeda Thornton. [G734-2]. See above: EVANS. [G319-1].

WOOD -- Embrey, Lucy Alexander. The Origin and Genealogy of the Woods Family. As Can Be Traced from 1649 to 1895. Kingsport, TN, Embrey, c1940. xxxviii p. D lists as WOODS. [L19038; D13903].

WOOD -- Alexander, K. W., Ed. The Wood - Woods Family Magazine. Columbia, TN, n.d. V. Quarterly. [S2760].

WOOD -- Wood, William L. Samuel Wood: His Seven Sons and Their Descendants: Virginia to North Carolina, Tennessee, Kentucky, Illinois and Beyond. 1755-1988. Strafford, MO, W.L. Wood, 1938. xii, 320, 134p. 1. Wood family. 2. Wood, Samuel, 1737-ca. 1800-Family. [G734].

WOOD -- Wood, Mary Parrott. Drifting Down Holston River Way, 1756-1966. Maryville, TN, 1966. 240p. [L19049].

WOODFIN -- Ravan, Fannie Maud (Woodfin). Woodfin, Clark. 1722-1952. South Pittsburgh [sic], TN, R.M. Woodfin, 1952. 33p. [L19061].

WOOLDRIDGE -- Frost, Wright Wilson. The Descendants of Josiah and Keziah Nichols Wooldridge and Their Ancestors - 1st ed. Knoxville, TN, 1973. vii, 221p. [S2767; DS775; NG104].

WORRELL -- Stahl, Faith Worrell & Estelle Worrell. The Worrell Family Living Time-Line

*Tableau.* Johnson City, TN, The Compilers, 1990. 18 leaves, 8p. Genealogical Table in file cabinet. [DC4034].

**WRAY** -- Wray,, Jewell E. *The Wray Family of West Tennessee.* NP, 1972. 70p. [D13958].

**WRIGHT** -- Steely, Skipper. *Six Months from Tennessee.* Wolfe City, TX, Henington, 1982. iv, 184p. [DS779].

**WRIGHT** -- Wright, Mildred S. *William Harper Wright and His Ancestry and Descendants and Allied Families of Stone's River Tennessee.* Decorah, IA, Anundsen Pub. Co., 1980. xiv, 172, 1 leaf of plates. Title on Spine: William Harper Wright of Stone's River, Tennessee. [C770].

**WYLY** -- Smith, Jonathan Kennon. *The Wyly Saga.* Memphis, TN, Padmoor Press, c1981. iii, 126p. [D14011].

## XYZ

**YADIN** -- Yadon, William A. *The Yadons of Camden County, Missouri: With Some Related Families of Claiborne, Grainger and Union Counties, Tennessee.* Tulsa, OK, L. J. Yadon, 1981. viii, 123p., 57 leaves of plates. [C772].

**YARDLEY** -- Upshur, Thomas Teackle. *Sir George Yeardley, Or Yardley, Governor and Captain General of Virginia and Temperance ( West ) Lady Yardley, and Some of Their Descendants.* Nashville, TN, 1896. "Reprinted from American historical magazine, Nashville, Tenn., Oct., 1896". VV lists as Yeardley. [L19215: VV207].

**YATES** -- Carpenter, Evelyn Yates. *John Yates, 1712-1779, and His Descendants to 1989: Includes the History and Genealogy of John Yates...* Clarksville, TN, Jostens Printing and Publ. Division, c1989. 424p. 1. Yates

157

family. 2. Yates, John, ca. 1713-1779 Family.
DC gives underscored part of title.
[G739-1; DC4051].

YEISER -- Wiley, Mary Louise Yeiser.
*Yeiser, Ledbetter, and Allied Families.*
Columbia, TN, P-Vine Press, 1977. 140p.
[D14045].
LC CALL NUMBER: CS71.Y393 1977

YORK -- York, William Alton. *A York Family
of North Carolina, Tennessee, Georgia and
Oklahoma and Allied Families.* Pittsburg, KS,
W.A. York, 1984. vi, 23 leaves. [C774].

YOUNG -- Armstrong, William. *Partial Family
History of Young - Galbraith - and Allied
Families of Pa., Va., and Tenn., from Various
Family Records.* NP, n.d. Various pagings.
[X1062-PH; VV207].

YOUNG -- East, Flora Evelyn, et al. *The
Young Families of Early Giles County,
Tennessee.* Fresno, CA, J. Young, 1986. xvi,
263, xliii p. 1. Young family. 2. Giles
County (Tenn.)-Genealogy. [G741-2].

YOUNG -- Young, Asher Leon. *Washington Young
of Wayne County, Kentucky, and His
Descendants.* Nashville, TN, Young, 1975.
217p. 1. Young family. 2. United States-
Genealogy. 3. Wayne County (Ky.)-Genealogy.
[G741-2; C774; X-FW/NY].

YORK -- York, William Alton. *A York Family
in North Carolina, Tennessee, Georgia and
Oklahoma and Allied Families.* Pittsburg, TN,
1984. iv, 23 leaves. [DC4055].

# BIBLIOGRAPHY

FILBY, P. William. Directory of American Libraries with Genealogy or Local History Collections. Wilmington, DE. Scholarly Resources. Inc., 1988. xiv, 319p.

GRUNDSET, Eric B. & Bebe, Metz. Library Catalog, Volume Three Centennial Supplement: Acquisitions 1985-1991. Washington, DC. NATIONAL SOCIETY of the DAUGHTERS of the AMERICAN REVOLUTION, 1991.

KAMINKOW, Marion J. Genealogies In The Library of Congress. Baltimore, 1972. 2. v. A-J and L-Z.

KAMINKOW, Marion J. Genealogies In The Library of Congress, Supplement 1972 - 1976. Baltimore. Magna Carta Book Company, 1976.

KAMINKOW, Marion J. Genealogies In The Library of Congress, Second Supplement 1976 - 1986. Baltimore: Magna Carta Book Company, 1987.

KAMINKOW, Marion J. A Complement To Genealogies In The Library of Congress. Baltimore: Magna Carta Book Company, 1981.

LIB. OF CONGRESS STAFF — Genealogies Cataloged in the Library of Congress Since 1986. Washington, DC, Cataloging Distribution Service, Library of Congress, 1991.

NGS LIBRARY STAFF — National Genealogical Society, Library Book List, 5th Edition. Arlington, Virginia, National Genealogical Society. 1988.

160

NGS LIBRARY STAFF  National Genealogical Society, Library Book List, 5th Edition Supplement. Arlington, Virginia, National Genealogical Society. 1989.

NEAGLES, James C. and Mark C. The Library of Congress: A Guide to Genealogical and Historical Research. Salt Lake City, UT, Ancestry Publishing Co., 1990. xi, 381p.

MICHAELS, Carolyn Leopold and Kathryn S. Scott. Library Catalog, Volume One, Second Revised Edition, Family Histories and Genealogies. Washington, DC, National Society of the Daughters of the American Revolution, 1983.

MICHAELS, Carolyn Leopold and Kathryn S. Scott. Library Catalog, Volume One - Supplement - Family Histories and Genealogies. Washington, DC, National Society of the Daughters of the American Revolution, 1984.

VIRDIN, Donald O. Virginia Genealogies and Family Histories. Bowie, Maryland, Heritage Books, Inc., 1990.

VIRDIN, Donald O. Pennsylvania Genealogies and Family Histories. Bowie, Maryland, Heritage Books, Inc., 1992.

# TENNESSEE GENEALOGIES IN THE
# LIBRARY OF CONGRESS
# CONVERTED TO MICROFILM

A list of the few older Tennessee genealogies and family histories in the United States Library of Congress which have been converted to microfilm follows this brief introduction to availability of microfilms and other material from the Library of Congress.

Where conversion to microfilm has taken place, there is often no original volume in the Library's collection. Microfilm reels in the Library are 35mm. All listings are on 1 reel unless otherwise indicated.

The list of microfilmed genealogies in this volume can be used as a borrowing tool for librarians and those doing research on a particular family name can purchase the microfilm reels directly or paper copies made from them.

Library policy does not allow circulation of genealogy on interlibrary loan, but microfilm copies may be circulated. The Library may be able to assist in purchasing photocopies of out-of-print items. The interested researcher may obtain free upon request a circular entitled Out-of-Print Materials and Reprinted Publications. Requests should be addressed to: Library of Congress, Humanities and Social Science Division, Washington, DC 20540.

Copies of microfilm listed below may be ordered from the Photoduplicating Service at the address given above at a cost of $30.00 per reel, which includes postage and handling. Requests for "Copyflow" prints on paper may also be ordered. The researcher needs to inquire regarding specific prices.

Provided there are no copyright restrictions, photocopies of any item in the Library's genealogical collections may be obtained under the conditions specified in the order form, which may be obtained from the Library of Congress Photoduplication Service, Washington, DC 20540. As an example of the cost involved The Library indicates that the charge for preparing an unbound photocopy of a 200-page book (page size 9" x 6") would be about $50. Note that in requesting photocopy services, the specific pages and material to be copied must be cited in the request.

The following short bibliographies on genealogical subjects are available without charge from the Library of Congress, Humanities and Social Science Services Division:

♦ Guide to Genealogical Research, a Selected List of Publications, which tells how to trace an ancestor.

♦ Surnames, a Selected List of References to books on family names and national origins.

♦ Immigrant Arrivals, A Short Guide to Published Sources, of possible help in identifying ships and passenger lists.

♦ Heraldry, a Selected List of References to books on the origins, use, design, and identification of coats of arms.

Note that there is some duplication between the works shown as being in the Library collection as those listed below as being on Microfilm. It is probable, that where duplication exists, the original work is no longer available other than in microfilm.

The cross-index of names at the end of this volume includes both those contained in microfilm form as well as in printed publications.

# TENNESSEE GENEALOGIES ON MICROFILM

## A-C

ALDRIDGE -- Aldridge, Franklin Rudolph. *Aldridge Family Genealogy and History [microform]:* Nashville, TN, Commercial Letter Shop, 1960. v, 95p. "The descendants of Jesse Alldridge and Rachel Cobb. MICROFILM 86/8770 (C) <MicRR>. [G1135-2].

BOLTON -- Bolton, Charles Knowles. *The Chief Slave-Dealing Family of the Old South. The Boltons of Tennessee [microform]:* NP, C.K. Bolton, 1937. ca. 100p. A collection of typewritten and manuscript material, including wills, deeds, correspondence and mounted photographs. MICROFILM 85/7933(C) <MicRR>. [G1138-3].

CALLAWAY -- Hoffmeyer, Bessie Dee Callaway. *The Calaway Clan [microform]:* Collegedale, TN, College Press, 1948. 98 (i.e. 100p., 1 folded leaf of plates. Genealogical table inserted at end of book. MICROFILM 86/6962(C) <MicRR>. [G1149-1].

CARSON -- Carson, Frederick Ton. *A History of the Carson Family and the Allied Families Cooke, Kimbrough and Henderson [microform]:* Being an account of the forebears and the Descendants of Doctor William Cooke Carson and Dorcas Elizabeth Kimbrough of Tennessee and Texas. Washington, DC, 99, 4p. 1 leaf of plates. Supplement to Carson family history follows p. 99. MICROFILM 86/6034 (C) <MicRR>. [G1150-3].

CHANCE -- Chance, Hilda Nancy Ersula Snowberger. *Chance of Ohio, Virginia, North Carolina, Georgia, Texas, Tennessee, Kentucky, Delaware, Maryland, Pennsylvania, Michigan, California, Indiana, New Jersey [microform]:* Liberty, PA, H.N.E.S. Chance, 1970. 19 l. MICROFILM 86/5007 (C) <MicRR>. [G1152-3].

CHARLES -- Charles, Clell E. *History of the Charles Family in Eastern Kentucky, Southwest Virginia [microform]:* Erwin, TN, 25p., 6 leaves of plates. MICROFILM 86/6309 (C) <MicRR>. [G1153-3].

CHRISTIAN -- Christian, Hubert C. *Record of the Families of Gilbert Christian and Moses Fish [microform]:* Chattanooga, TN, 1969. 95p.
MICROFILM 86/5691 (C) <MicRR>. [G1155-2].

CLODFELTER -- Ledbetter, Mrs. Henry B. *Genealogy of the Family of John F. Clodfelter, 1700-1791 [microform]:* Memphis, TN, Accurate Print., 1971. 95p. MICROFILM 85/7691 (C) <MicRR>. [G1158-3].

COOPER -- Cooper, Homer C. *Cooper, McKemy, Ferrell / Farrell, Wooddell, Gothard, Wilson, & Paton Families of Augusta & Rockbridge Counties, Virginia, York, & Adams Counties, Pennsylvania, Blount, Knox and Roane Counties, Tennessee, Pocahontas, Gilmer, & Ritchie Counties, West Virginia, Wayne County, Kentucky, Virgo & Sullivan Counties, Indiana, York County, South Carolina [microform]:* Athens, GA, 1969. 7 leaves.
MICROFILM 86/6311 (C) <MicRR>. [G1162-2].

CROCKETT -- French, Janie Preston Collup & Zella Armstrong. *The Crockett Family and Connecting Lines [microform]:* Bristol, TN, King Print. Co., c1928. 611p., 32 leaves of plates (Notable Southern families; v. 5).
MICROFILM 88/5750 (C). [G1123-1].

## D — H

DELAND -- Leete, Frederick Deland. *The Deland Family in America [microform]:* A Biographical Genealogy. Deland, FL, 1943. Nashville, TN, Parthenon Press, 414p., 16 leaves of plates. MICROFILM 87/5158 (C) <MicRR>. [G1169-2].

HART -- Young, Sarah Simpson Smith. *Genealogical Narrative of the Hart Family in the United States [microform]:* Memphis, TN, S.C. Toof, 1882. 83p. MICROFILM 7445. (C) <MicRR>. [G1194-1].

## J -- O

JOHNSON -- Johnson, A.M. *Genealogy of a Branch of the Johnson Family and Connections [microform]:* Incidents and Legends. Chattanooga, TN, W.f. Crandall & Co.., 1893. 154p., 15 leaves of plates. Contains also the Stell, King, and Whiteside families. MICROFILM 84/8039 (C) <MicRR>. [G1207-2].

OCHS -- Ochs, Grace Lillian. *Up From the Volga [microform]:* the story of the Ochs family. Nashville, TN, Southern Pub. Association, c1969. 128p. MICROFILM 86/8241 (C) <MicRR>. [G1234-2].

## R -- S

RUCH -- Ruch, Charles Orin. *Sarah Verena Ruch and Charles Orin Ruch, Jr., Ancestral and Family Records [microform]:* Showing lineage through the following families: Ruch, Fuller, Ross, Stalder, Bonham, Johnson: also partial family records giving Kempf, Bryan, Phillips connections. Chattanooga, TN, 1951. 74 leaves in various foliations. MICROFILM 86/6665 (C) <MicRR>. [G1251-3].

SMITH -- Smith, Wesley. *A Family History and Fifty-Two Years of Preacher Life in Mississippi and Texas. [microform]:* Nashville, TN, University Press Co., 1893. 167p., 19 leaves of plates. MICROFILM 85/8472 (C) <MicRR>. [G1265-1].

STEPHENSON -- Stephenson, J. C. *The Stephenson Family [microform]:* A genealogical

sketch of the Stephenson family from Henry
Stephenson of Scotland, to the present time.
Nashville, TN, The Author, 1906. 126p.
MICROFILM 87/6321 (C) <MicRR>. [G1271-3].

STURMAN -- Williams, Marguerite White.
*Thomas Sturman and Ann [microform]: Col.*
*William Hardwick and Elizabeth Sturman,*
*Jeffrey Johnson and Margaret of Virginia, and*
*Their Descendants of North Carolina and Knox*
*County, Tennessee.* U.S.A., 1974. 98 i.e. 118
leaves, p. 99-110.
MICROFILM 86/6779 (C) <MicRR>. [G1274-2].


T-Z


THRUSTON -- Thruston, Gates Phillips. *A*
*Sketch of the Ancestry of the Thruston -*
*Phillips Families [microform]:* With some
records of the Dickinson, Houston, January
ancestry, and allied family connections.
Nashville, TN, Press Brandon Print. Co., 1909.
viii, 64p., 17 leaves of plates.
MICROFILM 86/6892 (C) <MicRR>. [G1280-3].

WILLIAMS -- Williams, Joseph Vincent. *James*
*Tate Williams, His Family and Recollections*
*[microform]:* Kingsport, TN, Kingsport Press,
1938. xiv, 250p./, 20p. of plates.
MICROFILM 85/8764 <MicRR>. [G1301-1].

WINTERS -- Winters, Ralph L. *Historicl*
*Sketches of the Winters Family [microform]:*
Clarksville, TN, R.L. Winters, c1965-
v.<1 >.
MICROFILM 88/5340 (C) <MicRR>. [G1303-1].

YEARDLEY -- Upshur, Thomas Teackle. *Sir*
*George Yeardley, Governor and Captain General*
*of Virginia and Temperance ( West ) Lady*
*Yeardley, and Some of Their Descendants.*
Nashville, TN, 1896. 36p.
MICROFILM 85/9506 (C) <MicRR>. [G1308-1].

## SUPPLEMENTAL TENNESSEE FAMILY
## HISTORY AND GENEALOGY SOURCES

The following is a selection of Library of Congress reference material, with the Library's call numbers, related to Tennessee. Material cited is from the Library of Congress History & Genealogy Section Reference Collection, Subject Catalog, dated December 18, 1995. Similar, or identical material, is possibly available from historical society and major genealogical libraries in Tennessee and, occasionally, in other major collections.

TENNESSEE -- ADMINISTRATIVE AND POLITICAL
           DIVISIONS
  Siler, Tom.
  Tennessee Towns,      Knoxville, TN, East
  Tennessee Historical Society, 1985.  108p.
  976.8 19 bi 87-22035
  F436  .S58 1985 LH&G

TENNESSEE -- ADMINISTRATIVE AND POLITICAL
           DIVISIONS -- REGISTERS
  Alphabetical list of cities, towns, and
  villages in Tennessee.  Nashville, TN, The
  Department, 1984.  89p.
  917.68/003 19 bi 87-24313
  F434  .A44 1984 LH&G

TENNESSEE -- BIOGRAPHY
  Armstrong, Zella.  Some Tennessee heroes of
  the Revolution.  Baltimore, MD, Genealogical
  Pub. Co., 1975.  162p.
  973.3/4/0922 B  bi 87-7882
  F436  .A74 1975 LH&G

  Crutchfield, James Andrew.      Timeless
  Tennesseans.      Huntsville, AL,  Strode
  Publishers, 1984.  183p.
  920/.0768 bi 87-1196
  CT261  .C785 1984 LH&G

TENNESSEE -- BIOGRAPHY
  Gillum, James L. Prominent Tennesseans, 1796-
  1938. Lewisburg, TN, Who's Who Publishing Co.

TENNESSEE -- BIOGRAPHY 1940 (Cont).
  vii, 286p.
  920.0768  bu 87-1196
  F435  .G55 LH&G


  Speer, William S.  Sketches of Prominent
  Tennesseans.  Easley, SC, Southern Historical
  Press, 1980.  p. 228-514
  976.8/04/0922 B 19  bi 87-16782
  F435  .S74 1978  LH&G


TENNESSEE -- CENSUS
  Sistler,  Byron.  Tennessee  mortality
  schedules.  Nashville, TN, B.  Sistler &
  Associates, 1984.  v, 363p.
  929/.3768 19 bi  87-21069
  F435  .J27  LH&G


TENNESSEE -- CENSUS -- INDEXES
  Jackson, Ronald Vernon.  Early Tennessee.
  Bountiful, UT, Accelerated Indexing Systems,
  [1980-  v. <1  >
  929/.3768 19 bi  87-15184
  F435  .J27  LH&G


TENNESSEE -- CENSUS -- 1820 -- INDEXES
  Bentley, Elizabeth Petty.  Index to the 1820
  census of  Tennessee.  Baltimore,  MD,
  Genealogical Pub. Co., 1981,  x, 287p.
  929/.3768 19 bi  87-14841
  F435  .J3 1981  LH&G


  Jackson, Ronald Vernon.  Early Tennessee.
  Bountiful, UT, Accelerated Indexing Systems,
  1974.  [9], 150p., [1] 1 leaf of plates
  929/.3768  bi 87-11070
  F435  .J3 1974  LH&G


TENNESSEE -- CENSUS -- 1830 -- INDEXES
  Jackson, Ronald Vernon.  Early Tennessee.
  Bountiful, UT, Accelerated Indexing Systems,
  1976.  [56], 213p.
  929/.3768  bi 87-11122
  F435  .J32  LH&G


TENNESSEE -- CENSUS -- 1840
  Sistler, Byron.  1840 Census  -- Tennessee

Nashville, TN, B. Sistler, 1986.  iv, 592p.
929/.3768 20 bi  87-24348
F435  .S54 1986  LH&G

TENNESSEE -- CENSUS -- 1840 -- INDEXES
Jackson, Ronald Vernon.  Early Tennessee.
Bountiful, UT, Accelerated Indexing Systems,
1976.  [4], 260p.
929/.3768  bi 87-11113
F435  .J333  LH&G

TENNESSEE -- CENSUS -- 1850
Marsh, Helen Crawford.  1850 Mortality
Schedule of Tennessee.  Shelbyville, TN, Marsh
Historical Publications, 1982.  363p.
929/.3768 19 bi  87-16401
F435  .M59 1982  LH&G

Sistler, Byron.  1850 Census  -- Tennessee
Evanston, IL, B. Sistler & Associates, 1974-
1976.  8 v.
929/.3768 19 bi  87-16915
F435  .S55 1974  LH&G

TENNESSEE -- CENSUS -- 1850 -- INDEXES
Jackson, Ronald Vernon.  Tennessee 1850 Census
Index.  Bountiful, UT, Accelerated Indexing
Systems, 1977.  [56], 452p.
929/.3768  bi 87-9899
F435  .J333  LH&G

TENNESSEE -- CENSUS -- 1860
Sistler, Byron.  1860 Census  -- Tennessee.
Nashville, TN, B. Sistler & Associates, 1981 -
<1982  >  v. <1-3  >
929/.3768 19 bi  87-15209
F435  .S56  LH&G

TENNESSEE -- CENSUS -- 1870
Sistler, Byron.  1870 Census  -- Tennessee.
Nashville, TN, B. Sistler, 1985.  2 v.
929/.3768 20 bi  87-24347
F435  .S563 1985  LH&G

TENNESSEE -- CENSUS -- 1880
Sistler, Byron.  1880 Census  -- Tennessee.
Evanston, IL, B. Sistler & Associates, 1981?-

v.
929/.3768 19 bi   87-16699
F435   .S564 1981   LH&G

TENNESSEE -- CENSUS -- 1890
   Sistler, Byron.    1890 Civil War veterans
   census, Tennessee.   Evanston, IL, B. Sistler
   & Associates, 1978.    viii, 355p.
   973.7/6  bi  87-13598
   E494   .S59  LH&G

TENNESSEE -- GENEALOGY
   Acklen, Jeannette (Tillotson).
   Tennessee    records.    Baltimore,    MD,
   Genealogical Pub. Co., 1967.   2 v.
   929.3  bi 87-4456
   F435   .A34 1967  LH&G.

   Allen, Penelope Johnson
   Tennessee soldiers in the Revolution.
   Baltimore, MD, Genealogical Pub. Co., 1975.
   71p.
   973.3/4  bi 87-7673
   E263.N8 A374 1975  LH&G.

   Armstrong,   Zella.    Twenty-four   hundred
   Tennessee    pensioners.    Baltimore,    MD,
   Genealogical Pub. Co., 1975.   121p.
   973.3/4  bi 87-7673
   E263.N8 A374 1975  LH&G.

   Baker,   Russell   Pierce.    Obituaries   and
   Marriante notices from the Tennessee Baptist,
   1844-1862.   Easley, SC, Southern Historical
   Press, 1979.   127p.
   929/.376 19 bi 87-12142
   F435 .B34  LH&G

   Bamman, Gale Williams.   Tennessee divorcees,
   1797-1858.   Nashville, TN, G.W. Bamman, 1985.
   v, 121p.
   929/.3768 19 bi 92-11458
   F435   .B36 1985  LH&G
TENNESSEE   -- GENEALOGY (Cont.)
   Bates, Lucy Womack.   Roster of soldiers and
   patriots of the American Revolution buried in
   Tennessee / Rev. 1979.   Brentwood, Tennessee

Society. NSDAR, 1979.  196p.
973.3/6 bi 87-12112
E255 .525 1979 LH&G

Brock, Reid.  Volunteers.  Nashville, TN.
Kitchen Table Press, 1996.  2 vols.
973.6/24 19 bi 87-23325
E400.5.T4 B76 1996  LH&G

Burgner, Goldene Fillers.  North Carolina land
grants in Tennessee, 1778-1791.  [NP] Southern
Historical Press, 1981  196p.
929/.3768 19 bi 87-14696
F435 .B77 1981  LH&G

Daughters  of  the  American  Revolution.
Tennessee  membership  roster  and  soldiers.
Nashville, TN  1961-70.  2 v.
E202.5  .T22 LH&G

Eddlemon, Sherida K.  Genealogical Abstracts
from Tennessee newspapers, 1791-1808.  Bowie,
MD, Heritage Books, 1988.  379p.
929/.3768 19 bi 87-24174
F435 .E33 1988 LH&G

Eddlemon, Sherida K.  Genealogical Abstracts
from Tennessee newspapers, 1803-1812.  Bowie,
MD, Heritage Books, 1988.  239p.
929/.3768 20 bi 91-8520
F435 .E34 1989 LH&G

Fischer, Marjorie Hood.  Tennessee tid-bits,
1778-1914.  Easley, SC, Southern Historical
Press, 1986-  v. <1  >
929/.3768 19 bi 87-23357
F435 .57 1986  LH&G

Fulton Genealogical Society.  Bible Records of
Kentucky and Tennessee.  Fulton, KY, The
Society, 1975.  100 leaves.
929/.3768 19 bi 87-8275
F490 .84 1975  LH&G

Garrett, Jill L.  Obituaries from Tennessee
newspapers.  Easley, SC, Southern Historical
Press, 1980.  434p.

TENNESSEE --- GENEALOGY (Cont.)

929/.3768 19 bi 87-13332
F435 .G37 LH&G

Jackson, Ronald Vernon. Mortality schedule,
Tennessee, 1850. Bountiful, UT, Accelerated
Indexing Systems, 1979. 109 leaves.
929/.3768 bi 87-13652
F435 .J29 LH&G

Johnson, Robert Foster. Wilderness Road
cemeteries in Kentucky, Tennessee, and
Virginia. Owensboro, KY, McDowell
Publications, 1981. 282p., [8]p. of plates.
929.5/09769 19 bi 87-18268
F450 .J63 1981 LH&G

Lucas, S. Emmett. 35,000 Tennessee marriage
records and bonds, 1783-1870. Easley, SC,
Southern Historical Press, 1980. 434p.
929/.3768 19 bi 87-13332
F435 .G37 LH&G

Marsh, Helen Crawford. Tennesseans in Texas.
Easley, SC, Southern Historical Press, 1986.
vi, 402p.
929/.3764 19 bi 87-22240
F385 .M264 1986 LH&G

McCay, Betty L. Sources for genealogical
searching in Tennessee. Rev. ed. Johnson
City, TN, McCown, 1977. xi, 183p.
973.5/26 bi 87-10022
E359.5.T4 M3 1977 LH&G

McGhee, Lucy Kate. Tennessee Revolutionary
War pensioners and other patriotic records.
Washington, DC, McGhee, 1954. 73 leaves.
929/3768 bi 87-8300
E255 .M3 LH&G

Murray, Nicholas Russell. Tennessee.
Hammond, LA, Hunting for Bears. [1986 - v.
<1-7 >
929/3768 19 bi 87-22350
F435 .M87 1986 LH&G

Potter, Dorothy Williams. Passports of
southeastern pioneers, 1770-1823. Baltimore,
MD, Gateway Press. Nashville, TN, D.W. Potter,
1982. xi, 449p.
929/3768 19 bi 87-18506
F208 .P65 1982 LH&G

Pruitt, Albert Bruce. Glasgow Land Fraud
papers, 1783-1800. North Carolina
Revolutionary War, Bounty Land in Tennessee.
NC, A.B. Pruitt, 1988. 1 v. (various
pagings).
929/3768 19 bi 87-24203
F435 .P78 1988 LH&G

Ray, Worth Stickney. Tennessee cousins.
Baltimore, MD, Genealogical Pub. Co., 1966
[1950] viii, 811p.
bi 87-3644
F435 .P78 1988  LH&G

Sistler, Byron. Index to early Tennessee tax
lists. Evanston, IL, Sistler, 1977. 217p.
[2] folded leaves of plates.
929/3768 19 bi 91-2480
F435 .S57  LH&G

Sistler, Byron. Index to Tennessee wills &
administrations, 1779-1861. Nashville, TN,
Byron Sistler & Associates, 1990. vi, 409p.
929/3768 20 bi 94-5325
F435 .S573 1990  LH&G

Sistler, Byron. Tennessee mortality
schedules. Nashville, TN, Byron Sistler &
Associates, 1984. v, 363p.
929/3768 20 bi 87-21069
F435 .S577 1984  LH&G

Sistler, Byron. Vital statistics from 19th
century Tennessee church records. Nashville,
TN, Byron Sistler, 1979. v.
929/3768 bi 87-13579
F435 .S58  LH&G

Tennesseans in the Civil War. Knoxville, TN,
University of Tennessee Press, [1981, c 1965]

TENNESSEE -- GENEALOGY (Cont) v. <2  >

  973.7/68 19 bi 87-3547
  E579.4  .A53  LH&G

  Tennessee Civil War Veterans Questionnaires.
  Easley, SC, Southern Historical Press, 1985.
  5 v.
  973.7/468 19 bi 87-20668
  E494  .T46 1985  LH&G

  Tennessee Historical Society.  Guide to the
  processed   manuscripts   of   the   Tennessee
  Historical  Society.   Nashville  Tennessee
  Historical Commission [c1969].  viii, 70p.
  929.3 bi 87-6154
  CD 3524 .T36  LH&G

  Tennessee marriages.  Bountiful, UT, Precision
  Indexing Publishers, 1990.  xxi, 69p.
  929/.3768 20 bi 92-22268
  F435 .T365 1990  LH&G

  Tennessee State Library & Archives.  Marriages
  from early Tennessee newspapers, 1794-1851.
  Easley, SC, Southern Historical Press, 1978.
  538p.
  929.3768 19 bi 87-16778
  F435  .T37 1978a  LH&G

  Tennessee State Library & Archives. Obituaries
  from  early  Tennessee  newspapers,  1794-1851.
  Easley, SC, Southern Historical Press, 1978.
  415p.
  929.3768 19 bi 87-16777
  F435  .T37 1978  LH&G

  Trickett,   Annie   Sandifer.   Genealogical
  abstracts  of  marriages  and  deaths  from
  Nashville  Christian  advocate,  1846-1851.
  Dallas, TX, A.S. Trickett, 1985.  viii, 306p.
  929/.376855 19 bi 87-20674
  F444  .N253 A27 1985  LH&G

  Whitley,  Edythe  Johns  Rucker.  Tennessee
  genealogical  records.   Baltimore,  MD,
  Genealogical Pub. Co., 1980.  vii, 393p.

929/.3765 b) 87-13157
F435 .S59 1978 LH&G

TENNESSEE -- GENEALOGY -- BIBLIOGRAPHY --
CATALOGS
Fulcher, Richard Carlton. Guide to county
records and genealogical resources in
Tennessee. Baltimore, MD, Genealogical Pub.
Co., 1987. 199p.
929/.1/0720768 19 bi 91-2683
Z1337 .F85 1987 LH&G

TENNESSEE -- GENEALOGY -- DIRECTORIES
Bradshaw, R. D. Tennessee Directory of Family
Searchers and Genealogists. Cumberland Gap,
TN, Tennessee Genealogical & Historical News,
c1986. vii, 249p.
929/.1/025768 19 bi 87-2231
F435 .B73 1986 LH&G

Hathaway, Beverly West. Genealogy research
sources in Tennessee. West Jordan, UT,
Allstates Research Co., 1972, iii, 167p.
929/.3/025768 bi 87-6051
F435 .H3 LH&G

TENNESSEE -- GENEALOGY -- HANDBOOKS, MANUALS,
ETC.

Hailey, Naomi. A guide to genealogical
research in Tennessee. Hartford, KY, Cook &
McDowell Publications. 1979. 54p.
929/.1/0720763 bi 87-13567
CS16 .H34 LH&G

Schweitzer, George Keene. Tennessee
genealogical research. Knoxville, TN, G.K.
Schweitzer, 1986. 138p.
929/.1/0720768 19 bi 87-22210
F435 .S37 1986 LH&G

Sistler, Bryon. The yellow pages. Evanston,
IL, B. Sistler, 1978. iii leaves, 36p.
929/.1/0720763 19 bi 87-15159
F435 .S59 1978 LH&G

TENNESSEE -- GENEALOGY -- MICROFILM CATALOGS

Tennessee State Library & Archives. Guide to
microfilmed manuscript holdings of the
Tennessee State Library and Archives. 3rd ed.
Nashville, TN, The Library and Archives, 1983.
viii, ca. 200p.
016.9768 19 bi 87-19878
Z6621.T327 T47 1983 LH&G

TENNESSEE -- GENEALOGY -- SOURCES
Tennessee Historical Records Survey.
Inventory of the church and synagogue archives
of Tennessee. Nashville, TN, The Tennessee
Historical Records Survey, 1941. iv, 55 numb.
leaves.
296.09768 bi 87-1260
BM223 .T2 H5 LH&G

TENNESSEE -- GENEALOGY -- SOURCES --
 BIBLIOGRAPHY
Tennessee State Library and Archives,
Nashville. Tennessee county data for
historical and genealogical research.
Nashville, TN, [pref. 1966]. Nashville, TN,
50p.
bi 87-4974
F443.A15 A57 LH&G

TENNESSEE, EAST -- CENSUS, 1830
Sistler, Byron. 1830 Census, east Tennessee.
Nashville, TN, B. Sistler & Associates, 1983.
276p.
929./3768 19 bi 87-21072
F442.1 .S57 1983 LH&G

TENNESSEE, EAST -- GENEALOGY
Allen, Penelope Johnson. Leaves from the
family tree. Easley, SC, Southern Historical
Press, 1982. ix, 372 [81]p.
929./3768 19 bi 87-19661
F442.1 .C7 LH&G

TENNESSEE, MIDDLE -- CENSUS, 1830
Sistler, Byron. 1830 Census--middle
Tennessee. Evanston, IL, B. Sistler &
Associates, 1976, 294p., [2] leaves of plates.

929./37686 19 bi 87-16823
F442.2   .S57 1976 LH&G

Sistler, Byron.    Early   middle   Tennessee
marriages.  Nashville, TN, B. Sistler, 1988.
2 v.
929./37686 20 bi 87-24048
F442.2   .S58 1988  LH&G

TENNESSEE, WEST -- CENSUS, 1830
   Sistler, Byron   1830 Census--west Tennessee.
   Evanston, IL, B. Sistler & Associates, 1971,
   213p., [2] leaves of plates.
   929./37686 19 bi 87-16882
   F442.3   .S67 1971  LH&G

TENNESSEE, WEST -- GENEALOGY
   Sistler,   Byron.     Early   west   Tennessee
   marriages.   Nashville, TN, Byron Sistler &
   Associates, 1989, 2 v.
   929./37686 20 bi 91-2476
   F442.3   .S68 1989  LH&G

CROSS INDEX TO FAMILY & SECONDARY NAMES

# ACCESSING LIBRARY OF CONGRESS
# RECORDS VIA THE INTERNET

Access: The Library of Congress provides internet access to its Gopher-based information system, LC MARVEL, which can provide access to the Library of Congress Information System (LOCIS). LC MARVEL can be accessed on such a World Wide Web Browser at:

        gopher://marvel.loc.gov/ or through a gopher client at marvel.loc.gov.

        The LC MARVEL, Main Menu looks in part like this:

1.    About LC MARVEL
2.    Events, Facilities Publications,
            and Services
3.    Research and Reference (Public
            Services
4.    Library and Publishers (Tech Svcs)
5.    Copyright
6.    Library of Congress Systems

Entering Item 6. will take you to LOCIS.

        The Library also has a World Wide Web "homepage" or initial selection screen. Connections can be made by specifying a Uniform Resource Locator
of URL through your client software. The URL for the LC WEB is:

        http://www.loc.gov

At the "homepage" you should see a topic:

LC Online System
Search  LOCIS  (Library  of  Congress
Information  Information  System)  via
Telnet...

The Internet Address for the Library of Congress
Home  Page  is:  http://lcweb.loc.gov/home
page/lchp.html.

A — 1

HOURS:     The System is on Eastern Time and
           Hours of Access are:

    Monday-Friday  6:30 am to Midnight
    Saturday       8:00 am to 5 pm
    Sunday         1:00 pm to 5 pm
         This  last  option  may  not  be
         available  if  the  Library  remains
         closed on Sundays.

The following shows, for example, what we might
expect to see if we were searching for any
Library of Congress holdings about a West Family
in Tennessee.   The actual appearance on our
computer  screen  will  likely  be  somewhat
different because of differences between the
width of this page and the width of our computer
screen.  The data will be the same.

The following Menu will appear:

LOCIS:   LIBRARY OF CONGRESS INFORMATION SYSTEM

To make a choice: we type a number, then press
                      ENTER

1     Library of Congress Catalog
2     Federal Legislation
3     Copyright Information
4     Braille and Audio
5.    Organizations
6.    Foreign Law
7. - 11. Information about the Library
12.   Comments and Logoff
      Choice:              PRESS 1 & ENTER


Entering 1, we will see the Library of Congress
Catalog Menu:

CHOICE                                          FILE

1  BOOKS:  English language books 1968-.  LOCI
   French 1973-, German, Portuguese,
   Spanish 1975-, other European languages
   1976-77, non-European languages 1978-79.
   Some microforms 1984-.

2  BOOKS  earlier than the dates above.  PREM
   Some serials, maps, music, audio visual
   items

3  Combinations of files 1 and 2 above.
       (LOCI and PREM)

4  SERIALS....                                  LOCS

5  MAPS........                                 LOCM

6  SUBJECT TERMS and cross references    LCXR
   from Lib. of Congress Subject Headings.

12 Return to LOCIS MENU screen.

CHOICE/COMMAND                        ENTER 1

NOTE: We can comeback later and look for books
published earlier than 1968 by entering 12 to
return to the main menu and later entering 2
from this menu to take us to the Library's
holdings for the years before 1968.

Entering 1, we will see the screen shown on the
next page.

LOCIS—THE LIBRARY OF CONGRESS INFORMATION SYSTEM
is now available for your search

CONTENTS:   Books, some microforms:
English              1968-   Other European   1976-
French               1973-   Non-Europeans    1978-
German, French,              Microforms       1984-
      Portuguese 1975-

TO SEARCH.  USE FIRST
              WORDS OF              EXAMPLES
      subject------------>    browse solar energy
      author ------------>    b faulkner, william
      title or series-->      browse megatrends
      partial LC call #>      b call QA76.9
      LC record #------->     loci 80-14332

OR SEARCH INDIVIDUAL WORDS--> find internet

HELP:   Enter HELP for LOCI info, or
        HELP COMMANDS for command list.

READY FOR NEW COMMAND:
      Since we are looking for a book about the
West Family from Tennessee, we will TYPE west
family and tennessee and press ENTER.

We will see a list of 12 terms to browse.   I
show here only those pertinent to our search:

B05 West family//(TITL=2; SUBJ=29)
B06 West family data base//(TITL=1)
B08 West family history records//(TITL=1)

-EXAMPLES: s b6              (SELECTS     line    b6:
                             creates a SET for each
                             term type)
            f b6-b8/b10      (FINDS lines b6 thru b8
                             and line b10, combines
                             sets,       displays
                             results)
            r b6             (RETRIEVES b6; searches
                             text in some files)
            r subj=b6        (RETRIEVES      term
                             type...)

A - 4

Since these line numbers (65, 66 ...) and 66 of the previous page related most closely to what we are looking for, we will include them all by TYPING F 65-66/66 and PRESSING ENTER

That entry creates five sets of titles and shows us the first page of the last of the five sets on the screen, which looks like this:

ITEMS 1-3 OF 30   SET 5   BRIEF DISPLAY FILE: LCRI
                  (DESCENDING ORDER)
1. 95-19/184: Plemmons, Gladys.... The Plemmons and West families of Buncombe County, North Carolina ... [A West family; but not from Tennessee].
2. 94-195513: West, Howard E.  The West family data base / Bowie, Md : Heritage Books, 1994. [Possibly contains information about a West family from Tennessee *].
3. 92-339419....[No indication that this book is even about the West family *].

NEXT PAGE:          press transmit or enter key
SKIP AHEAD/BACK:    type any item # in set
                    EXAMPLE--> 25
FULL DISPLAY:       type DISPLAY ITEM plus an
                    item #
                    EXAMPLE--> display item 2*
READY:                        ENTER: HISTORY

    Typing "display item 2" will gives us more information about item 2, possibly indicating that a West family from Tennessee is included in that book.  Item 3 can be checked in similar fashion.

    Note that PRESSING ENTER will take us to the next several pages of listings and a total of 30 items under this heading.

    Entering History at the Ready Command will show us all the sets the system found and allow us to look at those sets individually.

A - 5

Thus when we enter History, we get the following
list of Sets:

*****SEARCH HISTORY*****          SETS 1 - 5 OF 5

Set 1             2:  SLCT LOCI/TITL/west family
Set 2            29:  SLCT LOCI/SUBJ/west family
Set 3             1:  SLCT LOCI/TITL/west family
                         data base
Set 4             1:  SLCT LOCI/TITL/west family
                         history records
Set 5            30:  COMB 1 OR...OR 4 $PERFORMED
                  BY THE "FIND" COMMAND.
READY FOR NEW COMMAND:         TYPE & ENTER:
                               DISPLAY 4

That entry displays SET 4, which deals with West
Family History Records.   We then see on the
screen:

ITEM 1 OF 1    SET 4 BRIEF DISPLAY    FILE: LOCI
                  (DESCENDING ORDER)
1. 88-159894:  Robbins,  Kathleen  West,   West
      family history records/Huntsville, TN, ...
      Scott County Historical Society, [1985] 37
      leaves...
NEXT PAGE:             press transmit or enter key
SKIP AHEAD/BACK:       type any item # in set
                         EXAMPLE--> 25
FULL DISPLAY:          type DISPLAY ITEM plus an
                         item #
                         EXAMPLE--> display item 2
READY:                 TYPE & ENTER: DISPLAY ITEM 1

     Since this looks like a direct hit, we
enter Display item 1 to get more details and we
get the information shown on the next page.

Robbins, Kathleen West

  West family history records / compiled by
Kathleen W. Robbins. Huntsville, TN, : ..... Scott
County Historical Society, [1985]. [?] leaves..

LC CALL NUMBER: CS71/.W52 1985


SUBJECTS:
     West family
     Tennessee -- Genealogy


ADDED ENTRIES:
     Scott County Historical Society (Tenn.)

DEWEY DEC:  929/.2/0973; dc 19

NOTES:
  "Presented to the Scott County Historical
Society on May 31, 1985." Imprint stamped on
t.p.

          and on the following page after we
               PRESS ENTER, we get:


GEOG. AREA CODE:  n-us-tn
LCCN: 88-129894
PAGE 2 OR 2.  READY FOR NEW COMMAND OR PAGE #

At this point we can type History to look at the
other sets and review them, or, if our search is
over, we can ENTER END to return to the main
menu.

At that point we can also select 2 (PREM File)
from the Main Menu to conduct a similar search
for books published before 1968, using
essentially the same search routine.

A WORD OF CAUTION:  A Library of Congress
staffer indicated to me that LOCIS "is about as
user-friendly as a saber-toothed tiger".

www.ingramcontent.com/pod-product-compliance
Lightning Source LLC
Chambersburg PA
CBHW070909270326
41927CB00011B/2505